French Politics, Society and Culture Series

General Editor: Robert Elgie, Paddy Moriarty Professor of Government and International Studies, Dublin City University

France has always fascinated outside observers. Now, the country is undergoing a period of profound transformation. France is faced with a rapidly changing international and European environment and it is having to rethink some of its most basic social, political and economic orthodoxies. As elsewhere, there is pressure to conform. And yet, while France is responding in ways that are no doubt familiar to people in other European countries, it is also managing to maintain elements of its long-standing distinctiveness. Overall, it remains a place that is not exactly *comme les autres*.

This new series examines all aspects of French politics, society and culture. In so doing it focuses on the changing nature of the French system as well as the established patterns of political, social and cultural life. Contributors to the series are encouraged to present new and innovative arguments so that the informed reader can learn and understand more about one of the most beguiling and compelling of all European countries.

Titles include:

Gill Allwood and Khursheed Wadia
GENDER AND POLICY IN FRANCE

Sylvain Brouard, Andrew M. Appleton and Amy G. Mazur *(editors)*
THE FRENCH FIFTH REPUBLIC AT FIFTY
Beyond Stereotypes

June Burnham
POLITICIANS, BUREAUCRATS AND LEADERSHIP IN ORGANIZATIONS
Lessons from Regional Planning in France

Jean K. Chalaby
THE DE GAULLE PRESIDENCY AND THE MEDIA
Statism and Public Communications

Pepper D. Culpepper, Bruno Palier and Peter A. Hall *(editors)*
CHANGING FRANCE
The Politics that Markets Make

Gordon D. Cumming
FRENCH NGOs IN THE GLOBAL ERA
France's International Development Role

David Drake
FRENCH INTELLECTUALS AND POLITICS FROM THE DREYFUS
AFFAIR TO THE OCCUPATION

David Drake
INTELLECTUALS AND POLITICS IN POST-WAR FRANCE

Graeme Hayes
ENVIRONMENTAL PROTEST AND THE STATE IN FRANCE

David J. Howarth
THE FRENCH ROAD TO EUROPEAN MONETARY UNION

Andrew Knapp
PARTIES AND THE PARTY SYSTEM IN FRANCE
A Disconnected Democracy?

Michael S. Lewis-Beck (editor)
THE FRENCH VOTER
Before and After the 2002 Elections

John Loughlin
SUBNATIONAL GOVERNMENT
The French Experience

Mairi Maclean and Joseph Szarka
FRANCE ON THE WORLD STAGE

Mairi Maclean, Charles Harvey and Jon Press
BUSINESS ELITES AND CORPORATE GOVERNANCE IN FRANCE
AND THE UK

Susan Milner and Nick Parsons (editors)
REINVENTING FRANCE
State and Society in the Twenty-First Century

Gino G. Raymond
THE FRENCH COMMUNIST PARTY DURING THE FIFTH REPUBLIC
A Crisis of Leadership and Ideology

Sarah Waters
SOCIAL MOVEMENTS IN FRANCE
Towards a New Citizenship

Reuben Y. Wong
THE EUROPEANIZATION OF FRENCH FOREIGN POLICY
France and the EU in East Asia

French Politics, Society and Culture
Series Standing Order ISBN 978–0–333–80440–7 hardcover
Series Standing Order ISBN 978–0–333–80441–4 paperback
(outside North America only)

You can receive future titles in this series as they are published by placing a standing order. Please contact your bookseller or, in case of difficulty, write to us at the address below with your name and address, the title of the series and the ISBN quoted above.

Customer Services Department, Macmillan Distribution Ltd, Houndmills, Basingstoke, Hampshire RG21 6XS, England

---

Gender and Policy in France

Gill Allwood
Reader in Gender Politics, Nottingham Trent University, UK

and

Khursheed Wadia
Senior Research Fellow in Ethnic Relations, University of Warwick, UK

First published 2009 by
PALGRAVE MACMILLAN

Palgrave Macmillan in the UK is an imprint of Macmillan Publishers Limited, registered in England, company number 785998, of Houndmills, Basingstoke, Hampshire RG21 6XS.

Palgrave Macmillan in the US is a division of St Martin's Press LLC, 175 Fifth Avenue, New York, NY 10010.

Palgrave Macmillan is the global academic imprint of the above companies and has companies and representatives throughout the world.

Palgrave® and Macmillan® are registered trademarks in the United States, the United Kingdom, Europe and other countries.

ISBN 978–1–4039–9331–1   hardback

This book is printed on paper suitable for recycling and made from fully managed and sustained forest sources. Logging, pulping and manufacturing processes are expected to conform to the environmental regulations of the country of origin.

A catalogue record for this book is available from the British Library.

A catalog record for this book is available from the Library of Congress.

10 9 8 7 6 5 4 3 2 1
18 17 16 15 14 13 12 11 10 09

Printed and bound in Great Britain by
CPI Antony Rowe, Chippenham and Eastbourne

Contents

List of Tables

Acknowledgements

Many people have contributed in all sorts of ways to the completion of this book. We would like to thank in particular Robert Elgie for playing an essential role in the project; Amy Mazur for constant support, encouragement and advice; Joyce Outshoorn for making her research available to us and for advice and information; Jan Windebank for her enthusiastic support and encouragement for this project; Marina Della Guista and Vanessa Munro for all their feedback on prostitution; friends and colleagues at Nottingham Trent and Warwick Universities for seemingly unending patience and understanding; all the editorial staff at Palgrave who have been involved in this book; and, of course, Rustom, Zubin, Dave, Kristina, Caitlin and Ben.

Introduction

In 2007, nearly fifty years after the creation of the French Fifth Republic, Socialist Party candidate Ségolène Royal reached the second round of the presidential election, where she won almost 47 per cent of the vote. Although there have been other women presidential candidates (there were three others in this election, and Arlette Laguiller (Lutte Ouvrière) has stood in every presidential election since 1974), this was the first time that a major party with a serious chance of winning selected a woman candidate.

The relation between women and politics has been the subject of public debate in France since at least 1992, when the campaign for parity was launched by women in and close to the centre-left Socialist Party. Ten years earlier, France had been in the international spotlight when it instituted a Ministry for Women's Rights under Yvette Roudy. In fact there have been women's policy agencies in place since 1974, although their title, structure and remit have changed repeatedly over the years. In 2000, a law on parity was introduced, following a revision of the Constitution in 1999 in order for this to be possible.

However, policy is still made in male-dominated institutions. The 2001 law on contraception and abortion was debated in a Parliament consisting of 89 per cent men. The 2006 law on domestic violence was debated in a Parliament consisting of 87.7 per cent men (Observatoire de la Parité 2008). Men decided whether girls could wear the Islamic headscarf to school, whether and in what conditions women in France could terminate a pregnancy, and what measures would be taken to increase the proportion of women involved in making these decisions.

The relation between gender and policy is far more complex than whether or not women participate in decision-making. The equal participation of women in policy-making would not necessarily bring about gender equality. Firstly, gender equality has multiple meanings which can encompass equality with men, equal opportunities, recognition of gender differences, protection in pregnancy and motherhood, or social recognition of caring. It can mean equality for all women or differential equality according to class and ethnicity. Women do not constitute a homogeneous group. Inequalities based on gender intersect with other structural inequalities of ethnicity, class, age, physical ability etc., and the study of intersectionality is of growing interest to feminist policy analysts.

Secondly, there is inconclusive evidence that women in decision-making act in the interests of women (and again, would this mean all women or just some women?). However, there are no valid arguments *against* the equal participation of women in decision-making, which can be seen as necessary, but not sufficient.

Public policy

The study of public policy has changed considerably since its appearance as an academic discipline. With its origins in the policy-making world and sustained links with it, policy studies for a long time sought to identify and recommend the best policy solution to particular problems. Later, perspectives introduced from other areas of the social sciences produced a more critical strand of policy studies, within which it was recognised that there is no value-free objective analysis of policy problems and their solutions. Instead, it was argued that interested parties competed to insert their definition of the problem into the policy debate, giving leverage to their proposed solution.

Drawing on social movement theory, researchers have investigated how social movements strategically frame issues in ways most likely to achieve their goals. Non-governmental or civil society organisations make strategic decisions about how to frame issues in order to add legitimacy to their demands and motivate collective action. They do this by presenting a problem in such a way that their proposed solution appears logical and appropriate (Geddes and Guiraudon 2004: 335). Their success depends on the dynamic interaction of, on the one hand, the political opportunity structure, which refers to the accessibility of institutions, the support of influential allies, and changes in political alignments or conflict, and, on the other hand, the mobilising structure or network which these civil society actors have at their disposal, including the presence of organisational entrepreneurs, an international constituency, and relevant experts (Joachim 2002: 2). The political opportunity structure privileges certain frames and marginalises others. This explains why actors target the most favourable venue for their action (Geddes and Guiraudon 2004: 335).

Policy proposals are usually incremental. The study of social movements tells us that demands are most likely to result in policy output when there is a confluence of meaning between policy advocates and institutional decision-makers. NGOs are most likely to succeed when their frames resonate with those of their targets and become part of the political culture. Meanings are normally steeped in history, tradition and institutional convention. Occasionally a radical change will be made, but policies most likely to succeed are those which fit with current ideas and values (Baumgartner, Green-Pedersen et al. 2006: 963).

Policy-making: global context and influences

Any wide-ranging discussion on policy-making must consider the global context. As decision-making at the international level becomes more extensive and influential, national governments are compelled to respond appropriately or risk being left behind. Since the end of the Second World War when the United Nations and the Bretton Woods institutions (originally only the World Bank and the International Monetary Fund) were established, the majority of independent nation-states have recognised there are advantages in participating in negotiations relating to the maintenance of a stable international (market) economy and in making sure that any loss of sovereignty that necessarily follows from this is compensated by decisions going at least partly their way.

Global policy-making occurs for reasons similar to those related to national policy-making. Governments, in consultation with non-state policy actors, institute policies as a means of changing existing distributive and social outcomes of economic activity. So redistributive mechanisms are used to achieve a more equal sharing out of available resources (aid to poorer countries, fair trade agreements etc.); regulatory parameters are set to indicate the responsibilities and duties of private social actors (business and financial organisations); and laws are passed to guarantee citizens' human rights.

In the global context, intergovernmental organisations work alongside international NGOs (such as International Women's Rights Action Watch and social movements such as Women in Black) and transnational private sector organisations (TNCs such as Nestlé) and formulate policies to bring about social redistribution, regulation and social rights on a global level. Global policy is also aimed at shaping the limits and possibilities of national policy. Within this context national governments constitute the most powerful decision-makers but non-state actors also play an important role in policy formulation and decision-making on the global stage. The terms under which the categories of policy actors come together within international policy-making forums vary but traditionally among the non-state actors NGOs are the least powerful and therefore least likely to hold formal powers of decision-making despite their enormous growth in the past few decades.

Over the last three decades, global social policy has been viewed by many in a negative light as processes of globalisation, driven by neo-liberal ideology, have undermined the importance of international development, protecting the environment and human rights of the world's citizens. Critics of global policy have pointed to the increasing wealth gap between North and South, the political disenfranchisement of the world's poorer populations, the commodification of politics and cultures and the unfettered growth of powerful TNCs which place constraints on the choices that socially and politically progressive governments and citizens may wish to make. The thrust of global policy, it is argued, has been to brush aside equality-producing measures in favour of so-called economic efficiency and competitiveness. However, the neo-liberal agenda has not been implemented without opposition from policy actors within national governments, intergovernmental agencies and from NGOs and social movements. Arguably, the latter groups have had some campaigning success in advancing human rights and mitigating some of the most extreme effects of neo-liberal policies such as the structural adjustment programmes imposed on developing countries under a 'one cap fits all' approach. Past successes have included the debt reduction campaign waged by Jubilee 2000, Oxfam, Action Aid and others.

One of the ways in which global policy is formulated in favour of human rights, a more just redistribution of wealth and regulation of state and private sector activities is through goal-setting and strategising at international events such as UN summits. The UN Millennium Summit of 2000, followed up by the Millennium +5 Summit in 2005, brought together key groups of policy actors to look at priority areas in policy-making – the eradication of poverty and the advancement of democracy and human rights among them. The summit adopted a number of Millennium Development Goals (MDGs) including policies to 'promote gender equality and empower women' (MDG3). The aim was for all 191 member states to achieve the goals set by 2015. It is certain that the majority of countries will only have achieved a few of the MDGs by 2015 even though several agreements to spend billions of dollars on achieving the MDGs were signed in 2005. Commentators will of course continue arguing about the usefulness or otherwise of such summits in policy-making given that the outcomes are at best modest. On the other hand, national governments, IGO representatives, NGOs and private interests will continue to lobby at the UN and in other international forums (the World Trade Organisation's 'Doha Development' negotiations launched in 2001 or the OECD's multi-stakeholder forums which take place each year) for the respective policy goals and outcomes of their choice.

Another intergovernmental level at which policy-making is carried out is the European level, more specifically within the EU and its institutions and within the Council of Europe (CoE). The CoE was set up to promote and protect human rights and the rule of law in Europe. It engages closely with European non-state policy actors and with EU institutions to produce reports, recommendations and guidelines on human rights issues and regulates CoE member-state activities through rulings issued by the European Court of Human Rights. Policy-making in the EU is carried out through a co-decision procedure whereby both the Council of the European Union (i.e. Council of Ministers) and the European Parliament amend, adopt or reject legislation proposed by the Commission. EU policy is expressed through regulations and directives which are binding on member states, through opinions and recommendations which are not binding and through decisions which are binding on particular parties within member states. There has been much discussion about whether European policy-making should be regarded as an element of global policy-making or as a separate, even perhaps counter-process.

For some, globalisation and Europeanisation may be seen as part of the same process of pressures being exerted on national welfare states, whereas for others, Europeanisation is a distinct process which can act as a brake on the seemingly unstoppable processes of globalisation. So Snyder, for example, argues that:

> Europeanisation and globalisation are both friends and rivals. EU law is an expression, a means, and an outcome of Europeanisation. At the same time certain aspects of EU law . . . respond to and encourage the development of global economic networks, which are among the basic features of economic globalisation. EU law thus is an integral part of global economic networks. But these networks have contradictory effects on the EU and its member states, tending both to strengthen and to fragment and partly restructure them as political organisations and polities. Europeanisation and globalisation thus are complementary, partly overlapping, mutually reinforcing, but also competing processes. (Snyder 2000: 319)

However, Andrew Jackson (2001) separates Europeanisation and its expression in EU policies and law from globalisation as expressed by neo-liberal ideology and practice. Hence:

> Europe offers . . . an outline of a different model of regional economic integration. The social dimension of the European Union can be exaggerated, but the fact remains that the EU does set some minimum social standards, including regulation of health and safety conditions and working time, and a requirement for trans-national corporations to establish works councils. Diversity of social policy is respected and indeed still paramount, but some agreed social policy objectives have been set for the EU as a whole . . . Social policy at the EU level helps explain why downward harmonization has been limited, and why advocates of minimalist social welfare policy, such as Margaret Thatcher, have viewed the EU projet de société with such distaste.

Whether one regards globalisation and Europeanisation as part of the same process or two distinct processes, the fact is that France and other EU countries are subject to diverse, often conflicting external pressures related to policy-making. Sometimes such pressures reinforce national policy priorities and laws and other times run counter to them. Hence national policy-making is never a straightforward exercise but can resemble a minefield through which governments cautiously pick their way between domestic lobbies representing different interests and pressures exerted by IGOs and other international policy actors. In the chapters which follow, we have tried to highlight where relevant the influence of global and/or European policy on French governments and policy actors.

Policy-making and politics in France

The current French political system dates from 1958 and was designed to resolve the problems of the Fourth Republic, which had a weak executive and unstable multiparty coalitions. It is semi-presidential, and the power of the president increased with direct election in 1965 and has been exercised in increasingly presidential fashion in recent years. French public policy is often a product of elite decision-making, with bureaucrats playing a significant part, although this varies according to policy sector (Reuter and Mazur 2003: 53). Comparativists categorise the French policy style as strong, centralised and relatively closed (Elgie and Griggs 2000; Kriesi et al. 1995; Reuter and Mazur 2003). Kriesi et al. found that the strength of the formal institutional structure of the French state means that it is able to ignore social movements or respond proactively to them if the aims of the movement correspond with the policy aims of the government. Centralisation also limits access to decision-making. They found that the political and administrative response to social movement demands in France is exclusive, meaning that protest tends to be explosive and radical, since moderate action tends to be ineffective. They also found that certain political parties and trade unions can act as allies, so it makes a difference whether the left or the right is in power (Bell 2001: 189).

The idea of French specificity is also often evoked, along with Republicanism, universalism and anti-Americanism. We find such exceptionalism as there is in the centrality of the Republican discourse of universalism and the discourse of French exceptionalism itself, although this is overstated, and globalisation and Europeanisation are diminishing it yet more (Elgie and Griggs 2000: 183–4). The expanding remit of the EU has meant that it is increasingly difficult to ignore the relationship between national and EU policy-making (Elman 1996; Hoskyns 1996; White 2004).

Gender and policy

Feminist political scientists, political theorists, sociologists and social policy experts have, since the 1980s, sought to integrate gender into policy analysis. They draw on the mainstream literature, methods and concepts in the various disciplines, reflecting major trends in social science research. This has included, for example, the growing insistence that institutions matter, the reintegration of ideas and discourse into policy analysis, and concern with the relative impact on policy processes and output of social movements and policy environment. They have explored how and why feminist, equality, or women's policy is made (Elman 1996; Gardiner 1997; Lovenduski 1986); the interaction between feminist movements, women's policy agencies and public policy (Charles 2000; Mazur 2001; Outshoorn 1996; Stetson and Mazur 1995); and the relation between gender and the welfare state (O'Connor et al. 1999). There is, for example, a vast literature on women and political representation, which asks why women have been excluded from sites of political decision-making, whether and how they can be included, and what difference, if any, this would make. It finds that women are underrepresented in policy-making processes, and that this appears to make a difference to the decisions that are made (Mazey 2000: 336–7).

There is also a substantial literature on gender and welfare state regimes, which examines the relations between states, markets and families. It concerns, for example, employment, childcare, eldercare, benefits and entitlements. These studies are often comparative, producing typologies of welfare state regimes.

There is a substantial feminist policy studies literature which sees the policy-making process as a pattern of argument among policy actors over which problems deserve attention, how these problems should be defined, and what should be done about them (Stetson 2001: 4). It examines strategic framing processes, engaged in by women's movements, which define problems and solutions in a way that advances their goals (Joachim 2002: 15). The conflict over the meaning of the issue is central, and when a group sees its frame incorporated into the dominant frame, it gains a legitimate place in the policy process (Stetson 2001: 4). Feminist policy analysis has tended to focus on framing, examining the links between issue definition and access to policy-makers and investigating the influence of dominant policy frames on feminist attempts to insert their meanings into the debates (Mazur 2007: 189).

Feminists have studied women as collective actors attempting to influence policy outputs and gain access to the policy process. This includes the study of women's movements and feminist movements (Alvarez 1998; Beckwith 2000; Charles 2000; Lovenduski and Randall 1993; Molyneux 1998; Randall 1987; and Threlfall 1996) and the study of the institutional structures and processes they come up against (Gelb 1989; Hoskyns 1996; Lovenduski 1986). These structures and processes determine strategic action, privilege certain interests over others in terms of access and influence, and reflect and reinforce a particular policy frame or view of the world. In this way, they act as opportunities or obstacles to policy change. Actors gravitate towards the arenas most favourable to their cause and their policy frame (Mazey 2000: 339).

Some feminist scholars have focused on the ability of social movements and civil society organisations to influence the policy agenda. These studies have found that in order to achieve policy change, social movements must be anchored in effective mobilising structures or networks, they must have access to political institutions, and they must have support from powerful actors in formal decision-making structures (Mazey 2000: 340). Amy Mazur (2002: 4), for example, found that one of the most important conditions for the production of 'feminist policy' was 'the presence of a "strategic partnership" or "triangle of empowerment" between women in elected office, feminist/women's movements and organisations and women's policy offices in the development of a specific policy'. Mazey states that these findings help explain 'why most social movements (including feminism), which emerge as radical, oppositional movements, eventually acknowledge the need to participate in mainstream politics' (Mazey 2000: 340).

These studies have found that women engage with the state and affect its outputs, but that public policy is made in male-dominated institutions, and this makes a difference. Studies have sought to establish whether the exclusion of women from policy-making also excludes women's interests and women's issues. Joni Lovenduski finds that, 'although expectations of women representatives are unrealistic, the impact of feminists on public policy has actually been underestimated' (Lovenduski 2005a: 2). Catherine Hoskyns (1996: 10) states that, 'Virtually all public policy-making on women's issues takes place within structures that are male dominated, in the sense that they reflect male life-patterns, are largely controlled by men, and support a process which presents different but essentially male views of problems and solutions.' Hoskyns uses Schattschneider's term 'mobilisation of bias' to refer to the way in which this can exclude both women and women's issues. Male policy gender bias means that women may be disadvantaged by a policy; that policy initiatives to redress inequalities may be poorly funded or lack prestige; and that such issues may be marginal to or absent from the agenda. The presence of women would not necessarily bring about change, but women can play a significant role in promoting women's issues. Hoskyns distinguishes between 'system women' who identify with prevailing norms, 'lone women' who can exert considerable influence as a result of personal conviction and commitment, and 'supported women' who are part of networks inside and outside the formal system. Georgina Waylen argues that the state has mostly reinforced women's subordination, but is nevertheless a space in which the opportunity exists to bring about change. Within this framework, state feminism becomes a potentially effective tool (Waylen 2002: 8).

A major ten-year comparative research project was conducted by the Research Network on Gender, Politics and the State (RNGS) (1995–2005) to examine the role of women's policy agencies in producing women-friendly public policy. The study asked to what extent frames of policy debates have become gendered; whether these frames lead to policies that coincide with women's movement perspectives; and to what extent policy-making processes have expanded to include participation of women and women's movements (Stetson 2001: 5). The RNGS project found that, through their women's policy agencies (WPAs), states have offered institutional resources that help achieve feminist goals as presented by women's movements. Factors which favour state feminism include the presence in power of left-wing parties when there are links between these parties and the women's movements; coherence within the movement around their demands; and high agenda status within the movement for the issue in question. When these conditions are not present, women's policy agencies with feminist leaders can still intervene effectively. In the absence of effective women's policy agencies and a left-wing government, it is still possible for strong movements to have some impact, but only when policy subsystems are open or moderately closed, rather than closed (Stetson 2001: 295).

Feminist policy studies have also attempted to expose the deeply embedded assumptions about gender that are contained in policy proposals and debates, whether these policies are aimed specifically at women, deal with relations between men and women, or are ostensibly gender-neutral. Constructivists have looked at the impact of ideas, norms, knowledge and beliefs about gender upon politics and policy-making. Relations between men and women reflect and reinforce deeply embedded norms and assumptions. For example, the assumption that men are breadwinners and women are primary carers is present throughout politics and society and is responsible for a range of political and socio-economic inequalities. Policy proposals and debates rest on these assumptions (Mazey 2000: 337). As Jeff Hearn and Fiona McKie write, 'gender constructs policy, as policy constructs gender' (Hearn and McKie 2008: 75).

Gender equality policy and mainstreaming

Gender mainstreaming means incorporating gender at all stages of all public policy-making. It is an approach to gender equality which emerged from the area of women in development and was espoused initially by agencies associated with the UN, including UNESCO and UNDP, and later by the EU and some of its member states. The Commission first made a formal commitment to gender mainstreaming in 1996. The EU's Roadmap for Equality between Women and Men 2006–2010 'reaffirms the dual approach of gender equality based on gender mainstreaming and specific measures' (Commission of the European Communities 2006: 2).

Gender mainstreaming is not uncritically accepted by all feminists, not least because it has proven itself a highly malleable concept. Its potential lies in the way in which it forces policy-makers to consider gender at all stages and in all areas of policy-making. Feminist disagreements, however, are rooted in their fundamentally different views of what gender equality is and how to achieve it. Is the goal of feminism to achieve sameness with men, equality through difference, or to transform gender relations? (Walby 2005: 455–6). Is this best achieved through gender-neutral policy, gender differentiated policy, or gender mainstreaming, which in some interpretations, transcends this dichotomy? Equal treatment risks ignoring the realities of the different demands which are placed on women and men, particularly with regard to domestic labour and caring. Demands for different treatment, however, risk accentuating, legitimising and perpetuating these differences. Some argue that mainstreaming, by focusing on the gendered impact of policies, may offer a way out of the impasse which the difference debate has reached. However, while theoretically this may be the case, in practice mainstreaming is likely to prove difficult to implement and monitor (see Beveridge et al. 2000). For example, how should gender impact be assessed and how would it take into account differences between women? In an analysis of the impact of mainstreaming initiatives in the devolved institutions of Scotland, Wales and Northern Ireland, Beveridge et al. (2000) argue that 'if mainstreaming is to be effective, it must spearhead a radical reform of policy-making procedures and a radical reconfiguration of power relationships'.

Gender and policy in France

The study of gender and policy in France has focused to a large extent on the relation between gender and the welfare state, and, in particular, on family, employment and reconciliation (or work–life balance) policy. Major contributions have been made by authors in France and elsewhere, including Janine Mossuz-Lavau, Jane Jenson, Jacqueline Heinen, Jeanne Fagnani, Jan Windebank and Linda Hantrais. Recent studies of gender and policy in France have included those conducted as part of the RNGS project; Kimberley Morgan's excellent research on French childcare policy; Linda A. White's work on family and employment policy (White 2004); and Jan Windebank's many publications on women's employment and domestic labour.

France has international obligations on gender as a result of signing UN Conventions, including the Beijing Platform for Action and CEDAW. The requirement to submit data and periodical reports on progress towards the goals set in these Conventions has proved an important incentive in a country in which it has only recently become acceptable to collect disaggregated data.

France has low representation of women in Parliament, although higher representation in government. Elite women have played an important role in raising the profile of some issues, especially in the early years of Mitterrand's first presidency (1981–8) and during the Jospin governments 1997–2002. France has a long history of women's policy machinery which has played a role in much policy-making explicitly concerning women. There has been some kind of government department responsible for women's issues or women's rights since 1974. The status and title of the department and of the individual responsible for it have changed, as have its funding and potential influence on decision-making. The government department has at its service the administrative Service des Droits des Femmes which has a central office in Paris and a network of offices throughout the country. Two parliamentary delegations were created in 1999 in order to advise Parliament on issues relating to women's rights and to ensure the implementation of laws in the area. Interestingly, the composition of the delegations must not only be representative of the parliamentary political groups and permanent committees, but must also be made up of an equal number of women and men (République française 2006: 6). In addition, there is the Observatoire de la Parité, created in 1995 and responsible for commissioning, undertaking and publishing research on women's status, studying gender inequalities and obstacles to political, social and economic equality, and advising the government.

France has a strong and proudly defended tradition of universalism, which has played an important role in excluding women and women's movement issues from the public and political sphere. This has been achieved partly through the construction of the universal subject, identical to all other subjects and equal in rights. Elected representatives do not represent a social group or a constituency, but form part of the body intended to represent the interests of the nation as a whole. Their sex, ethnicity and other markers of social identity are deemed irrelevant to their ability to do this. The denial of the relevance of sex in the falsely gender-neutral republic makes it difficult for women's claims for representation to be heard and for policy debates and outputs to be gendered. Mazur writes, 'Ultimately, with its emphasis on universal citizen rights, universalism prevents gendered approaches to equality from being introduced in public policy' (Mazur 2001: 161). At the same time, this 'gender-neutral' universalism hides the gender-biased approach of many actors and the underlying assumptions about gender on which policy is built (Mazur 2004: 137). These include the assumption that women are primarily responsible for the family and are therefore expected to combine work with family life (Mazur 2001: 161). In equal employment policy, Reuter and Mazur claim that gender-biased universalism may be breaking down, not least because of the impact of the EU in this area (Reuter and Mazur 2003: 54). Also, the parity reforms of 1999 and 2000 introduced gendered approaches to equality on the basis of the argument that humanity is universally gendered and that representative bodies should reflect this (Scott 2005).

References to gender mainstreaming became systematic in documents produced by the various women's ministries or government departments and by the administrative Service des Droits des Femmes et de l'Egalité in 2000, with the first reference appearing in Nicole Péry's document outlining government action on gender equality, which was published on 8 March 2000 (Dauphin 2008: 142). Since 2001, a gender budget has been appended to the annual budget (Dauphin 2008: 146). This requires each government department to detail the actions and resources committed to gender equality. However, Dauphin points out that an appendix to the budget is not the same as gender mainstreaming the budget, which implies evaluating and adjusting all aspects of public income and expenditure to take into account the needs and priorities of women in the same way as those of men in order to attain gender equality (Dauphin 2008: 147). In 2004, an Equality Charter, presented to the Prime Minister by the Minister for Parity and Equality at Work was based on a commitment to a dual approach, combining, on the one hand, gender mainstreaming and, on the other hand, measures which target women specifically in order to address existing inequalities.

What does the book do?

This book is not about women as a stable group affected sometimes differently and sometimes similarly by policy outputs. It is about the relation between policy and gender, which is a construct created in part within, and by, policy debates and also reflected in them. Policy debates, proposals and decisions contain assumptions about gender. They reinforce, or less frequently, challenge notions of gender. Drawing on feminist post-positivist policy studies, we reject the idea that there are pre-existing problems 'out there' waiting to be solved by the application of the 'best' policy solution. Instead, we ascribe to the constructivist position that policy problems are constructed by the various actors in the policy debates and that the way in which they are constructed and the interactions between the various constructions are objects of study in their own right. This is not to say that policy debates are only constructs with no material effects. The impact of the constructs, the debates and the policies themselves is hugely important for individuals, particular groups, or society as a whole, and this is one of the central themes of this book.

This book explores the relations between gender and policy in France, by examining:

- the extent to which gender-motivated lobbies, including feminists, have tried to influence policy debates and outcomes;
- the role of the feminist movement, elite feminists and the women's policy machinery;
- the way in which issues are framed by the various actors involved;
- the gendered assumptions that underlie policy proposals and debates;
- the gendered impact of particular policies.

It takes six issue areas as case studies: employment, parity, abortion, prostitution, violence and headscarves. The chapters focus on specific policy proposals or debates. In each of the cases examined, we ask:

- who the main actors were;
- how they framed the issue;
- which solutions appeared acceptable, logical and effective, and which were excluded from the debate;
- how the issue was brought onto the political agenda;
- how the battle to control definitions played itself out;
- how the outcomes fitted with the original demands;
- what impact this has on constructions of gender and on women in France.

Focusing on major legal reforms or parliamentary debates does not tell the whole story about policy in each of these areas. Much of this is made at the local level, is remade and remodelled in day-to-day interactions, in implementation, in struggles over funding, resources and priorities. Some of the chapters will focus on these issues, but none of these case studies provides a comprehensive and conclusive analysis. Instead, each one illustrates a number of aspects of the relation between gender and policy and together they will enable us to draw a number of tentative conclusions.

The selection of the six issue areas enables us to explore a number of broader themes. French gender debates are embedded in a discourse of Republican universalism which denies the public and political relevance of all differences at the same time as it rests on a highly symbolic gender dichotomy. The headscarf debates provide an added complexity to the binary opposition of gender by requiring us to engage with the intersections of gender and ethnicity and by emphasising the impossibility of representing women as a homogeneous category. Abortion, as an issue which is clearly gendered in that it, like headscarves, affects only women, raises a specific set of questions about who has access to policy-making and who has the power to define the issue in an area which impacts directly on women's bodies. Violence and prostitution raise different questions, concerning the construction of gender in policy debates. Both of these issues can be defined as gendered or gender-neutral, and we examine the struggle around these definitions and the impact that these debates and the resulting policies have on real women's lives. The case studies also enable us to look at the relative influence of the international, regional (in this case EU), national and local on policy debates.

The link between normative debate and policy debates is not clear, and this is demonstrated in many of the case studies. For example, how can feminist ideas of gender justice be translated into effective public policy? Feminists could argue that it is not worth trying and could fundamentally reject the state and any idea of reform. However, many feminists have sought state reform or legislation, not necessarily as an alternative to revolution. Examples can be found in debates around parity, violence and abortion, amongst others. Feminists have found that it is not necessarily most effective to frame the issue in feminist terms (see Michel 2002) and that it can sometimes be more effective to remain in the shadows and allow other social actors to lobby on behalf of other interests. The danger, however, is that the results may be mixed, and feminists may end up in alliances with unlikely partners.

This book can be expected to show us something about:

- who makes policy;
- what opportunities there are for women and/or feminists to intervene in the policy process;
- how gender is constructed in policy debates;
- how women's issues and/or interests are excluded from or included in policy-making;

- how women are themselves excluded from or included in policy-making.

All of this takes place in a broader policy context that has political, social, economic and cultural elements. The complex mix of these factors has an influence on those issues that make it onto the policy agenda; the actors that succeed in inserting their frame into the policy debate; the decisions that result; and their implementation, successful or otherwise. Although it is usually impossible to determine the relative influence of any particular aspect of this complex mix, it is nevertheless important to try to sketch as detailed a picture as possible of the broader context in which policies are made and implemented. Part of this endeavour is to try to expose the opportunities and constraints for influencing policy.

The presence of a left- or right-wing majority is likely to be of relevance to gender and policy. Janine Mossuz-Lavau (2002: 409) reminds us, for example, that in France, eleven of the twelve major reforms between 1967 and 2001 related to sexuality were supported by left-wing groups in Parliament, and right-wing groups supported only two of them.

Why a single-country study?

Focusing on a single country enables us to provide a contextual richness which is difficult to achieve in comparative studies. We nevertheless draw on the work of comparativists, such as Kriesi et al. (1995), whose typologies are a useful starting point for understanding despite the limitations of these general theories (Charles 2000: 60; Waters 2003). A different comparative approach has been adopted by the RNGS project, which takes the policy debate, rather than the nation-state, as the object of study and constructs a comparative typology on this basis, thus avoiding over-generalised national stereotypes assumed to apply to all policy subsystems. It finds that differences are not consistently found between states, but cut across states according to the policy debate. It nevertheless finds some national characteristics, for example, in the case of France, the combination of Republican universalism and masculine gender bias and the high occurrence of symbolic reform.

By focusing on France, we can consider the similarities and differences across the six issue areas. These similarities and differences might derive from the relative influence of the international, European, national and local context; the political salience of the issue; public opinion; resource implications; relative strength or weakness of the state and civil society actors; and unintended consequences or issue perversion.

Limitations

It would clearly be impossible in a book of this length to investigate all possible aspects of the relation between gender and policy for each of the issues selected. Limits have had to be imposed, firstly, in terms of timescale. Even if we were only to outline briefly policies on a particular issue since, for example, the start of the Fifth Republic (1958), it would result in an unsatisfactorily superficial description with little room for analysis. We have chosen, therefore, to focus instead on particular debates, proposals or outcomes in each chapter in order to highlight specific aspects of gender and policy in France. The object of study is not just top-down decisions, but also bottom-up actions or interventions. This highly selective approach is necessary in order to produce any worthwhile analysis, but highlights the fact that much fruitful research remains to be done in these broad areas.

1
Women, Employment and Gender Equality Policy

Although women have made important advances in the labour market and the principle of equality between male and female workers has been established in the employment policies of successive French governments since 1946, gender inequalities in relation to rates and patterns of economic activity, salaries, job status, career advancement and work-time issues persist. A snapshot of female employment based on figures provided by the French Ministry of Employment, Social Relations and Solidarity shows that women workers are present in only 10 occupational clusters out of 86; they are amongst the lowest paid in the workforce; they are more likely to find themselves unemployed than men; they represent 80 per cent of the 3.2 million workers paid below the minimum wage; and they constitute 81 per cent of the part-time workforce (Ministère du Travail, des Relations Sociales et de la Solidarité 2007). However, it is not the intention, in this chapter, to explain the social relations and processes which give rise to such inequalities as such accounts have been provided elsewhere by scholars in France and the UK (see, for example, Cockburn 1991; Daune-Richard and Devreux 1992; Delphy 1998; Hirata and Rogerat 1988; Kergoat 1982, 1998, 2005; Windebank 1994; Windebank and Gregory 2000). What will be examined here is policy aimed at women in the labour market including policies designed to correct inequalities between male and female workers as well as those which intend or claim to 'protect' women's right to determine a balance between work and other aspects of life or a reconciliation which favours their interests. In doing so, we will focus on: the development of equal employment policies in France; the institutions and actors responsible for formulating and implementing such policies; and selected examples of 'gendered' policy and its expression in legislation. This chapter also examines aspects of what many would consider 'gender-neutral' employment policy and argues that all policy including that on employment is gendered.

Equal employment policy may be considered as policy which aims to dismantle hurdles faced by women in the labour market and the workplace so that they are able to participate on the same terms as men. Hence equal employment policy has to do with (equality) issues surrounding recruitment, wages, material working conditions, vocational training, career advancement, dismissal and lay-offs and bullying and (sexual) harassment. It also concerns issues of work and time, such as part-time employment, length of the working week, paid holiday time and rest periods. In other words, equal employment policy considers what are termed 'direct' rather than 'indirect' hurdles to women's equality in the labour market and workplace. Indirect hurdles consist of the practical constraints imposed on women in the home and family and of policies in spheres other than employment which impact on their capacity to participate equally with men in the world of waged work (Steinberg-Ratner 1980: 41–2). While it is crucial, from a feminist perspective, that equal employment policy-makers take account of the ways in which indirect hurdles, particularly non-employment policies (on taxation, benefits or childcare for instance), produce inequalities for women in the labour market and workplace, for feminist scholars of policy there are difficulties involved in trying to combine an analysis of direct and indirect hurdles to equal employment. The examination and analysis of indirect hurdles to women's full integration into the labour market and workplace can mean that there are too many issues and actors to consider and that focus on the direct hurdles to equal employment becomes diffuse. Besides, trying to include an analysis of indirect hurdles entails going beyond employment policy, into areas such as social welfare or childcare and early years education which will inevitably be covered more comprehensively elsewhere. For this reason, this chapter focuses on policy which addresses the direct hurdles women face in the labour market and workplace although indirect hurdles will be referred to where relevant. The examination of equal employment policy is preceded by an overview of women's participation in paid employment.

Women in paid work

French women's participation in the labour force has a long history. Several studies have documented this participation and its expansion over several generations from both historical (for example, Roux 1966;

Stewart 1989; Sullerot 1968; Toutain 1963) and contemporary perspectives (Batagliola 2004; Huet 1982; Maruani 1998, 2006, among others). While quantification of women's employment before the Second World War is problematic,[1] there is agreement among scholars that even when discounting the movement of women out of the agricultural sector (where they were not always counted) into the growing commercial and industrial sectors, their numbers in the labour force increased between the mid-nineteenth century and the beginning of the interwar period. Although the overall increase was unspectacular (from 34 per cent of the working population in 1851 to 36.1 per cent in 1921), it was in the non-agricultural sectors of the economy that women became most visible (INSEE 1995: 115). In 1856, women constituted 35.7 per cent of the non-agricultural labour force; this figure had increased to 48.5 per cent by 1906 before falling to 42.5 in 1921, 34.1 in 1936 and to an average of 35 per cent over the next thirty years (Roux 1966: 45). The increase in women's employment outside agriculture, in the second half of the eighteenth century and up to 1906, was due to rapid industrialisation, urbanisation and economic growth. During this period, women took up jobs in the textile and garment industry, retailing, handicrafts and the expanding white-collar sector. Conversely, the decline which started in the post-1918 period may be explained by the 1930s economic crisis which intensified sex discrimination practices against female workers and, after 1945, by the drive by successive governments to push women back into the domestic sphere in an attempt to reverse France's demographic shortfall. On the positive side, one may associate a proportion of the decrease in women's employment with increased access to education for girls and young women and earlier retirement opportunities for older women.

It was the late 1960s, however, which marked a real turning point in women's employment history and in the eight years following the events of May 1968, a million more women (baby-boomers for the most part), representing 75 per cent of the increase in the working population, became part of the labour force as they took up jobs in the light manufacturing, white-collar and professional sectors of the economy (Bard 2001: 216). By the end of the 1970s, women's overall representation in the working population had reached almost 40 per cent (INSEE 1995: 115). There are several reasons – economic and social – why this occurred. First, by the late 1950s, France had achieved stable economic growth with approximate annual increases of 3.5 per cent in productivity and 4.5 per cent in GNP (1950–1960) (Trotignant 1985: 436). The 1960s represented a decade of economic development unhindered by the financial difficulties of previous years and as the economy and job market expanded, particularly in the white-collar service sector, acute motivational problems occurred at the bottom of the employment pyramid. The most Taylorised jobs in disagreeable workplace conditions were left unfilled as they carried no status. In order to maintain productivity, employers recruited workers for whom earning any wage rather than position or role in the workplace hierarchy was of primary consideration and women (along with male migrant workers) filled this gap.

A second important reason relates to the sharp bifurcation of the French labour market in the 1960s. During this period, emerging industries in the primary economic sector (e.g. nuclear, petrochemical and oil refining), and to a lesser extent the heavy end of the secondary sector (aerospace, car and telecommunications), began to meet the demand for materials and goods through investment and use of fixed capital rather than labour, hence introducing semi-automated and automated techniques to generate productivity and expansion. This led to the creation of a capital-intensive sector in which specialist skills, knowledge and experience were well remunerated and where workers with sector or firm-specific expertise enjoyed stable employment conditions. The latter sector was distinct from a labour-intensive one (light manufacturing and services) in which low-paid, semi/unskilled jobs multiplied in response to the rising consumption of goods and services but which could be sharply reduced during periods of economic stagnation. Skilled French workers, of which the majority were male, rejected labour-intensive employment to secure jobs within the capital-intensive sector. The shortfall of workers within the labour-intensive sectors of the economy was made up by women first and labour migrants subsequently.

The economic factors which determined women's massive entry into the 1960s and 1970s labour force were accompanied by other significant social factors which produced a change in women's behaviour. The most notable of these were the democratisation of education and the influence of a thriving women's movement. The widening of access to education, raising of the school leaving age from 14 to 16 years and the establishment of mixed secondary schooling led to greater numbers of girls and young women succeeding at school, progressing to further and higher education, attaining better qualifications and consequently wanting to establish a career (see Baudelot and Establet 1992; Duru-Bellat 1990; Ourliac 1988; Terrail 1992a, 1992b). Furthermore, women's growing ambitions to participate in post-secondary education and training were fuelled by a women's movement whose ideas, campaigning militancy and slogans became more resounding and visible as the 1970s progressed (see Duchen 1986; Picq 1993; Rémy 1990 for the development and impact of the MLF – Mouvement de Libération des Femmes). Not only did women, particularly those married with children, wish to fulfil aspirations of upward mobility through work, but for many work also represented a means of independence, an escape from the humdrum of domestic life and a path towards the achievement of equality with men. In the 1970s, women began to make inroads into salaried professions, in particular teaching and research, medical science, the legal system, journalism and the civil service.

A final contributory factor in the growth of women's employment during the 1960s and 1970s which warrants mention is that of immigration into France. Early postwar immigration, from Southern Europe and North Africa (France's ex-colonies), was composed mainly of men. However, family immigration[2] became favoured government policy from the mid-1960s as concern over declining births persisted. The application of family immigration policy coupled with an unofficial policy of cultural preference,[3] meant that large numbers of Spanish and Portuguese families arrived in France throughout the 1960s. For instance, Portuguese migrants (the fastest growing group of newcomers) constituted only 2 per cent of the total immigrant population in 1962 but went on to make up 8.8 per cent in 1968 and 16.9 in 1975 (INSEE 1997: 19). While 27 per cent of Portuguese immigration into France was due to family immigration (ibid.: 27), hence consisting mainly of women, a sizeable number of those who came to find work were also women. The population of Spanish immigrants also expanded between 1962 and 1968 with 37 per cent of the increase attributable to family immigration, that is, women and minors, but Spanish women accompanying husbands also entered the labour market in large numbers once they were settled. Finally, the character of North African and other non-European immigration to France before 1975 remained overwhelmingly male and the proportion of non-European women (particularly those from France's ex-colonies) only increased significantly after 1975 when labour immigration from non-European countries was halted and family reunification became the primary type of immigration. This remained the case until the late 1980s when it was overtaken by refugee immigration. The feminisation of the immigrant population in France, since the mid-1970s (from 38.2 per cent in 1962 to 40.1 in 1975 and 48 per cent in 1999), has meant that increasing numbers of immigrant women have entered the world of work, overwhelmingly at the bottom end of the labour market (Chaib 2001: 4). For example, between 1990 and 1999, an increase of 121 per cent was recorded in jobs related to childcare and 361 per cent in the small and medium-sized retail sector. Much of the demand for care and low-level retail work has been met by women from migrant backgrounds (Bezat 2001; see also Condon 2000; Merckling 2000; Samir et al. 2002 on the history of immigrant women and employment in France).

Since the 1970s the growing representation of women in the workforce has become an unstoppable phenomenon. By 1979 women constituted 39.7 per cent of the working population. This figure rose to 42.5 per cent in 1988, 44.7 in 1994 and 46.7 in 2005 (INSEE 1995: 115; 2006). While the proportion of women in the working population is now similar to that in other major EU states, France has always exceeded the European (EC/EU) average. In 2008, only Sweden, Finland, Denmark and the East/Central European countries which joined the EU after May 2004 had a higher proportion of women in their respective working populations.

Equal employment policy: development and institutional architecture

Development

Employment policy-making in relation to women may be traced back to the nineteenth century, referred to as the 'siècle de l'ouvrière' (century of the working-[class] woman) due to the fact that record numbers of women took up paid work in the industrial sector. The large presence of women in the most poorly paid, dead-end jobs captured the attention of nineteenth-century feminists and social reformers who sought to raise public awareness of the situation of this new urban class of working women. For example Julie-Victoire Daubié's work, *La Femme pauvre au XIX siècle* (see Thiercé, 1999), which caused controversy amongst social commentators and economists, catalogued and analysed the working life of women in factories and workshops and called for measures (for example, equal pay for equal work, professional training) to lift these women out of exploitation and poverty. Alongside advocates such as Daubié, working women spoke out for themselves and made radical claims during the revolutionary upheavals of 1830, 1848 and 1870 for equal citizenship with men. These claims concerned rights accruing to the status of worker which have formed an essential component of the French Republican model of citizenship since 1789.

The state's response to such claims was ambiguous given the deep divisions in public and political opinion over women's status as workers. In order to be seen to take issues of women's employment seriously while at the same time wishing to deflect attention away from substantive claims to equal citizenship and concomitant employment rights, the state responded by placing an emphasis on protecting women from long working hours and from unhealthy and hazardous working conditions. Under the mantle of this protectionist logic, employment legislation passed in the late 1800s and early twentieth century, in relation to women, included a ban on working in mines (1874), on night work (1892) and limiting the working day to ten hours (1900). Although certain rights were conceded due to mounting pressure from socialist feminists and a labour movement growing in confidence – the right to take up to eight weeks of unpaid maternity leave (1909); to control their pay packets without interference from husbands (1907); and to participate in works council (Conseil du Travail) elections (1901) – highly paternalistic attitudes prevailed among policy- and law-makers.

A disruption, albeit brief, of protectionist logic in employment policy occurred as a result of the First World War during which time women 'served the nation' by working in sectors that were key to the war effort and hence the survival of France. Their increased visibility as public-spirited workers and citizens coupled with various strike actions calling for their participation to be recognised meant that the state was compelled to treat them as independent, legal beings in their own right. The early interwar period saw women gain further rights such as the right to join a trade union without husbands' consent (1920) and the right to equal pay for female teachers (1927). However, the economic depression in France and the rest of the industrialised West which followed the boom and bust cycles of the 1920s brought with it a reassertion of protectionist logic (reflected in laws on social security benefits including family allowances) encouraging women to return to the 'safety' of hearth and home and measures designed to keep them out of the labour market (for example, a bar on certain types of civil service entrance exams and posts). This logic persisted throughout the 1930s, up until the outbreak of the Second World War.

The early years of the war saw an intensification of protectionist logic, expressed in official ideology and discourse as defence of the family in the interests of the nation. The Vichy regime promoted measures and enacted laws designed to (re)assign the 'natural vocation' of wife and mother to women. An entire institutional framework was put in place to formulate and implement measures (the development of family allowances and incentives for large families and nursing mothers, the extension of maternal salary to single mothers and so on) in support of the family. Although there are few if any reliable statistics available on women's employment during the war, there is little doubt that these policies would have had the desired effect of pushing more women into the home and thereby reducing female participation in the labour force. For example, in 1940, 19,000 women were laid off in the post and communications sector alone (Bard 2001: 234). However, the striking gap between the extreme family ideology of the state and the reality of labour market shortages created by the absence of an estimated 1.5 million men meant that after 1942, women in occupied France were called back to work in certain key sectors of the economy, notably post and communications. However, this call for women to take up work in the war economy did nothing to weaken the state's targeting of family-first policies towards them, and the return of full male employment during the first 25 years of the postwar era meant that women failed to become part of the 'standard employment' model (predicated on the male worker, employed full-time by the large company) in spite of constitutional recognition, in 1946, of the principle that women were citizens equal to men and legislation, in the same year, that provided for equal pay for equal work (see Table 1.1). In fact, at the same time as women and men were declared equal citizens, the postwar welfare state consolidated pre-1945 systems of family allowances thus ensuring that gendered divisions of labour within the family were maintained. Throughout the 1950s and until the mid-1960s, successive French governments deemed that the need for labour power and reproductive power, in reconstructing French society and economy, would be met respectively by men and women.

It was only in the 1970s after the challenges posed by the events of May 1968 and the development of a highly visible and dissenting women's movement (Mouvement de Libération des Femmes) that a programme of liberal socio-political reform began to formally address policies motivated by a women's rights logic and which promoted equality in employment between men and women. Starting with the Equal Pay Act of December 1972, various laws passed during the 1970s under the presidency of Giscard d'Estaing and under the Socialist presidency of Mitterrand in the 1980s were aimed at preventing discrimination against women in processes of recruitment and dismissal, training and promotion and in relation to paid maternity leave (see Table 1.1). However, even the most 'feminist' of laws during this period, driven by the Socialist Ministry for Women's Rights under Yvette Roudy, had a limited impact on the working life of the majority of women because state funding of equal employment initiatives amounted to a paltry fraction of the total employment budget at any given time and also because the radical Socialist programme announced by Pierre Mauroy's first government in 1981 was weakened progressively after 1983 and eventually jettisoned during the premiership of Laurent Fabius.[4] Consequently, the state agencies responsible for implementing these laws were neither effective nor willing to make recalcitrant employers fulfil their legal obligations towards their female employees.

By the early 1990s, the French Socialist government had decided unambiguously to adapt socialism to the market economy. This decision, followed by the return of the right to power in 1993,[5] had a significant effect on public policy generally and a particularly damaging one on equal employment policy which endured throughout this decade. The so-called 'neutral' (as opposed to women's rights) approach to policy-making that was adopted marked a setback for women's employment rights. The only 'feminist' legislation relating to women and work, passed in the 1990s, was the sexual harassment law (see Table 1.1), seen by its supporters as a further step in the advancement of women's workplace rights. However, as it stood, the law was criticised by many women's rights activists and scholars for submitting to a very narrow definition of sexual harassment which detracted from the notion of sexual harassment as sexual discrimination (see Louis, 1999; Saguy, 2000, 2003).

Policies which had a deleterious effect on women's employment status and conditions were guided by two objectives. The first was the reduction of employment costs while the second was the promotion of 'reconciliation of work and family life' (*conciliation travail et famille*) or 'work–life balance' as it later came to be known (*articulation vie familiale–vie professionnelle*).[6] First, policies to reduce employment and other costs by governments of both the left and the right were motivated by the triumph of neo-liberalism in many of the world's major economies (USA, UK, Japan, Germany) leading to market deregulation, the progressive retreat of the state from the social-welfare sphere and economy and to huge cost-cutting operations by large companies in the name of modernisation and competitiveness. Second, the focus on 'work–life balance' policies from the 1990s onwards stemmed from EU employment strategy which, at its inception in the 1970s, aimed at an equal redistribution of domestic duties and workload between men and women but which developed into a strategy concerned with encouraging women, rather than men, to combine work and family commitments efficiently (for a detailed account of the evolution of the concept of work–life balance and its incorporation into EU employment policy-making, see Stratigaki 2004). During the 1990s, the EU objective of achieving a work–life balance increasingly shielded the cost-cutting objectives of French employers, supported by government, through the introduction of part-time[7] and other 'flexible' forms of labour. Government justification for atypical work was that it would meet women's social demand ('demande sociale des femmes') for a better balance between family and working life and that at the same time it would reduce unemployment amongst women, young people and other economically vulnerable groups in French society. The 1990s were marked by a protectionist logic in policy-making and the downplaying of women's equal rights. The importance placed by the state on protecting the family was also reinforced through a raft of measures put in place by the 1994 Family Law which boosted family income and support for home-based childcare arrangements through increased social security allowances.

The 2000s may be described as a decade in which a certain equal rights/opportunities dynamic has developed within the framework of parity equality, beginning with the left's return to power in 1997. The Jospin government (1997–2002) launched a series of initiatives including revision of the Constitution in 1999 to integrate the principle of gender parity in political representation, followed by the Parity Law of 2000, a reactivation of the 1983 Roudy Law in 2001 (Génisson Law – see Table 1.1) and the commissioning of numerous reports on equality including equal employment (Génisson 1999). This 'return' to equal opportunities and rights at the start of the decade reflected in part the desire of Lionel Jospin to present himself and his government as revivers of a Socialist project that was ditched in 1983/4. It is also indicative of the right's acceptance from 2002 onwards of the parity approach and discourse which encompasses certain notions of equal rights and opportunities for women, which coincided well with the shift in the EU's gender equality strategy from one of positive discrimination in the 1980s and 1990s to the more amenable one of mainstreaming.[8] However, apart from the brief years of the Ministry for Women's Rights in the 1980s, no French government has been willing to decouple issues of women's position and role in the economy and society from that of their relationship with home and family, and French government in the 2000s has been no different in this respect. So the acceptance of parity principles and discourses, by recent governments of the right, has been strongly tempered by a continued emphasis on protecting children, hearth and home through the consolidation of work–life balance policies. The Ameline Law of 2006 demonstrates this contradiction perfectly (see Table 1.1 and discussion of the law further on).

The necessary overview of women's employment and equal employment policy above shows that a number of social, economic and political factors, not all of which have been mentioned here, have influenced

Table 1.1 Equal employment legislation 1945–2006

Date	Key components
1946	• Croizat Decree abolishes lower rates of pay for women and introduces principle of equal pay for equal (same) work. Lifting of restrictions on public sector jobs. Certain functions excepted for 'service reasons'.
1966	• Law allowing women to undertake paid work without husband's consent. Law prohibiting employers from dismissing women for reasons of pregnancy up to 12 weeks after delivery date.
1971	• Introduction of maternity pay to the value of 90 per cent of gross salary.
1972	• Legal establishment of the principle 'equal pay for work of equal value' although 'equal value' remains undefined.
1975	• Law against sex discrimination in job recruitment except on 'legitimate grounds'.
1977	• Introduction of parental leave for women employed in private sector firms of over 200 employees.
1979	• Partial revocation of law on night work for women occupying managerial, supervisory and highly specialised posts.
1983	• Roudy Law on equal employment defines work of 'equal value'; places the burden of proof in pay discrimination cases on the employer so that the latter must justify pay differentials deemed discriminatory; requires employers to provide essential social and economic/financial information to a company's works council in order to promote principles of fairness and equal employment into collective bargaining; introduces principle of positive action, derived from the 1976 European Community directive on equal treatment of men and women.
1987	• Further lifting of restrictions on night work for women.
1989	• Law encouraging employers to introduce or reinforce catch-up measures for women workers.
1992	• Law on sexual harassment.
1994	• Extension of parental leave to women part-timers in the public sector.
2001	• Génisson Law reinforcing certain provisions of the 1983 Roudy Law. Total revocation of ban on night work for women in all sectors including industry.
2006	• Ameline Law on equal employment sets up a framework of compulsory negotiations in order to eliminate the gender pay gap by 31 December 2010. Further, it contains measures to promote a better work–life balance. In addition, it incorporates: the EU directive on workplace discrimination where the 'burden of proof' in (direct or indirect) sex-discrimination cases rests with the employer accused of discrimination; strengthens entitlement to maternity leave; and aims to promote women's access to all jobs, apprenticeships and in-service vocational training.

equal employment policy-making and legislation in France. Among the most important of these are: the growth in women's labour force participation from the late 1960s onwards; the emergence and growth of the women's movement from the mid-1960s to the late 1970s; the evolution of parts of this movement into state feminism[9] as symbolised by the Ministry for Women's Rights, during the 1980s; and the development of a policy and legal framework for equal employment at EU level from the 1990s onwards.[10] While these conjunctural factors have given rise to various initiatives and pieces of legislation in relation to women's employment between 1945 and 2006 (see Table 1.1), a constant tension between protectionist attitudes and an equal rights-based approach, or what Commaille (1993) and others (Morgan 2003) have characterised as *politique familialiste vs. politique féministe*, has underpinned French equal employment policy-making. French public policy has sought to improve the status of women while at the same time preserving women's capacity to reproduce and provide care. This two-pronged approach has been characterised at times by a positive attitude (deriving from feminist ideology) towards equality between women and men in the labour market but also by the resolve (reflecting familialist ideology) to maintain gender divisions in the labour market through an ongoing affirmation that women's presence in the private/domestic sphere is essential for the continuation of the family, considered as the foundation stone of French society and symbolic of a stable political order since the Revolution. Familialist ideology has been reinforced by recurrent concern since the 1800s over demographic decline and measures designed to boost birth rates have contributed to familialist policy. On the other hand, feminist arguments in favour of equal employment have been helped by the admission of policy-makers that women's employment is a contributory factor of economic growth. However, it is the combination of social, economic and political conjunctures that constitutes a powerful context for the orientation of policy towards either more familialist or feminist goals at any given time.

Institutional architecture

Table 1.2 presents a profile of institutions located at central state level with responsibility for issues of women's employment in France. These institutions may be placed into one of two main categories: consultative structures and ministerial structures. Consultative structures have included the Comité du Travail Féminin (CTF) which replaced the Comité d'Etude et de Liaison des Problèmes du Travail Féminin (CETF) in 1971 and was superseded by the Conseil Supérieur de l'Egalité Professionnelle (CSEP), created under the Roudy Law of 1983. In addition, the Observatoire de la Parité (OP) was established in 1995.

Consultative structures: the CETF, the CTF and the CSEP

The CETF was set up as a standing research and advisory group and included among its prime movers equal rights feminists such as Madeleine Guilbert, Communist Party activist and sociologist; Jeannette Laot and Chantal Rogerat, both sociologists and prominent trade unionists belonging, respectively, to the Socialist-affiliated CFDT (Confédération Française Démocratique du Travail) and the Communist CGT (Confédération Générale du Travail); and Marcelle Devaud, a well-connected Gaullist who had held parliamentary and mayoral mandates prior to 1965. It was because of Devaud's association with the then Secretary of State for Employment, Gilbert Grandval, that the CETF was established within his department. Although the CETF produced an impressive number of studies and organised various meetings and conferences around the theme of inequalities between women and men in employment and despite official acknowledgement of its lobbying and advisory role within government, its policy recommendations were ignored by ministers and senior civil servants. Its establishment immediately after the presidential elections of 1965, the first by direct universal suffrage and in which de Gaulle emerged victor in the second round by a modest 55.2 per cent of the vote, indicates that it had never been regarded as more than a token gesture to women voters who, according to electoral soundings, had contributed largely to the high abstention rate. Its insignificance in the government's view was also confirmed by the fact that it was not given funds or office staff.

However, by 1971, and following ever-growing feminist demands for equality and freedom, Devaud had managed to persuade government ministers that the CETF should be supported by concrete resources. It was therefore elevated to committee status, given a budget and office staff. For the following three years the CTF continued to publish reports on various equal employment issues including recruitment, training, pay and state childcare provision. It was also used increasingly by equal rights feminists in the trade unions and old-style women's associations to channel through demands for equal pay to government. The CTF had few if any connections with the newer feminist groups which made up the MLF. In 1974, the creation of a new Secrétariat d'Etat à la Condition Féminine under Françoise Giroud marked the beginning of the decline of the CTF. Although technically the CTF was consulted by government over measures contained within the Seventh Economic Plan (1976–1980) to lessen social tensions through the reduction of income inequalities and job hierarchies, Giroud herself was far more interested in courting some of the newer women's groups and activists of the MLF. During the 1970s, the CTF was either systematically sidelined by Giroud or ignored due to the indifference of Pasquier and Nonon. In 1983, it was finally broken up by Yvette Roudy, the Minister for Women's Rights, who preferred working on issues of equal employment and commissioning studies through her personal contacts in the CFDT and the Socialist Party.[11]

The end of the CTF in 1983 made way for the founding of the CSEP and its administrative wing the Mission d'Egalité Professionnelle (MEP), later to be replaced by staff from the Service des Droits des Femmes et de l'Egalité (SDFE). The CSEP has had a stop-start history as a result of several government changeovers during the 1980s and 1990s. Its first phase of operation lasted from 1983 until 1986. During this time it took over the CTF's research functions and acquired the role of implementing government equal employment policy. However, when the Socialists lost the 1986 legislative elections, the CSEP was left to collapse by the new Chirac government. It disintegrated easily because it had essentially worked as a relay belt for Roudy's ideas and actions and when the new government abolished the Ministry for Women's Rights, the CSEP found it stood for little else. Women's affairs were delegated to Hélène Gisserot. Although the CSEP was revived between 1988 and 1993, on the return of the Socialists to government, it served merely as a talking shop and met with increasing irregularity. Over the following ten years, the CSEP continued its existence but fulfilled very little purpose even under the Socialist government of Lionel Jospin (1997–2002) whose equal rights agenda was dominated by the issue of gender parity in elected assemblies. In any case, by 1995, a new consultative body – the Observatoire de la Parité (OP) – had been created under Prime Minister Juppé.

The Observatoire de la Parité

The OP was set up in 1995, following the presidential elections of that year and promises made by the main candidates to set up an official body, as recommended by parity campaigners, to monitor the implementation of gender equality measures, produce studies and make policy recommendations. Headed by a *rapporteur(e)*, the OP's membership which originally comprised 18 'experts' and expanded to include 33, works in three commissions in charge of: parity in political institutions; parity in the social, economic and private domains; and raising public awareness of parity issues and the production of studies on equality between women and men in France and beyond. While the OP is better off than previous government research and advisory bodies on gender equality, it is still relatively poorly funded and staffed and has not met expectations or impacted meaningfully on equal opportunities and rights.

Ministerial structures

The brief for women's status and rights has been given to various types of ministerial officeholders, over the past four decades, ranging in importance from ministre,[12] to ministre délégué,[13] to secrétaire d'état,[14] down to the simple délégation.[15] However, on a number of occasions in the 1990s and 2000s, women's status and rights have become part of the general responsibility of particular government departments (such as the present Ministère du Travail, des Relations Sociales et de la Solidarité) rather than being allocated to a discrete departmental structure (see Table 1.2).

The position, within the hierarchy of government, of a particular ministerial structure responsible for women's affairs has not necessarily influenced the capacity of the politicians and civil servants working within it to advance women's position and employment and other rights. So, for example, Nicole Pasquier's Délégation à la Condition Féminine (1976–8) had less clout than did the same type of structure headed by Hélène Gisserot (1986–8). This may be explained by the fact that Pasquier seemed distinctly less interested in women's issues than Gisserot which in turn impacted on the level of resources that each of these leaders could garner and how much influence they could exert on ministerial colleagues in other government departments. Pasquier was given a small budget and her office was moved to Lyon, away from the corridors of power, but she was also mocked for being a government stooge and not having any opinions on women's rights and feminism (see Storti 1976 and editorial in the Trotskyist *Rouge* 1976). Gisserot, on the other hand, benefited from being located in Paris and having a bigger budget but it was also recognised that she punched above her weight.

As is to be expected, a factor which has influenced the capacity of any given structure to improve women's position and opportunities in employment and other domains is resourcing. The majority of ministerial structures responsible for women's status or rights have consisted of small cabinet offices with few administrative resources. The exception to this was the Ministry for Women's Rights which, in 1981, received a budget of 94.28 million francs and a staff of 5,000. Although the MDF's finances amounted to next to nothing (0.025 per cent) as a proportion of the government's overall budget (Duchen 1986: 128) and were modest even in comparison with those of other smaller government departments, Roudy had a spending power that was far in excess of anything her predecessors had known. The resources put at her disposal coupled with Roudy's personal reputation as a strong champion of women's rights meant that despite certain policy failures (see below), Roudy and the MDF succeeded in promoting other equal employment measures, such as the piloting of training schemes and access courses for women in information technology, electronics and other career fields from which women were largely absent.

As far as the administration of women's affairs is concerned, one of the legacies of Michèle André's term as Secrétaire d'Etat aux Droits des Femmes was the reorganisation of administrative services at central government level for the resourcing of women's affairs which led to the establishment of the Services des Droits des Femmes in 1990 (later Services des Droits des Femmes et de l'Egalité). However, the way in which the SDFE has been conceived has been more helpful to those dealing with women's employment rights issues than to those responsible for delivering on social and individual rights.

Finally, a factor which indicates the approach of different governments to questions of women's status and rights relates to the titles given to structures responsible for women's affairs. It is possible to pick out a naming pattern between 1974 and 2002 where the right has tended to use the term 'condition féminine' or women's status to describe the work of ministerial structures dealing with women's affairs (including employment) while the left has preferred 'droits des femmes' or women's rights. It may be argued that women's rights have to be fought for and won in order to achieve an improvement in women's status. Thus the term 'women's rights' suggests the need for action which is contestatory and which fits in with the political culture of the left but which is eschewed by the right. The term 'women's status' on the other hand carries no connotation about the nature of action to be taken and suggests perhaps that changes in women's status will occur through the gradual evolution of mentalities – an approach traditionally favoured by the right. Since 2002, however, governments of the right have favoured the term 'parity' to cover equal employment and other equal opportunity and rights initiatives in respect of women because it can be presented as a French concept rather than one that belongs to left or right and at the same time serves as a useful (French) alternative to the English term 'gender mainstreaming' used throughout the EU. One last comment in relation to the naming of structures relates to the linking of women's issues (mainly by the right) with those of family (1980–1), consumer affairs (1992–3) and social cohesion (2005–7) among others. The fact that the women's affairs brief has been slotted into various structures with so many different types of issues indicates its relative unimportance in government agendas.

Table 1.2 Institutional architecture

Structure	Dates	Type	Remit and priorities	Composition
1. Comité d'Etude et de Liaison des problèmes du Travail Féminin (CETF) *Headed by:* *Marcelle Devaud*	1965–1971	Research and advisory group reporting to the Secretary of State for Employment.	Production of studies on women's employment including recommendations on equal employment policy.	State, women's organisation and trade union representatives; special advisers.
2. Comité du Travail Féminin (CTF) *Headed by:* *Claude du Granrut*	1971–1983	Research and advisory committee reporting to the Secretary of State for Employment.	Raise awareness of issues related to women's employment and formulate equal employment policy recommendations.	State, trade union and management representatives, and four to five permanent administrative staff members.
3. Secrétariat d'Etat à la Condition Féminine *Headed by:* *Françoise Giroud*	1974–1976	Political office reporting to the Prime Minister.	Identify and recommend policies to improve women's status in French society, as encompassed in the Giroud report *Cent mesures pour les femmes* (1976).	Small cabinet office[16] including the minister in charge, a few senior civil servants and personally known collaborators/advisers called upon when required.
4. Délégation à la Condition Féminine *Headed by:* *• Nicole Pasquier* *• Jacqueline Nonon*	1976–1978	Political office (based in Lyon) reporting to the Prime Minister.	As above.	As above.

5. Secrétariat d'Etat à l'Emploi Féminin *Headed by:* *Nicole Pasquier*	1978–1981	Political office reporting to the Secretary of State for Employment.	Raise awareness of women's employment situation and promote equal employment policy.	As above.
6. Ministère Délégué à la Condition Féminine *Headed by:* *Monique Pelletier*	1978–1980	Political office reporting to the Prime Minister.	Raise awareness of women's position and promote the advancement of women's status alongside family values.	As above.
7. Ministère Délégué à la Famille et Condition Féminine *Headed by:* *Monique Pelletier*	1980–1981	Political office reporting to the Prime Minister.	Raise awareness of and promote advancement of women in society. Promote pro-natalist and family policies.	As above.
8. Ministère Délégué aux Droits de la Femme *Headed by:* *Yvette Roudy*	1981–1985	Junior ministry reporting to the Prime Minister.	Raise awareness of women's rights as separate from those of the family. Formulate and implement equal employment and other equality policies and legislation to improve women's position in society.	Cabinet office including the minister in charge, a number of collaborators/advisers and administrative (civil service) staff.

(*Continued*)

Table 1.2 (Continued)

Structure	Dates	Type	Remit and priorities	Composition
9. Conseil Supérieur de l'Egalité Professionnelle (CSEP) *Convened by minister in office of women's rights*	1983– 1986 1988– 1993 2003–	Consultative body reporting to various government departments over the period of its existence.	To monitor implementation of the 1983 Roudy Law and successive equal employment policies; recommend equal employment policy; advise on the Code du Travail;[17] commission research and studies aimed at progressing equal employment policies.	Ministers, trade union, employers' and women's organisation representatives; office staff drawn from the Mission d'Egalité Professionnelle and later from the Service des Droits des Femmes.
10. Ministère des Droits de la Femme (MDF) *Headed by:* *Yvette Roudy*	1985– 1986	Government department.	Legislate in favour of women's rights, particularly in the area of equal employment rights, and ensure that legislation is applied. Institutionalise feminist ideas and principles within state structures in order to combat sexism in society.	Cabinet office including the minister in charge, political collaborators/advisers and administrative staff at central, regional and departmental levels.
11. Délégation à la Condition Féminine *Headed by:* *Hélène Gisserot*	1986– 1988	Political office reporting to the Prime Minister.	Promote and protect the status and 'double mission' of *mères de famille* as key agents in the production process and in the family.	Small cabinet office including the minister in charge, some advisers and clerical/administrative assistants.

12. Secrétariat d'Etat aux Droits des Femmes *Headed by:* *Michèle André*	1988–1991	Political office reporting to the Prime Minister.	Promote work and family strategies in order to improve equal opportunities for women in society generally and in the workplace.	As above.
13. Service des Droits des Femmes/Service des Droits des Femmes et de l'Egalité (SDFE)	1990–	Equality and women's rights central administrative services office reporting to the ministry or ministries under whose authority it is placed.	Implement measures to correct gender-based inequalities and promote policies aimed at achieving equality between women and men in decision-making processes and in all domains of public life. However, emphasis is placed on equal employment policy and issues.	Central administrative service comprising two policy sections: equal employment; women's individual social rights. It also included a communications section, a human resources and general affairs staff and administrative offices at regional and departmental levels.
14. Secrétariat d'Etat aux Droits des Femmes et à la Vie Quotidienne *Headed by:* *Véronique Neiertz*	1991–1992	Political office reporting to the Secretary of State for Employment.	Promote strategies to help women and men achieve a better work–life balance and to increase women's equal employment prospects.	Small cabinet office including the minister in charge, a number of collaborators/advisers and administrative staff.
15. Secrétariat d'Etat aux Droits des Femmes et Consommation *Headed by:* *Véronique Neiertz*	1992 – 1993	Political office reporting to the treasury department (Ministère de l'Economie et des Finances).	As above.	As above.

(Continued)

Table 1.2 (Continued)

Structure	Dates	Type	Remit and priorities	Composition
16. Ministère des Affaires Sociales, Santé et Ville *Headed by:* *Simone Veil*	1992– 1993	Government department whose portfolio includes women's rights.	Promote the family as a means to protect women's interests.	Small number of ministry staff assigned to women's rights and issues. The Service des Droits des Femmes is placed under the ministry's authority.
17. Ministère de Solidarité entre les Générations *Headed by:* *Colette Codaccioni*	1995	Government department whose portfolio includes women's rights.	Defend parents' (i.e. women's) 'freedom to choose' between paid employment and looking after the home and children.	As above.
18. Ministère Délégué à l'Emploi *Headed by:* *Anne-Marie Couderc*	1995– 1997	Junior ministry reporting to the Secretary of State for Employment whose portfolio includes women's rights alongside employment.	Work on inequalities between men and women in the workplace, focusing on pay differentials and professional training. Enable women to achieve a work–life balance.	As above.
19. Observatoire de la Parité (OP) *Rapporteur(e) nominated* *by Prime Minister*	1995–	Consultative body responsible to the Prime Minister's office.	Raise awareness of parity issues, recommend policy and report every two years on the advancement and implementation of parity reforms.	Special advisers nominated by government and general administrative staff.

20. Délégation Interministérielle aux Droits des Femmes *Headed by:* *Geneviève Fraisse*	1997–1998	Interministerial office with responsibility for women's rights, reporting to the Prime Minister.	Mainstream or integrate equal opportunities for women into all policies across all government departments. Act as a source of policy proposals in favour of women and as a driver of government action.	Dependent on availability at (infrequent) meetings of staff from various government departments.
21. Secrétariat d'Etat aux Droits des Femmes et à la Formation Professionnelle *Headed by:* *Nicole Péry*	1998–2002	Political office reporting to the Secretary of State for Employment and Solidarity.	Improve training opportunities for women and help them attain a better 'articulation' between work and family life (*articulation entre vie professionnelle et vie familiale*).	Small cabinet office including the minister in charge, a number of collaborators/advisers and administrative staff.
22. Ministère Délégué à la Parité et à l'Egalité Professionnelle *Headed by:* *Nicole Ameline*	2002–2005	Junior ministry reporting on parity and equal employment to the Secretary of State for Social Affairs, Employment and Solidarity.	Promote equal employment (among other equality/parity policies) as a factor of growth in and a reflection of a modern economy.	Small cabinet office including minister in charge, collaborators/advisers, clerical/administrative assistants.

(*Continued*)

Table 1.2 (Continued)

Structure	Dates	Type	Remit and priorities	Composition
23. Ministère Délégué à à la Cohésion Sociale et à la Parité *Headed by:* *Catherine Vautrin*	2005–2007	Junior ministry reporting on parity and social cohesion to the Secretary of State for Employment, Social Cohesion and Housing.	Ensure women's access to positions of responsibility in political, economic and socio-cultural life (parity). Advance equal employment measures and those related to work–life balance.	Small cabinet office including minister in charge, collaborators/advisers, clerical/administrative assistants.
24. Ministère de Travail, des Relations Sociales et de la Solidarité *Headed by:* *Xavier Bertrand*	2007–	Government department whose portfolio includes women's rights alongside employment, social relations and solidarity.	As above.	Small number of ministry staff assigned to women's rights and issues. The Service des Droits des Femmes is placed under the ministry's authority.

The above profiling and examination of institutional structures shows that equal employment has over a long period constituted a privileged area of government action in contrast with issues of women's social and individual rights (see Table 1.2, particularly columns relating to names of structures and policy brief). It also reveals that the majority of structures have had to make do with small budgets, few human resources and powers, which has implications for influencing policy-making and implementation. With the exception of the MDF, these ministerial structures have acted as 'administrations de mission' (similar to a task force) which have public awareness-raising, lobbying and coordination functions rather than those of policy development, preparation of legislation, budget-setting and enforcement of regulations which are proper to 'administrations de gestion' typified by government departments responsible for employment, education or social security for example. Robert Poujade, Ministre Délégué and Ministre pour la Protection de la Nature et de l'Environnement in the 1970s, and whose position was comparable with that of Giroud and her successors, named these ministerial structures 'missions impossibles' in view of the meagre resources allocated to them and the impossibility of promoting change and improvements through them (Poujade 1975). Consequently, it has been easy for incoming governments to disband such structures set up by predecessors and replace them with new ones while also tinkering around with name changes.

The following sections examine the development of certain important equal employment initiatives leading to legislation set against the interplay of social, economic and political factors. As it is neither useful nor possible to provide an account of all equal employment issues and policy over the past 60 years, we focus on certain constituent parts in order to demonstrate the tensions between the competing protectionist or familialist and feminist ideologies which underpin them. We explore the main arguments which shape particular policies and accompanying legislation and identify the principal players involved. The components of equal employment policy considered below are the 1983 Roudy Law and the more recent Ameline Law, passed in 2006.

Equal employment policy: the Roudy Law of 1983

The Roudy Law is selected here because it represents policies and a piece of legislation inspired by a classic equal rights logic. It made a break with previous legislation based on conceptions of women as passive beings in need of protection because of their sex and their role as mothers and carers in the family. Hence its treatment of women in the labour market and workplace is not tied in with the fact that women also play a crucial family role. In terms of Commaille's classification of familialist/ protectionist vs. feminist policy-making, the Roudy Law falls squarely into the latter category. Moreover, the law's (equal rights) feminist inspiration was openly emphasised by Roudy as was the idea that the MDF was in the business of encouraging laws for women, made and implemented by women.

The Equal Employment Law of 1983 was passed two years after Yvette Roudy launched her state feminist project in the face of criticism and personal insults from both anti-feminist and feminist camps including grassroots non-statutory organisations, media commentators, trade unionists and politicians. While the former camp accused her of introducing measures equal to a symbolic emasculation of French men the latter berated the co-opting of certain prominent movement feminists to the cause of the Ministry and the neutralisation of long fought for feminist principles. However, the passage of the equal employment bill into law ultimately proved uneventful for a number of reasons.

First, before meeting approval by the Conseil des Ministres and reaching its first reading in Parliament, some of the bill's most authoritative sections – i.e. ones which would have legally obliged employers to tackle inequalities at work – were cut out or diluted. For example, clauses associated with (10 per cent) minimum quotas for women on all technology-related national training programmes were rejected by employers, trade unions and the Minister for Employment and Training as were those relating to compulsory company annual reports and equality plans (see below) as tools for monitoring and reducing inequalities between men and women in the workplace. Other important clauses removed from one of the earlier drafts of the bill related to the creation of an independent statutory body (similar to the former UK Equal Opportunities Commission) with powers to check on the performance of companies in reducing gender inequalities and to advise women who had sex discrimination complaints. However, the idea of an independent body to check on employers' gender equality procedures and actions and to advise women in sex discrimination cases was vociferously opposed by the Ministry for Employment and by the Inspection du Travail (the statutory agency tasked with the enforcement of employment law in the workplace) on the basis that it would weaken existing arrangements for the implementation of the Code du Travail. Two further omissions from the final draft which was presented to Parliament concerned: the use, by female employees, of representatives from feminist organisations in the prosecution of employers in discrimination cases; and the application of heavy penalties on employers found guilty of sex discrimination. Opposition to the use of feminist organisation representatives in prosecution cases against employers came from the trade unions which argued that, in the workplace, they were the only credible advocates of workers' interests based on their long history of struggle for the rights of working people and that therefore only they could make legal representations on behalf of their members. As far as the punishment of bosses guilty of discrimination was concerned, it was deemed that fines and prison sentences proposed in earlier drafts of the bill were too harsh. The pressure to soften punishment in this case came from the Ministry for Justice (for a useful and detailed discussion of the Roudy bill see Mazur 1995: 210–16). Finally, while numerous omissions were made, the bill's architects failed to eliminate the 'special conditions' (*dispositions particulières*) connected with women's working hours, particularly those barring night work which had been in effect, in some form or other, since 1882.

Second, the bill was presented in Parliament four months after the enactment of the Socialists' showpiece Auroux Laws of August 1982 which aimed at improving workers' rights in the workplace through increased collective bargaining, stronger works councils and trade union representation in the workplace. The Auroux reforms had received prolonged consideration from politicians, trade unions and employers, all of whom subsequently approached the equal employment bill with a certain amount of indifference or at best saw it as an add-on, at worst as entirely unnecessary. In any case, the equal employment bill was also eclipsed by the anti-sexist bill, launched by Roudy in March 1983, for which the most vitriolic confrontations were reserved.

Finally, the equal employment bill was uncontentious in the sense that the social partners concerned were aware that French law had not complied with EC employment legislation and that it would eventually have to be brought in line with the EC 1976 equal treatment directive.

Equal employment constituted one of the main items on the MDF's agenda and included various measures. The provisions of the 1983 Equal Employment Act can be grouped under two main aspects: equal rights and equal opportunities.

As far as equal rights were concerned, the Roudy Law reaffirmed the general principle of non-discrimination on grounds of sex in all domains of workplace relations (that is recruitment, pay, promotion, training and so on) and within this logic, firstly, it established a legal definition of 'work of equal value',[18] thereby plugging the loophole of the 1972 Equal Pay Act. Second, it quashed the principle of 'legitimate grounds' (*motif légitime*) used in refusing women certain jobs while providing a shortlist of jobs where it was possible to favour one sex above another. Lastly, in sex discrimination prosecution cases, the law provided for the onus to be placed upon the employer to prove that unequal treatment on grounds of sex had not occurred. However, this was not an automatic provision and it was left to the tribunal judge to decide whether or not an employer was obliged to present proof of non-discrimination. Where an employer was found guilty of discrimination on the grounds of sex, tribunals were given recourse to certain 'soft' penalties.

The 1983 law also contained various provisions pertaining to equality of opportunity, premised on principles of (temporary) positive action deemed necessary if women were ever to catch up with men, in matters of qualifications and experience, pay and promotion, in order to accede to higher posts. First, positive action measures required employers in firms of 50+ employees to produce an annual report for works council or employee representatives which would include data on gender equality (related to recruitment, training, promotion, work organisation and conditions) within the company and how these could be incorporated into collective bargaining procedures. Annual reports were also required to present information about how gender inequality was being tackled and key areas of action in the future. The annual report, which was supposed to be debated by all the social partners within a company, was aimed at strengthening the position of employees in annual processes of collective bargaining.

Second, and linked to the annual report was the Equal Employment Plan (*plan d'égalité professionnelle*) the production of which was left to employers' good will. It was hoped that Equal Employment Plans would serve as a vehicle for positive action and which, if successfully negotiated between an employer and the trade union representatives within the company, could attract state funding to partially cover the costs of special training schemes for women and the salaries of women accessing such schemes.

Third, a Higher Council for Equal Employment (Conseil Supérieur de l'Egalité Professionnelle), responsible to the MDF and the Ministry for Employment and Training, was set up to ensure that equal employment policies were implemented, to monitor the results of Equal Employment Plans and to contribute to the further development of equal employment principles and measures. In addition to the CSEP, the 1983 Act also created the Mission de l'Egalité Professionnelle to administer the work of the CSEP.

The indifference or lack of enthusiasm that surrounded the passage through Parliament of the 1983 Equal Employment Act was essentially reproduced by the social partners involved when it came to implementation of the act. For example, knowing that penalties could not be imposed, the majority of employers simply did not complete the company annual report. Where reports were submitted, they were often incomplete or inadequate. Nor did the majority of employers produce equality plans, the quality of which depended on good annual reports. The undertaking of reports and equality plans was seen as an unwelcome administrative burden by employers and the additional fact of having to negotiate equality plans with the trade unions was a disincentive to many (for an assessment of the implementation of annual reports and equality plans see Colclough 2004; Laufer 2003; Mazur 1995: 216–21; and Sarde 1988). Over a twenty-year period following the 1983 Act, only 35 equality plans have been agreed in mainly large companies (Colclough 2004) while only one-third of employers have drafted annual reports (Rehfeldt 2007).

The responses of the two main trade unions to implementing the 1983 Act were different although both demonstrated a common lack of interest or antagonism. While supporting principles of equal employment, the CFDT argued that the best way of implementing and achieving equal employment was through direct union–employer negotiations at company level, taking a case-by-case approach whether it involved unfairly treated women individually or collectively. The union was unwilling to mobilise wage-earners generally, using relatively modest resources, to make blanket equal opportunities demands for all women throughout the economy. The CGT, on the other hand, continued to claim that the Roudy reforms would best serve the interests of middle-class, professional women while ignoring working-class women in poorly paid, unstable jobs. After 1984, following the end of the Communist Party's participation in Socialist government, the CGT withdrew support from implementation of the 1983 Equal Employment Act, amidst accusations that the CSEP served as Yvette Roudy's personal office and that it would deliberately disadvantage working-class women by working towards the elimination of 'special conditions' provisions.[19]

Finally, despite the fact that the 1983 Act had broken with past legislation in terms of its broadly feminist motivation, it failed to draw support from feminist organisations which were disappointed with the retention of 'special conditions' relative to night work, the lack of penalties applicable to employers who failed to abide by the law at company level and the trade union-led refusal to allow women's organisations to act on women's behalf in cases of workplace discrimination.

The failure of the 1983 Equal Employment Act to impact positively on women workers, coupled with further EU directives on gender equality,[20] has provoked further legislation and measures to reinforce provisions on the equal treatment of women and men in France. Amongst these are:

- The 1989 Equal Employment Law which extended special parental rights (including leave for the care of newborn babies and sick children) to working fathers and which gave employers further opportunity to introduce catch-up measures for women workers.
- The 2001 Génisson Law which introduced: compulsory negotiation of gender equality in the workplace every three years; the mainstreaming of gender equality and equal pay in collective bargaining; specific equality indicators to be used in annual reporting at company level; and the principle of gender parity in elections to bodies comprising workers' representatives (see Laufer and Silvera 2005 for an analysis of the impact of this law).
- The signature, in 2004, by trade unions and employers of a national intersectoral agreement on gender equality with emphasis on achieving a gender balance in the workforce, narrowing the gender pay gap, preventing maternity leave from impacting negatively on women's career advancement and addressing labour market segregation (Meilland 2004).
- The introduction, in 2004, of an equality kite mark awarded to companies, statutory and non-governmental organisations 'which demonstrate unquestionable commitment to equal employment' (see Vautrin 2005).
- The 2006 Ameline Law discussed below (also see Table 1.1 above).
- Launch of a consultation process (involving trade unions, employers and state actors), in November–December 2007, on future equal pay and occupational equality reforms among various other social policy issues.

In spite of the three pieces of legislation passed since 1983 (i.e. in 1989, 2001 and 2006), there still remains a substantial pay gap of about 19 per cent between women and men on the whole[21] and although there exists a relatively strong framework of anti-discriminatory provisions, women still experience discrimination in matters of recruitment, training and promotion as well as segregation within the labour market.

Equal employment policy: the 2006 Ameline Law

The Ameline Law merits consideration here because, unlike the Roudy Law (and its reinforcement through the Génisson Law), which was premised on the notion that family responsibilities undermined women's rights and their equal participation with men in the labour market, the Ameline Law exemplifies a compromise between promoting an aspect of gender equality (elimination of the gender pay gap) and achieving a work–life balance in order to protect women's role as mothers. The law's focus on work–life balance alongside equal employment rights reflects not only the traditional French statist reflex of preserving a protectionist logic within policies aimed at women but also fits in with EU discourses on equality opportunities for women within the demographic and labour market requirements of European economies.

Nicole Ameline presented her equal employment bill to the National Assembly on 10 May 2005 as a 'modern' and 'unifying' text resulting from principles of negotiation and social dialogue within the workplace. The bill had four main aims: to eliminate, within five years, the existing pay gap between men and women; to encourage the achievement of balance between work and parenthood; to promote gender parity in voting and administrative structures at company level; and to improve access for women to apprenticeship and employment training schemes. In common with the Roudy bill of 1983, its passage through Parliament was relatively noiseless. Unlike the Roudy bill, it was neither well-publicised nor widely known but arguably faced less indifference from employers and trade unions who had demonstrated a certain acceptance of equal employment principles in signing the national intersectoral agreement on gender equality the previous year. Nevertheless, the bill did not escape critical comment from the main social partners.

The Ameline bill was criticised by the Socialists as one which fell far short of expectations, resembling more a petition of principles rather than a law aimed at generating change. Furthermore, Catherine Génisson, author of the 2001 equal employment law, widely considered a dead duck, accused her successor of simplistically reducing questions of gender inequality to those of pay differentials between men and women (*Le Nouvel Observateur*, 10 May 2005). However, the position of the CFDT was hard to gauge as the union failed to provide a meaningful response to the bill's announcement. A press release from executive bureau member, Annie Thomas, merely stated that a new law could not absolve the social partners involved of their responsibility in bringing about equality and that the CFDT would fulfil its duty in that respect (CFDT 2005).

The Communist Party's Muguette Jacquaint, along with the CGT, accused Ameline of shying away from substantive issues such as the inequalities embedded in part-time contracts and compulsory penalties on employers who failed to observe the law (*Le Nouvel Observateur*, 10 May 2005). As far as the employers were concerned, the bill represented yet more meddling by legislators who they felt would have done better to trust the good will of the main negotiating parties in the workplace (MEDEF 2006). Finally, the bill provoked some reaction from women's organisations and feminists. The Collectif National pour les Droits des Femmes (representing well over a hundred local centres for women's rights) as well as individuals such as prominent feminist sociologist Margaret Maruani questioned the utility of a new law when three existing pieces of legislation (the 1972 Equal Pay Act, the 1983 Roudy Law and 2001 Génisson Law) had never been enforced properly, particularly in respect of employers' duties and when other government policies related to labour market deregulation and so-called flexible contracts had impoverished women even further (CNDF 2005; Grémillet 2005). Despite the criticisms outlined, all the social partners were aware that opposing the bill could be a waste of effort as it also constituted a response to EU requirements that member states should comply with directives on the equal treatment of men and women in employment and training. In addition, the wave of urban protests and violence which took place at the end of 2005, coupled with the fact that 2006 was a pre-election year (for presidential and legislative elections), meant that by the time the equal employment bill reached committee stage and public sitting, most politicians contesting elections in 2007 as well as the main social partners had become more absorbed with the introduction of measures, including a new equal opportunities law, designed to counter the many discriminations experienced by young people in deprived inner city neighbourhoods.

The Ameline Law which was finally adopted by the National Assembly in March 2006, ended up focusing only on the two themes of equal pay and work–life balance. Most of the important clauses relating to the two other themes, namely gender parity in company level voting and jurisdictional bodies and increased access for women to apprenticeship and vocational training schemes, were declared unconstitutional by the Conseil Constitutionnel either for reasons of procedure or in the name of (the French conception of) equality as opposed to 'Anglo-Saxon' notions of positive discrimination or affirmative action. Furthermore, proposals for coercive financial measures against companies were also dropped in favour of a review process and further legislation at the end of five years

if necessary. In the following paragraphs, we consider the issue of work–
life balance which constitutes one of the law's main themes in order to
demonstrate the competing ideologies (of protectionism vs. feminism)
at play. The law's content on equal treatment in the matter of pay is also
outlined briefly.

Where measures related to equal pay are concerned, the Ameline Law
aims at closing the gap between male and female salaries by 31 December
2010. This aim is to be realised through annual company level negotiations undertaken between employers and trade unions resulting in
the production of documentation which identifies where a company is
failing in respect of equal pay, the specific measures which should be
taken in favour of achieving equal pay as well as indicators of progress
made on a year to year basis and of the eventual elimination of the pay
gap. In addition, companies are responsible for ensuring that women
on maternity leave are not treated unfavourably and that they too
benefit from across the board, nationally negotiated pay increases or
from those awarded within branches or companies unless acceptable
equivalent alternatives are set out in company level collective bargaining
agreements. Finally, the law makes provision for a review and assessment process of the measures undertaken by companies to eliminate
the gender pay gap. If insufficient progress is made within five years,
then further legislation will be formulated and introduced in order to
impose penalties (unspecified) on employers. While the review process
began in November 2007 with the first of three conferences on equal
employment and equal pay, it is difficult to assess the effect of the 2006
law in terms of the number of companies working concretely towards
the elimination of pay differences between male and female workers.
However, it is entirely reasonable to suggest that the 2006 equal employment legislation is unlikely to make more of an impact on employers
than previous legislation given that they do not face punitive action
for non-compliance and given that the government's equal pay initiatives are counterbalanced by other employment measures (as part of
an increasingly ultra-liberal economic policy) such as the replacement
of long-term contracts (*contrats à durée indéterminée*) by single employment contracts (*contrats de travail unique*) which, argue the trade unions,
will effectively lead to the demise of stable jobs generally, particularly
in those sectors of the labour market affected most by the vicissitudes
of the economy and in which women form a significant part of the
workforce.

As with equal pay, employers and trade unions are obliged to include
issues pertaining to the reconciliation between work and family life in

their annual negotiations and to undertake measures which improve the balance between the two areas. These might include maternity, paternity or parental leave for the care of newborn babies, newly adopted or sick children, leave to care for elderly or disabled family members, the provision of care facilities for children, or flexible working arrangements such as job-sharing, flexible working hours, term-time working or teleworking.

In addition, the law contains specific clauses in favour of achieving a work–life balance. For example, where annual negotiations result in the provision of vocational training courses outside working hours, companies are promised at least 10 per cent of training costs of participating employees in order to enable the latter to cover extra childcare expenses incurred. Second, companies employing fewer than 50 staff are entitled to apply for financial assistance, to replace one or more workers on maternity or adoption leave. Third, companies cannot expect workers to participate in more than 80 hours of overtime work and out-of-hours training combined in any given year. Again, it is justifiable to suppose that these measures, if applied, will be directed primarily at women and that they will be used to increase the number of non-standard contracts with the aim of making such contracts the norm.

The Ameline Law's endeavour to link issues of gender equality with those of work–life balance in a single piece of legislation is the result of two developments. The first development is that of parity politics (see Chapter 6) in France and the acceptance of parity during the 1990s, by parties of the left and then the right, which reduced polarisation between feminist and familialist approaches to women's employment thus producing a cross-party consensus over the issue. The second development occurred at EU level in the mid-1990s amidst growing concern over unemployment in a number of member states and the realisation that the concept of reconciliation of work and family life or work–life balance could be co-opted to support labour market policy and 'flexibility' measures to combat unemployment in particular. Hence the rather questionable arguments in favour of linking equal opportunities for women with labour market and demographic concerns included among others that: EU member states are experiencing declining birth rates and that evidence demonstrates that countries offering possibilities for a healthy work–life balance have the best chance of maintaining a stable demographic structure; the EU's ageing population profile and escalating retirement budgets demand that the whole of the working population should be made as productive as possible; all available talents, abilities and experience should be used, including those of women who make up 50 per cent of the population; most new jobs are to be found in the service sector where women have traditionally constituted the majority of the workforce; new technologies (e.g. teleworking) offer opportunities for the reconciliation of work and family life.

In order to address labour market, demographic and equal opportunity concerns, EU policy-makers encouraged the creation of a social infrastructure for achieving work–life balance and at the same time argued that the way to provide such a (necessarily costly) infrastructure was through 'flexibilisation' of the labour market.[22] Labour market flexibility would ostensibly maximise job opportunities for women while allowing them (and men) to work and spend time with family. Thus the dominant model of women's employment has evolved from that which took for granted women's integration into the primary labour market of full-time, permanently contracted jobs linked with full employment and social security benefits to that which promoted their integration into the secondary labour market characterised by non-standard jobs linked with few or no employment or social benefits (see Stratigaki 2004 for a more detailed account of this evolution). There is little doubt that in a country such as France where unemployment rates have been among the highest in the EU, that governments will continue to use arguments and measures in favour of work–life balance to support the creation of non-standard jobs – a strategy which runs counter to the safeguarding of women's employment rights and promoting real equality of opportunity, in particular for women from (disadvantaged) working-class and immigrant backgrounds.

'Gender-neutral' employment policy and its impact on women

In the sections above, the content and impact of selected equal employment policy and legislation on women in the labour market and workplace have been discussed. However, it is equally important to examine policy considered 'gender-neutral' and to assess the effects, if any, of such policy on women. In other words, can any employment policy be justifiably deemed neutral and can any employment policy produce the same outcomes for all labour market participants regardless of factors such as gender and class? In this final section, we look at policy aimed at the creation of new jobs through the reduction of working hours, namely the Aubry Laws which produced the 35-hour week.

The 35-hour week

The first Aubry Law on the 35-hour week (Loi d'Orientation et d'Incitation à la Réduction du Temps de Travail) was passed by Parliament in May 1998. In a context of high unemployment (at 12.3 per cent for women and 9.2 per cent for men, see INSEE 2007), the law aimed to create new jobs through a reduction in work time by setting the statutory working week at 35 hours. The introduction of the 35-hour week was also touted as an additional vehicle for the achievement of work–life balance.

Employers were encouraged to immediately include the question of working hours in collective bargaining with the trade unions before those provisions of the law pertaining to the achievement of a 35-hour week came into force in 2000 for companies employing more than twenty staff and 2002 for those with under twenty employees. Incentive grants were payable to all companies (apart from state-run organisations drawing the major part of their financial resources from government budgets) which reduced working time and which, as a result, either recruited new staff or saved previously threatened jobs before the deadlines set. The terms of the law which affected all employees within the private and public sectors (bar civil servants) stipulated that company employers, in negotiation with trade unions, needed to ensure that: working time was reduced by at least 10 per cent of its original length; any new collective timetabling had to allow space for a maximum 35 hours of work time to be completed; the reduction in working time had to be accompanied by an increase in jobs which could provide employment to at least 6 per cent of a company's total workforce; employers had to commit themselves to the protection of staffing levels attained through new recruitment for at least two years; and incentive awards to companies would take the form of reductions in employers' national insurance contributions. Because the 35-hour week proposals had provoked so much controversy and employer-led resistance when first launched at the 1997 national conference on employment, the law aimed to act as an incentive in attaining working time reductions and both employers and trade unions were urged to find the most workable solutions for the particular circumstances of their company or sector.

The 35-hour proposals met with fierce criticism from the employers' representative body (the Confédération Nationale du Patronat Français – CNPF[23]) which, for a period of time, made opposition to the parliamentary bill its main issue. However, the ferocity of such opposition was unsustainable and eventually a *modus operandi* was found whereby the CNPF refrained from advising its subnational sections to boycott negotiations at company or sector level on purely ideological grounds.

The main trade unions were divided on this issue. The CFDT was most committed to the 35-hour week, making clear its intention of signing up to 25,000 company agreements during the first eighteen months and of going further to champion a 32-hour week. The CGT was initially more circumspect but eventually backed the law in the hope that it would provide the union with the opportunity to regain power it had lost in the workplace, through tough negotiations on more jobs, higher pay and transforming work patterns for the better. The CGT-FO (Confédération Générale du Travail-Force Ouvrière) was least convinced of the viability of the 35-hour week and claims that it could create hundreds of thousands of new jobs.

As far as feminists and women's organisations were concerned, the first Aubry Law produced mixed reactions. Many feminists felt bound to defend the law and more importantly its proposer Martine Aubry, then Secretary of State for Employment. Immediately after announcing her proposals for the new law, Aubry became a figure of misogynist contempt in employer circles. At an employers' rally against the 35-hour week, organised by the MEDEF in October 1999, one speaker fulminated, 'The problem with Martine Aubry is that she is dogmatic. She's frustrated and . . . what she needs is a good fuck' (Monnot 1999). Other feminists, while condemning the attacks on Aubry, denounced the fact that the proposals for the law did not pay attention to its gendered consequences; for instance the use of the law by employers to impose part-time work on (women) employees (see Cette 1999). It was as a result of feminist lobbying by women trade unionists and the Collectif National pour les Droits des Femmes amongst others that certain provisions, to counter negative effects on women employees, were incorporated into the second Aubry Law of January 2000. Measures relating to part-time work were instituted and these were intended to directly benefit women who made up over 80 per cent of the part-time workforce in France. For example, exemptions on employers' national insurance contributions applying to part-timers were done away with, part-time workers were accorded some rights (holidays, sick leave, for instance) in line with their full-time counterparts; there was to be a clamp-down on employers imposing part-time hours; and the possibility of moving more easily from a part-time position to a full-time one and vice versa. Also, employees were given the opportunity to accumulate time, gained from a shorter working week, in order to build up substantial blocks to be used in case of family illness or other reasons. However, the second Aubry Law did not put the brakes on the development of part-time work; it just provided a framework for managing it better.

Studies on the 35-hour week have shown that it has had a varied impact on men and women (CFTC 2000; Estrade et al. 2001; Fagnani and Letablier 2004; Hayden 2006; Lurol and Pélisse 2001; Oliveira and Ulrich 2002). Early soundings suggested that the majority of employees had welcomed the law, believing it to have had a positive effect on their working conditions and time. A TNS-Sofres poll of June 2000, commissioned for the Ministry for Employment and Solidarity and undertaken among 500 private sector employees, indicated an overall satisfaction rate of 80 per cent with the 35-hour week arrangements negotiated in their respective companies. Furthermore 83 per cent of those polled claimed that they had no wish to return to previous working time arrangements. The poll indicated high satisfaction rates with the law's implementation and outcomes regarding improved work–life balance and hence quality of life (85 per cent) and the creation of new jobs or preservation of existing ones (78 per cent) (Marcel 2000). However, later soundings and studies have painted a different, more nuanced picture which shows that the benefits of the 35-hour week have been derived most by employees in stable jobs who enjoy a certain amount of control over their own working rhythms, patterns and environment as well as the freedom to do as they please in their private life. Hence, professional middle-class women employees did relatively well out of the Aubry Laws but mainly in organisations where non-standard working arrangements had already been established. Workers in such organisations made good use of their experience of exploiting such arrangements in order to gain from the 35-hour week. But in contrast with male employees from similar occupational and class backgrounds, even professional, middle-class women face far more constraints in their private life due to family commitments and have tended not to use as much of the time gained from implementation of the Aubry Laws for leisure and personal development as they may have hoped for.

Those who have benefited least from the Aubry Laws are women from disadvantaged working-class and immigrant backgrounds working in poorly paid jobs without long-term prospects, in companies or sectors which have had little or no experience of non-standard working patterns. It is in these sectors that employers have demanded the most trade-offs for a reduced working week. The biggest 'compensations' demanded by employers in return for reducing working time were flexibility in the sense of being able to call on employees whenever and wherever they were required and wage restraint. The lowest paid workers were made to accept yo-yo shift patterns. Shifts were shortened but multiplied so that working patterns fitted in with management ideologies of permanent availability while workers hung around in between shifts, particularly in the care home, hotel, catering and supermarket sectors. There are countless examples of large, well-known companies such as Renault and Peugeot where managers tried to abolish tea and lunch breaks or introduce compulsory Saturday working in return for reduced hours (Bulard 1999). At Michelin, unskilled manual workers came in on Saturdays while managerial and supervisory staff took extra days as 'supplementary work time reduction days' (Bensoussan 2007).

Wage restraint was the other trade-off for acceptance of the 35-hour week which the Socialist government did not expect. According to Dominique Strauss-Kahn, Minister for Economy, Finance and Industry at the time, if there was one thing all the social partners were agreed upon it was that the 35-hour week would create jobs as long as the competitiveness of companies was not compromised and that therefore, in exchange for a four-hour reduction, employers would demand either flexibility of work or a wage freeze (*Libération*, 2 February 1998). The Socialists expected employers to opt for flexibility, using the slogan '35 hours paid at 39' to reassure workers that reduced working time would not entail wage cuts. Again the wage restraints that employers imposed affected those at the bottom of company wage hierarchies most. Those who had previously benefited from overtime pay were forced to accept extra weekend work at normal rates or reduced overtime rates. The annualisation of hours, introduced by the second Aubry Law, has allowed employers to avoid overtime payments during periods of increased production when the maximum working time may be increased to 48 hours, balanced out by a reduction in hours or time off when demand slows down. In these circumstances, many women workers on low wages, subjected to stop-start working patterns and family unfriendly hours have opted to go part-time or leave employment altogether rather than suffer stress and ill-health as many have done (Flottes 2006).

The formulation and application of the Aubry Laws shows that policies which fall outside the category 'equal employment' are far from neutral. Women constitute almost half the workforce and operate in a labour market marked by gendered and classed divisions of labour which produce unequal power relations. Consequently, and generally, any policy which fails to explicitly consider such divisions will impact differently on men and women, reproducing inequalities embedded in those divisions. The first Aubry Law's reliance on negotiated solutions between employers' and trade unions, rather than on tough prescriptions based on equality principles, meant that the former were given a free hand to drive hard bargains and demand trade-offs that contributed to the entrenchment of unanticipated inequalities particularly for women from disadvantaged socio-economic backgrounds.

Conclusion

Within the space allowed, this chapter has attempted to give as full a picture as possible of the development and main features of policies and initiatives directed towards women in employment and the labour market. In doing so, it has taken into account the ideological motivations and actions of policy-makers and the main social actors in the field; it has also considered the influence of institutional arrangements and wider economic, social and political factors. It has shown that employment policy towards women in France has been historically shaped by two opposing ideologies – that of familialism and that of equal rights feminism – and that the ascendancy of one over the other has been largely dependent on the political character of the government in power. However, more recently, the development of parity politics in France, coupled with the influence of certain equal employment strategies adopted in the EU, has minimised the ideological gap between governments of left and right on the approach to equal employment policy-making. This chapter shows that while there has been an acceptance among politicians, employers and trade unions of women's presence in the labour force and of their right and struggle to achieve equal pay and treatment, women, and particularly those from disadvantaged social classes, will continue to suffer multiple discriminations in the workplace. This situation will remain unchanged for as long as policy-makers overlook the possible gendered implications of their decisions and the goals and outcomes of one policy area (equal employment) conflict with and are overridden by priorities in other policy domains such as family welfare or even within the area of employment policy itself.

Notes

1. This is because the definition of agricultural activity in which large numbers of women were involved, varied between censuses. Also, many women were seen as helping husbands/fathers rather than performing important jobs and were consequently recorded as inactive on census forms.
2. Family immigration policy allowed male migrants to send for wives and children to join them (i.e. family reunification) but also provided for entire migrant families to enter and eventually settle in France.

3. Contained within the logic of immigration as a means of repopulating France, was the thinking that the most assimilable, therefore desirable, migrants were from countries bordering France as they least threatened to dilute *éthnie française*.
4. Pierre Mauroy's government was weakened in a context where a series of political leadership changes in EC member states led to the dominance of conservative government or coalitions headed by conservatives adopting neo-liberal economic policies. In addition, the quickening pace of European integration which demanded the convergence of economic goals and strategies meant that France was pressured to abandon 'its course of national, socialist economic policy' (Leicke and Schreiber 1989).
5. Socialist government in the 1980s and 1990s was interrupted by the return of governments of the right from 1986 to 1988 (known as the first 'cohabitation' period of the Fifth Republic when a Socialist presidency under Mitterrand operated alongside a government of the right) and from 1993 to 1997 (which included a second period of cohabitation under Mitterrand between 1993 and 1995).
6. Geneviève Fraisse, interministerial delegate for women's rights, favoured the concept of *articulation vie familiale–vie professionnelle* over that of *conciliation travail et famille* on the grounds that the notion of reconciliation between work and family (two opposing domains) suggested having to make compromises. *Articulation vie familiale–vie professionnelle* (analogous to 'work–life balance'), on the other hand, sounded neutral and could be seen to address both women and men equally. In this chapter, for convenience, we use the term 'work–life balance' to cover both terms which suggest the bringing about of an equilibrium between the amount of time spent at work and that given to other aspects of life and which relate to flexible working and family-friendly policies.
7. Unlike the UK and certain northern European countries where one of the main components of the female worker model has long been part-time work, in France atypical jobs have not been used extensively by employers due to historical restrictions on non-standard employment contracts. In 1992, 34.8 per cent of the Dutch and 22.9 per cent of the UK workforces were engaged in part-time work compared with only 13.1 percent of the French workforce (EFILWC 2007: 3). The latter figure reached a peak in 1998 at 18 per cent. As far as women are concerned, part-time work represents 31 per cent of women's employment today compared with 12.5 per cent in 1990 (Conseil Economique et Social 2008: 4).
8. Mainstreaming is defined as 'the (re)organisation, improvement, development and evaluation of policy processes so that a gender equality perspective is incorporated in all policies at all levels and at all stages, by the actors normally involved in policy-making' (Council of Europe 1998).
9. The term 'state feminism' has been variously defined to constitute either public policy, dominant thinking or the presence of individuals (feminists/'femocrats') within certain state structures whose aim is the advancement of women's rights and interests. However, there is growing consensus around the view that state feminism entails the advocacy of women's movement claims, within state bodies, in order to carry out a feminist policy agenda (see Lovenduski, 2005b).

10. Prior to the 1990s, the EC aimed to regulate equal employment policy in member states with regard to the equal treatment directive (1976), the promotion of positive action for women (1984) and the equal treatment of self-employed men and women (1986). In the 1990s, the EU took on a coordinating and monitoring role, recognising the importance of gender equality for employment policy and ultimately its economic objectives. Its European Employment Strategy was launched in 1997 and included equal opportunities between men and women as one of its four main pillars.
11. For a fuller history of the CETF/CTF and its work see Révillard (2007).
12. The British equivalent would be a secretary of state in charge of a government department.
13. This would be equivalent to minister of state in Britain.
14. The closest British officeholder to the secrétaire d'état is the parliamentary under-secretary, normally given less important briefs.
15. In Britain this structure would equate to the office of parliamentary private secretary (PPS). Both the délégation and the PPS act as administrative units, implementing policy.
16. In common with most Western governments, France has a split system of central government where an elite layer of 'politicised' top advisers (drawn from academia, private industry, business and finance or the public sector) or senior civil servants, personally appointed to a cabinet by the minister in charge, coexists with a permanent administration of 'classical' or 'neutral' civil servants. This system responds to the two main objectives of preserving political neutrality and professionalism in the implementation of policies and legislation and creating a politically loyal group of supporters on whom government ministers can rely to push forward particular policies and legislative proposals. With the exception of Yvette Roudy, ministers for women's status/rights could count on neither a substantial politicised staff nor a classical administration.
17. The Code du Travail is the compendium of all legislative and regulatory texts applicable to France's employment law.
18. Work of equal value was defined as work that required equivalent qualifications, experience, level of responsibility or physical/mental workload. Moreover, all of these criteria had to be taken together in determining work of equal value. See Article 5.1, *Journal Officiel*, 14 July 1983.
19. The special conditions in relation to night work were finally revoked in 2001 (see Table 1.1), following several challenges by the European Commission, requiring French law to comply with the EC 1976 equal treatment directive, and the imposition of financial sanctions in 1999 by the European Court of Justice.
20. Further EU directives include the 1997 'Burden of Proof Directive' (97/80/EC), the 2002 'New Gender Directive' (2002/73/EC) on the equal treatment of men and women in employment and vocational training and the 2007 'Framework Employment Directive' (2000/78/EC) on the equal treatment of men and women in employment and occupation.
21. See Ministère du Travail, des Relations Sociales et de la Solidarité, http://www.femmes-egalite.gouv. fr/le_ministere/le_dispositif_daction/sdfe/index.htm#, accessed 20 February 2008.

22. The gender mainstreaming framework through which this was promoted included large programmes, such as EQUAL (and RACINE – Réseau d'Appui et de Capitalisation des Innovations Européennes – in France), funded by the European Social Fund.
23. The CNPF became the MEDEF (Mouvement des Entreprises de France) in October 1998 as part of a makeover, initiated by its then new head Ernest-Antoine Seillière, intended to show that French employers formed a dynamic organisation capable of delivering a more 'modern' (in other words liberalised) economy capable of competing in world markets.

2
Gender Parity Reform

The 'parity law', on women and men's representation in political institutions, was passed by the National Assembly in 2000 and has since then been applied to all the relevant election types (legislative, senatorial, European, regional, cantonal, municipal) at national and subnational levels. A significant literature on parity has developed over the past eighteen years, focusing on the following themes: the history of the parity campaign/movement; the debates surrounding the adoption of parity; the implementation of the parity law; and the effects of parity law on political structures and processes (Agacinsky 2001; Allwood 1995; Allwood and Wadia 2000: 213–25; Amar 1999; Baudino 2005; Bereni 2007; Bird 2003; Delphy 1994,[1] 1995[2]; Gaspard 2001; Gaspard et al. 1992; Krook 2007; Lépinard 2006; Martin 1998; Mossuz-Lavau 1998; Murray 2004, 2008; Opello 2006; Ramsey 2008; Scott 2005; Sénac-Slawinsky 2008; Sineau 2008). Far more of the literature covers the first two themes mentioned above although recent work has concentrated on the last two. Given the constraints of space and the extensive literature on parity, it is not the intention, in this chapter, to examine all of the themes mentioned above. Instead, we will comment on parity law and progress made towards the goal of increasing women's representation over the last decade; and give consideration to the question of 'the completion of French democracy' which figured as one of the main justifications for the law. A brief outline of the progress of women's political representation in history is presented first.

Gender and political representation in history

When universal suffrage was proclaimed in 1848, women did not form part of the picture for, along with children, they were considered minors.

They were only granted the right to vote in 1944 and yet the question of women's political representation, whether indirectly through suffrage or directly via election to a legislative assembly, had been debated for over 150 years before that time, sporadically sometimes and without a great deal of vigour and intensely and extensively at other times. Table 2.1 presents key dates in the struggle for women's representation over the last two centuries and shows that until the beginning of the twentieth century, few attempts were made to push for women's direct or indirect representation.

Up until the end of the eighteenth century, claims for women's political rights were made by individuals, mainly women, such as Olympe de Gouges and Hubertine Auclert. It was only in the run-up to the First World War that a systematic campaign waged by a growing movement of mainly left-wing feminists began to exert some influence on Socialist members of Parliament. For example in 1906, Henry Chéron, deputy for Calvados, formed a parliamentary group of about 100 members in favour of women's political rights. In addition, suffragette campaigns were having some effect on public opinion via progressive newspapers run by editors such as Gustave Téry of *Journal* who publicised arguments for women's right to vote and to sit in elected assemblies. The end of the First World War gave a huge boost to the French campaign for women's political representation not only because of the role that French women had played in victory over the Axis powers but also because of the momentum gained by suffragette campaigns in Europe and elsewhere, where the vote was accorded to women (e.g. in Britain, Sweden, Germany, USSR and Poland, in 1918; Canada and the USA in 1919). Consequently, enough French deputies were persuaded of the justness of votes for women and between 1919 and 1936 the lower house (Chambre des Députés) voted six times in favour of according women the right to vote but were countered each time by conservative senators in the upper house (Sénat). It was only after the Second World War that women finally gained the right to vote and be elected to legislative office in France. Several histories of women's representation are available to the interested reader; for example, Le Bras-Chopard and Mossuz-Lavau's *Les Femmes et la politique* (1997), Klejman and Rochefort's *L'Egalité en marche* (1989) and Latour et al.'s *Femmes et citoyennes* (1995).

Although French women gained the right to vote and be elected in 1944, their numbers in office have remained low over the past 65 years. They constituted only 5 per cent of National Assembly deputies in 1945, and by 1996 this figure had increased to a mere 6 per cent although they made up 53 per cent of voters. The factors accounting

Table 2.1   The history of women's representation

Date	Key event
1791	Publication of Olympe de Gouges's 'Declaration of the Rights of Women and the Citizen', declaring that 'mothers, daughters and sisters who represent the nation demand to be part of the National Assembly'.
1793	Declaration of a new Constitution, including establishment of 'universal suffrage' but without women; the Constitution fails to be applied.
1795	Women excluded from political arena.
1804	The Napoleonic Code of 1804 reinforces the idea that women, like children, should be placed under the care and supervision of their closest male relative. They are refused all political rights.
1848	Formation of the Second Republic and re-establishment of 'universal suffrage' but without women.
1849	Jeanne Deroin presents herself as candidate at the legislative elections of May. The press humiliates her.
1875	Constitutional recognition of the fact that women do not possess political rights.
1876	Foundation, by Hubertine Auclert, of the first suffragette group Droit des Femmes (later Suffrage des Femmes).
1901	First parliamentary (Gautret) bill in favour of female suffrage (for single women, widows and divorcées over 21).
1909	Creation of the Union Française pour le Suffrage des Femmes (UFSF).
1914	Coordination of a women's blank votes campaign in the run-up to the legislative elections. Half a million women submitted blank votes.
1916	Maurice Barrès's bill in favour of wives or mothers (in the absence of a father) to inherit the right to vote of husbands and sons killed in war.
1919	The Chambre des Deputés votes for the first time in favour of women's political rights but the bill is rejected by the Senate.
1920	Parliamentary bill, proposed by Jules Guesde, in favour of civil and political equality for women.
1922	Rejection of Guesde's bill by the Senate which instead revives the Barrès bill giving wives and mothers the votes of soldiers killed in service.
1925	• In April, the Chambre des Députés votes by 389 to 140 in favour of a bill establishing women's right to vote at municipal elections. • At the municipal elections of May, using a loophole in the electoral rules, the Communist Party places female candidates in winnable seats, in the Paris region. Those elected take up their seats until their election is annulled by the courts.
1927	The Chambre des Députés votes by 396 to 94 votes asking the government to push the Senate to debate the 1925 bill on women's direct representation in municipal elections.
1935	The Chambre des Députés votes for the fifth time for women's right to vote.

Table 2.1   (Continued)

Date	Key event
1935–6	A number of municipalities organise a campaign to elect extra women onto their local councils. Six women are elected to the Socialist-run council in Louviers.
1936	• Louise Weiss and suffragettes from the organisation Femme Nouvelle launch their 'socks' campaign telling the Senate that their socks would be mended despite women gaining the vote. • Deputies vote in favour of women's vote for the sixth time. • Léon Blum's Popular Front government appoints three women as junior ministers – Cécile Brunschvicg (UFSF leader) to the Ministry of Education, Suzanne Lacore to the Ministry of Public Health and Irène Joliot-Curie to Science and Research.
1942	De Gaulle promises women the vote once the war is over.
1943	Lucie Aubrac is nominated member of the provisional consultative national assembly and takes up her seat alongside Marthe Simard in 1944.
1944	• Article 17 of the ordinance on the postwar reorganisation of political power provides for the right of women to vote on an equal basis with men. • Ten women take up seats in the provisional consultative national assembly.
1945	• Women vote for the first time at municipal elections. • Women vote for the first time, at national level, for the national constituent assembly.
1947	Germaine Poinsu-Chapuis becomes the first woman to hold a full ministerial position.
1982	A parliamentary bill providing for 25 per cent minimum quotas for women candidates on party lists passes into law. The law is annulled by the Constitutional Council.
1996	Publication of the parity manifesto ('Le Manifeste des dix pour la parité') demanding that political parity be enshrined in the Constitution.
1999	Articles 3 and 4 of the Constitution amended by an Act of Parliament.
2000	Adoption of the 'parity law' on equal access for men and women to elected positions.

Sources: Assemblée-Nationale.fr (2008); Latour et al. (1995: 126–7).

for this underrepresentation are many and wide-ranging and have been the subject of numerous debates. For example, history points to facts and events such as the fourteenth-century Salic law which prevented women from succeeding to the French throne or the Napoleonic Code of 1804 which reduced women to the position of minors and which cumulatively contributed to an aggressive masculine political culture blocking the entry of women into politics. Environmental factors, on the other hand, have included the historically gendered social division of labour which has meant that the majority of women have devoted their time to home and family welfare, subsequently gaining little or no opportunity to accumulate the resources (time, money and political training or experience) required for effective political participation. Finally, among political-institutional factors, the following are highlighted: the type of electoral system and its impact upon party selection procedures, the role of political parties and the influence of successive women's movements in history, particularly that of the 1970s (Allwood and Wadia 2000).

The myriad obstacles to increasing women's direct representation led to the conclusion, amongst a group of women (politicians and academics), that the equal representation of women, or parity, would only come about if it was enforced by law. The idea of legally enforced parity was not new. Campaigns in favour of gender quotas had been waged since the late 1970s and early 1980s in a number of European countries. In France, the idea of a 15 per cent gender quota, to be applied to the municipal elections of 1977, had been floated unsuccessfully by Françoise Giroud. In 1982, the National Assembly voted in favour of a 25 per cent quota for women, in elections run according to the system of proportional representation. However, this law was later annulled by the Constitutional Council on the basis that it categorised citizens and was therefore against the Republican conception of the abstract citizen upheld by the Constitution. The emergence of the idea of parity, the debates and legislation surrounding it are discussed in the next section.

Parity debates and legislation

Claims in favour of gender parity in French political institutions emerged at the beginning of the 1990s mainly amongst feminist academics, journalists and activists. They argued that there was an urgent need for state action and legislation to promote the entry of women into political decision-making arenas which had remained male strongholds despite the fact that women had gained the right to vote and stand for election in 1944. The demand for 'parity' (equal representation of women and men in decision-making positions) appealed to a large number of women's organisations and individual women's rights champions in France. It can also be located within a broader, international framework of campaigns for gender equality. Since 1985, a series of UN conferences on women had drawn up a timetable for reaching specific targets as far as women's rights were concerned. Most notably, the 1995 Beijing Platform for Action (PFA) had declared that the achievement of parity in political decision-making constituted a cross-cutting goal of all initiatives aimed at achieving real equality between men and women and that, across the world, women should occupy at least 30 per cent of political decision-making positions (Karam 2000: 17; United Nations 1995). In addition, a number of international conferences and meetings were held specifically on women and political participation, bringing together female parliamentary, government and civil society representatives who focused on how to increase women's representation in political institutions while recognising that this question was inseparable from those of female poverty, labour market participation and the removal of barriers against women's economic independence. Women's political representation also reached the EU agenda during the early 1990s and equality between men and women in decision-making became one of the six objectives of the European Commission's Fourth Programme of Action (1996–2000).

The wider French public responded to the idea that gender parity in politics would lead to a break-up of established, self-perpetuating elite groups seen to make political decisions in their own interests and therefore to a general cleansing of political structures and processes steeped in decades of questionable if not corrupt practices. The popularity of the parity concept took many leading politicians by surprise and forced them to integrate it into their political agendas within a relatively short period of time. Jacques Chirac adopted it as a campaign theme during the 1995 presidential elections and on becoming president, he created the Observatoire de la Parité entre les Femmes et les Hommes (OP) (see Chapter 1, p. 31). The return of the Socialists to government, in 1997, saw Prime Minister Lionel Jospin give a personal undertaking to inscribe the principle of parity into the French Constitution. He was eventually supported by Jacques Chirac in this aim.

The introduction of the idea of parity provoked a wide-ranging theoretical and political debate around the themes of Republican universalism and the essentialisation of difference. The parity idea caused divisions within both the left and the right and amongst feminists. A fundamental division occurred between 'hard-line' or orthodox Republicans and pragmatists within mainstream political parties and civil society organisations over the conception and redefinition of Republican universalism while another interconnected debate took place within the feminist camp between equal rights and 'difference' feminists. Orthodox Republicans rejected moves to enshrine the principle of parity in French constitutional law. They argued: that the French nation comprised a citizenry (*le peuple*) undivided in public life by class, religion, sex, 'race' etc;

and that because 'the citizen', as an abstract concept, is unmarked by difference it may be equally applied to all citizens (voters and political representatives alike) whose duty it is to express the common will and interest of the nation. It was claimed, therefore, that by undermining the indivisibility of the nation, the neutrality of representation and equality between citizens, parity struck at the very foundations of Republican universalism. Further, the recognition of difference and suggestion of 'positive discrimination' raised the spectre of 'Anglo-Saxon' multiculturalism or communalism and, it was argued, risked destabilising French society through the creation of separate communities and a splintering of interests (Badinter 1996; cited by Fassin 1997).[3] Pro-parity pragmatists, on the other hand, rejected charges that parity opened the door to American-style multiculturalism and dismissed doom-laden predictions about the disintegration of the French nation:

> Parity should be a mix of 'national representation' as a whole, to represent the mix of the nation's humanity as a whole . . . parity does not operate in a 'communitarian' way . . . (it allows for) a representation of the dual profile of the people, just as men and women are the two faces of humanity. (Sylviane Agacinsky cited in Sineau 2002: 129)

Hard-line Republicans were accused of espousing a national rhetoric which obfuscated struggles against discrimination and inequalities. It was argued that their demonisation of multiculturalism as a perverse Anglo-Saxon import prevented a close examination of the everyday realities of political, economic and social disadvantage which dominated the lives of certain populations in France. Parity, it was claimed, was not a question of preferential treatment, which is how many Republicans saw it, but a compensatory measure designed to reverse the historical failure of Republicanism to include women, in theory and in fact, in political decision-making (see Guigou, National Assembly debate, 15 December 1998). Hence parity epitomised equality and provided a means of realising it.

As far as the debate within the feminist camp was concerned, two arguments were presented against constitutional-legal recognition of parity. The first, more simple contention was that parity involved feminist engagement with the state in a way that was anathema to those who had cut their teeth in the women's liberation struggles of the 1970s. The second, more substantive argument was that the inscription of the parity principle into law would lead to the biological essentialisation of politics and hence to a tendency to attribute the political words and deeds of political representatives to their biological sex rather than to ideology and political beliefs, founded on one's life experiences. Pro-parity feminists countered the first contention with the view that feminists, including 1970s women's liberation activists, had always engaged with the state in one way or other in order to achieve women's rights (whether it was the right to vote or the right to abortion) and improve their position in society. The second argument was considered erroneous. It was asserted that far from reducing differences between men and women to biological sex, parity was supporting the shift from a biological foundationalist paradigm to a social constructionist one. Hence, parity was about recognising the unequal power relations and constraints imposed by the social institution of gender (which compelled one to see differences between men and women as biological) and about removing those constraints and establishing equal power relations between women and men in the polity. It was while such internal debates were continuing that certain events created the dynamic for constitutional change. Both Lionel Jospin, the Socialist Prime Minister, and President Jacques Chirac decided to back constitutional reform, noting the value of parity as a marketing tool in their respective, competing visions for modernising French society and politics.

The enshrinement of gender parity in public law brought the seven-year campaign for parity to a close. For pro-parity campaigners, the constitutional reform would mark a symbolic break in Republican culture through substitution of the nation as an abstract universalist (but *de facto* masculine) entity with a 'polyversalist' order, while the parity law would bring about women's equal presence in politics in order to ensure that France no longer languished at the bottom of the EU league table on women's political representation. France would also become the first country in the world to pass a parity law.

On 28 June 1999, a special congress of both houses of the French Parliament voted by 745 votes to 43 in favour of a Constitutional Reform Bill on gender parity which proposed recognition, within the 1958 Constitution, of 'equal access for women and men to electoral office and elective functions' ('l'égal accès des hommes et des femmes aux mandats électoraux et aux fonctions électives' – see Loi constitutionnelle no. 99-569 du 8 juillet 1999 relative à l'égalité entre les femmes et les hommes, amendment to Article 3 of the Constitution, *Journal Officiel*, 9 July 1999: 10175). In addition, political parties were made responsible for the implementation of parity (amendment to Article 4 of the Constitution, ibid.). The principal and symbolic target of this reform was the National Assembly. The amendments to the Constitution did not apply to political executive bodies at any level. It is interesting to note that the word 'parity' was not actually used in amended Articles 3 and 4.

As a result of the constitutional reform of 1999, legislation passed on 3 June 2000, by the National Assembly, obligated political parties to field equal numbers of male and female candidates at national and subnational elections fought under a proportional representation system. Such elections included municipal council elections in *communes* (local government and electoral districts) of 3,500-plus inhabitants, regional and European elections and senatorial elections in constituencies returning three or more senators[4] (see Table 2.2). Additional legislation has been adopted since then to reinforce the 2000 parity law. In 2003, a new law provided for the application of stricter rules in the construction of party lists for regional, European and senatorial elections in order to further the goal of true parity between male and female candidatures. In 2007, another law provided for the application of parity to regional and municipal council executives; increased penalties to be imposed on parties which ignored parity rules in selecting candidates for legislative elections; and the introduction of 'mixed ticket' rules for cantonal elections. Finally, a law adopted in 2008 extended the mixed ticket rules (see Table 2.2).

Since 2000, the question of women's equal presence in political assemblies has raised moments of interest among media pundits, politicians and the public – mainly during an election period. Interest was high in 2001 when the law was first tested out in local council elections (*élections municipales*) and arguably highest at the 2002 legislative elections given that the parity campaigners' main target had always been the National Assembly. The question of gender parity in politics made headlines more recently, in 2007, in the run-up to the presidential election, as pro-parity factions within the main parties of the left and the right – the PS and the UMP respectively – identified credible female presidential candidates in Ségolène Royal for the Socialists and Michèle Alliot-Marie for the majority UMP. For the first time, therefore, a real possibility existed for French voters to elect a woman – an event, it was argued, that would impact positively on the legislative elections also to take place that year. In the event, Alliot-Marie did not step forward as UMP candidate and Royal, although eventually selected by her party, was defeated in the election by Nicolas Sarkozy. The most eager discussions at such times of interest have revolved around the numbers of women candidates, eventual elected representatives and the concrete barriers (mainly related to party attitudes and processes) to women's representation. What is seldom reflected upon these days is the question of the extent to which parity reform has

Table 2.2   Parity legislation 2000–2008

Date	Law	Key points
2000	**Loi no. 2000-493** du 6 juin tendant à favoriser l'égal accès des femmes et des hommes aux mandats électoraux et fonctions électives (*Journal Officiel*, 7 June 2000: 8560).	– Political parties to apply parity principle to mixed candidate lists in elections fought under a proportional representation system, alternating strictly between male and female candidates in single-round elections and by tranches of six candidates in two-round elections. – Parties to present as many women as men (with a maximum 2 per cent gap allowed) in legislative and other FPTP elections. – Financial penalties to be imposed on parties failing to respect parity principle in legislative elections.
2003	**Loi no. 2003-327** du 11 avril 2003 relative à l'élection des conseillers régionaux et des représentants au parlement européen (*Journal Officiel*, 12 April 2003: 6488).	– Parties to apply strict alternation in respect of male and female candidates on regional election lists as opposed to alternation of male and female candidates in tranches of six names. – Introduction of shortened regional lists through division of each list into sections (based on *départements* per region). – Creation of eight 'super-regions', hence eight lists (for each party) in European elections.
2007	**Loi no. 2007-128** du 31 janvier 2007 tendant à promouvoir l'égal accès des femmes et des hommes aux mandats électoraux et fonctions électives (*Journal Officiel*, 27 2007: 1941).	– Extension of the parity principle to regional executives and those of municipal councils covering fewer than 3,500 inhabitants. – Imposition of more severe financial penalties on parties refusing to respect parity law in selection of candidates for the legislative elections. – Introduction of a 'mixed ticket' where a candidate and his/her stand-in (*suppléant/e*) are of the opposite sex. In case of a candidate's death, the stand-in automatically takes up the vacant office of general councillor without having to undergo a by-election process.
2008	**Loi no. 2008-175** du 26 février 2008 facilitant l'égal accès des femmes et des hommes au mandat de conseiller général (*Journal Officiel*, 27 February 2008: 3370).	– Extension of the conditions under which a general councillor may be replaced automatically by her/his opposite sex stand-in without having to trigger a by-election. Extended conditions include death; resignation upon gaining a parliamentary or European mandate; presumed absence as defined in law.[5]

Source: Observatoire de la Parité entre les Femmes et les Hommes (OP) (2008a).

achieved its expected task of completing French democracy. In the following section we consider the first question – the application of parity law and increases in women's representation in legislative and executive bodies – before going on to discuss that of parity and the completion or 'fixing' of a (post-) liberal democracy.

Women's representation in legislative bodies

Table 2.3 sets out the evolution of women's representation in various elected assemblies. A number of broad developments are noteworthy and warrant some comment. First, in none of the elections listed has absolute gender parity (i.e. a 50/50 male-female split) been achieved. This is because the constitutional reform law was framed in such a way as to admit only the limited goal of equal access to electoral mandates rather than the more radical one of parity in the outcomes of elections. In other words, political parties, constitutionally nominated to implement parity, have not been in any danger of being compelled to use every means possible to achieve equal representation in numerical terms. Second, in all types of election where parity law has been applied since 2000, the proportion of women in representative assemblies has increased, although more significantly in some (e.g. municipal and regional elections) than in others (cantonal and legislative elections). Third, the smaller parties on the left and far left (Les Verts, Lutte Ouvrière, Ligue Communiste Révolutionnaire), followed by the mainstream left (Socialist Party – PS and Communist Party – PCF) have been more proactive in advancing the goal of parity than the parties of the right and far right (Union pour un Mouvement Populaire – UMP, Mouvement Démocratique – MoDem, Front National – FN). Fourth, and this leads on from the second point, application of the parity law is most successful where elections are fought under a proportional representation system with mixed member party lists and where stipulations are laid down in respect of how mixed lists should be constructed in order to promote equality between male and female candidates. So, for instance, French women have generally fared better in European Parliament elections where PR has been used since 1979 when women took up 22.2 per cent of the 78 seats allocated to France. In the 1990s this figure improved significantly – to 40.2 in 1999 and to 43.6 in 2004 as a result of the imposition of alternation of male and female candidates on each list (OP 2008b: 3).

As far as municipal council elections are concerned, the proportion of women representatives increased from 21.7 per cent in 1995 to 33 per cent in 2001 and 35 per cent in 2008 (Zimmerman 2008: 4). Municipal

Table 2.3   Women in elected assemblies 1995–2008

Election year	Election type	Number of women	Total number of seats	%
1995	Municipal (local councils)	107,979	497,208	21.7
1997	Legislative (National Assembly)	63	577	11
1998	Senatorial (Senate)	17	321	5.6
1998	Regional (regional councils)	517	1,880	27.5
1998	Cantonal (*conseils généraux*)	175	2,045	8.6
1999	European (European Parliament)	35	87	40.2
2001	Municipal	156,393	474,020	33
2001	Cantonal	189	1,932	9.8
2001	Senatorial	34	321	10.6
2002	Legislative	71	577	12.3
2004	Cantonal	222	2,034	10.9
2004	Regional	895	1,880	47.6
2004	Senatorial	56	331	16.9
2004	European	34	78	43.6
2007	Legislative	107	577	18.5
2008	Senatorial	75	343	21.9
2008	Cantonal	264	2,020	13.1
2008	Municipal	181,608	519,417	35

Source: Observatoire de la parité entre les femmes et les hommes (OP) (2008b: 8–9).

council elections are run on a combined FPTP and PR mixed list system where councils representing small districts of under 3,500 inhabitants (and which constitute 88.8 per cent of all France's municipal councils) are elected according to a FPTP system while those covering larger districts over 3,500 inhabitants use a PR mixed list system. The uneven effects of parity law here are clear. The proportion of women councillors representing small districts rose from 21 per cent in 1995 to 30 per cent in 2001 and 32.2 per cent in 2008 (ibid.). This is in sharp contrast with the figures relating to the larger districts (3,500+ inhabitants) where the proportion of women representatives went up from 25.7 per cent in 1995 to 47.4 per cent in 2001 and 48.5 per cent in 2008 (ibid.; Zimmerman 2005: 18). The latter pattern of scores is replicated in the regional elections which, again, are run on a mixed list PR system. Table 2.3 shows ascending figures for women elected as regional councillors between the pre-parity 1998 elections (27.5 per cent) and the post-parity 2004 elections (47.6 per cent). Parity, as defined in law, has been reached in the larger municipal councils described as 'the vanguard of the parity revolution' (Zimmerman 2008: 3) and the likelihood is that it will be attained by regional councils at the elections of 2009.

The smallest increases in the number of women elected representatives are registered at legislative and cantonal elections where the proportion of women deputies and general councillors (*conseillères générales*) respectively has never reached the 20 per cent mark (see Table 2.3). Even the Senate, whose conservative-minded members were among those most resistant to parity reform, now has a higher proportion of women than the National Assembly (21.9 per cent as opposed to 18.5 per cent). This can be attributed to the fact that senatorial elections are partly run according to a mixed list PR system. However, it would appear that the strongest bastions of resistance to parity are the general councils where women account for only 13.1 per cent of councillors. Even though the law of February 2008 is designed to facilitate access to general councils, it is estimated that if the rate of progress since 2001 remains the same, it will take another 70 years before numerical parity between women and men is achieved in the membership of general councils (Zimmerman 2008: 5).

While women have begun to constitute a substantial presence in sub-national legislatures, in particular regional and municipal councils, they remain a long way from making an impact, through sheer force of numbers, at national level. A number of causes have been identified and analysed for this lack of progress. The main ones are: disinterest or indifference on the part of large parties who prefer to pay penalties than to respect parity of candidatures; the predominance of the single constituency FPTP election system which encourages political parties to *de facto* reserve safe seats for male candidates; the continuance of the practice of holding multiple mandates which discourages the renewal of elites and perpetuates the masculine character of the *notable*. The barriers facing women's progress in elected assemblies are not reviewed here but the interested reader may refer to Bird (2002); Bird and Dubesset (2003); Murray (2004, 2008); Opello (2006, especially Chapters 4–6); and Sineau (2002).

The feminisation of elected assemblies: the rise of new inequalities?

While many parity supporters in government and the parties have hailed the municipal and regional election results as the beginning of the 'parity revolution', it may be argued that success measured only in terms of numerical parity attained in local and regional assemblies (and in future in other elected bodies) may conceal processes which do not favour women's advancement (Reskin and Roos 1990). The processes in question are those of occupational resegregation[6] and possible eventual ghettoisation which occur when feminisation of a field traditionally dominated by men takes place. In the highly centralised French state, municipal councils have not enjoyed the autonomy in policy and decision-making that their German or English counterparts have. However, the construction of an integrated Republican bourgeoisie (*la république des notables*) from the national level downwards, originally designed to resist anti-revolutionary forces, has meant that historically, local representatives have enjoyed strong links with the centre and have derived much of their power and prestige through these links and by acting as a direct relay for national ideologies and policy orientations. However, the links between the centre and local *notables* have been eroded over the last twenty years, for example due to the Socialist decentralisation programme of the mid-1980s which included creating alternative layers of subnational government and due to increasing European integration. Consequently, the centre has many more interlocutors today through which policies are transmitted and power may be wielded and the result is that the influence and prestige of local representatives have declined. It may be argued that the seepage of power away from municipal authorities in particular has made it easier for women to enter local assemblies and that, at the same time, the continuing entry of women into this arena, since the application of the parity laws, may empty it of men even further.

It would appear that men seeking political career advancement are increasingly setting their sights on other posts at the level of subnational government: for example, mayorships, regional and general council leaderships and other executive positions to which parity law has not been applicable so far and which offer greater opportunities for the acquisition of influence and power, not only in political but also in economic terms. Posts in EU institutions are also of greater interest – for instance the European Economic and Social Committee in which the French delegation numbers 26 councillors of which 6 (23.1 per cent) are women (Conseil Economique et Social 2007: 13). This means that fiercer competition is being created further up the political ladder, particularly where a nexus of political and economic interests occurs and this makes it more difficult than ever for women to move upwards from municipal assembly membership. These processes of occupational resegregation may be reflected in the figures relating to the proportion of women present in executive posts at subnational level (see Table 2.4).

Table 2.4   Women in executive bodies 1995–2008

Year	Total	Number of women	%
Municipal councils – mayoral office			
2001	36,709	3,998	10.9
2008	35,147	4,866	13.8
General councils – leader			
2001	99	1	1.0
2004	99	3	3.0
2008	99	5	5.0
General councils – deputy leader			
2001	812	64	7.9
2004	1,052	132	12.5
2008	Figures unavailable at time of writing		
Regional councils – leader			
1998	26	3	11.5
2004	26	1	3.8
Regional councils – deputy leader			
1998	265	40	15.1
2004	338	126	37.3

Sources: Départements (2008: 24); OP (2008b: 8–9); Zimmerman (2008: 8).

While municipal councils have been hailed as the vanguard of the 'parity revolution', the proportion of women mayors has remained low in the 2000s and has been linked with the small percentage of women heading electoral lists in 2001 and 2008. And while the larger municipal councils (governing areas of more than 3,500 inhabitants) have reached parity in terms of assembly membership, it is here that women become even less visible in executive positions – in 2008 only 9.6 per cent of mayors of larger towns and cities are women (Zimmerman 2008: 4). The majority of women mayors are to be found heading the municipal executives of smaller towns and districts. A similar picture emerges as far as general and regional council executives are concerned. In 2004, only one women – Ségolène Royal for Poitou-Charentes who is a 'star politician' – made it to the leadership of a regional executive while five women reached leadership positions in general councils. These figures suggest that the top executive responsibilities (linked with leader, deputy and assistant leadership positions) are being maintained as a male preserve while women directly serve their constituents through surgeries and lower level committee work. This impacts on political training opportunities for women.

If executive leadership positions at municipal, general and regional council level serve as an important training ground and launch pad for a political career at the next level up, then women are not benefiting. So women remain untrained within a political arena which consequently becomes unspecialised, devoid of power and hence increasingly unattractive to men. According to Marie-Jo Zimmerman, chief *rapporteure* of the Observatoire de la Parité, women councillors do not feel sufficiently integrated in decision-making and many quit after just one term in office (Malle 2008). A report on municipal councils in the *département* of Allier (Fayol 2006: 45) corroborates this view with the finding that only 27.1 per cent of women councillors intended standing for re-election while a majority of 41.4 per cent said they would not do so. In the *département* of Haute Loire, the findings were similar with 23.7 per cent of women councillors stating they would seek re-election, 37.7 saying they did not intend to stand for re-election and 35 per cent remaining undecided (Fayol 2007: 5). The main reason cited by the women for standing down (other than those of a personal nature) was 'lack of decision-making power' while an overwhelming majority of those questioned felt they needed political training (on administrative and financial issues as well as on how to communicate with other politicians and voters), alongside men, in order to perform well and effect real change (ibid.). While those who decide not to stand for re-election are likely to be replaced by other women (thus maintaining parity of numbers between men and women), the high turnover of female councillors, with each cohort lacking experience and political skills, will only exacerbate the occupational resegregation of politics.

At the 2001 municipal elections, in many areas, a large number of women who gained seats came in with little political experience and few skills. The reason for this is that the major political parties opted to select, for their lists, not women party activists with political experience but women with voluntary sector experience. In the *département* of Allier the majority of women (54.8 per cent) elected to municipal councils were first-time councillors. Only 20.3 per cent of female councillors had gained their seats in the previous election, in 1995. Furthermore, among the 2001 cohort, a majority (60 per cent) had not had any party political connections before their recruitment as candidates, while 80 per cent had been previously involved in community and voluntary sector organisations. Of these 40.7 had experience of heading up such organisations (Fayol 2006: 31–2). So, it would appear that another consequence of focusing on numerical parity is that it does not always benefit women activists in the main political parties. Instead, it may encourage the cooptation of token women ('femmes alibis' as referred to in sections of the media) whose lack of political experience and skills coupled with reduced opportunities for training leads to a lack of strong, direct challenges or competition against party men in charge at local level. Where numerical parity does not translate into equal decision-making power and in increasing women's substantive representation (in the sense of involving women and women's concerns in decision/policy-making), it will not have a positive impact on policy-making regardless of the policy areas concerned.

Parity and the completion of '(post-)liberal' democracy

By the time the parity campaign had emerged in the early 1990s, neo-liberalist ideology had made deep inroads into the policy orientations and actions of Western governments. As communist regimes crumbled across East and Central Europe, the liberal democratic political model, underpinned by neo-liberal economics (characterised by market deregulation, a greater orientation towards competitiveness and cost-cutting 'modernisation' operations by companies), was acclaimed triumphantly as the most workable model for the world in order to progress towards democracy. The promise of so-called economic freedom was accompanied by a discourse on individual political and civil rights, individual responsibilities and autonomy in opposition to group rights as pertaining to trade unions, cooperative movements and other collective organisations. However, by the early 1990s, the actual experience of neo-liberal reform in the West was that privileging the individual had led to a deterioration of collective social and economic gains made after 1945 (e.g. the welfare state, workplace rights of free collective bargaining and minimum wage laws, women's rights such as equal pay for equal work, etc.) and consequently to increasing social degradation and disadvantage. Not only that, but promises of protecting individual rights through holding business, industry and public institutions to account had also failed. The hopes of citizens for a democratisation of politics were dashed as elites in all these sectors seemed ever more to work in their own interests and become embroiled in corrupt exchanges of one sort or other. The task of improving, 'fixing' or completing the liberal democratic model (the best of many imperfect ones) undertaken by the neo-liberal project had simply not been accomplished.

In this context, and from the point of view of disadvantaged populations, it became difficult to accept the argument that there is a single humanity embodied within the abstract individual. Calls for a differentiated citizenship model which provides space for different groups to participate, be represented and make their voice heard emerged in a number of nation-states including France. Such calls amounted to what many have referred to as the (post-liberal) challenge to the prevailing neo-liberal citizenship regime (for example, see Bowles and Gintis 1987; Gray 1996). 'Post-liberalism' may be understood as a variant of political liberalism which interrogates and succeeds the neo-liberal project. Given the failure of the latter to protect individual rights and progress towards greater democracy, post-liberals demand that the state steps back firmly into the public arena and that it redevelops its relationship with citizens not only by recognising different (collective) voices and identities but also by ensuring that traditionally excluded groups are given space in civil society and state institutions to participate, to represent and be represented. The post-liberal demand for greater state intervention in social and political life, for guaranteeing the protection of citizens against overbearing private interests and hence for completing or 'fixing' democratisation processes is the *quid pro quo* for accepting the state's reduced role in the economy, in the name of efficiency. In the words of Suzanne Berger, a sympathetic yet serious critic of post-liberalist theory, 'the visions of Locke, Marx and the radical democrats would all at last be realized' in a post-liberal democracy (Berger 1986).

It may be argued that the demands of the parity movement were typical of a post-liberal challenge to the French state which was being asked to take up and execute policies to enable women (half of humanity) to be heard, to represent and be represented. Parity was therefore put forward as a means for democracy to be completed. As far as the parity campaigners were concerned completing democracy actually meant including women's voice(s) and hence reconstructing the French citizenship model to consist of both halves of humanity. The spin-offs of this, many argued, would be the reduction (or possibly even the end) of political scandals and corruption (*les affaires*)[7] through the renewal of political elites who had become more and more resigned to transgressions and injustice; and the enhancement of a pluralist political culture through the revival of feminist forms of action. We will limit ourselves to briefly considering the first spin-off, not because the question of whether or not there is a causal link between women's increased presence in political institutions and the diminution of political corruption (hence the 'fixing of democracy') can be answered here but because it offers fresh possibilities for future research on the impact of parity reform in France. The question of the effects of increased feminist action, through the parity campaign and reform, is considered by a number of scholars (e.g. Baudino 2008; Le Doeuff 2000; Lépinard 2007; Saint-Crin and Dauphin 2001) although it is not necessarily framed in terms of improving the pluralist nature of the liberal democratic state.

The effect of women's political participation and representation on political corruption

Several studies have explored the relationship between levels of corruption and women's political participation, particularly in relation to the developing world where development actors and scholars have argued that governments should legislate to promote more women in decision-making as a means of fighting corruption and advancing the cause of democracy (Dollar et al. 2001; Goetz 2007; Sung 2003; Swamy et al. 2001). Proponents of the view that women are less corrupt than men often begin by considering psycho-social research on women's behaviour in decision-making which has shown that women conduct themselves in a more open, fair and public-spirited way than men. The hypothesis that women promote honest government is then tested by comparing the findings about women's behaviour and evidence of the extent of corrupt practice in government (measured against an international corruption index) with data relating to women's representation in political institutions of the country concerned. Other country-specific variables such as tolerance of civil liberties, openness to trade and levels of education are also factored in to produce more nuanced analyses. Conclusions such as 'women may have higher standards of ethical behavior and be more concerned with the common good' may then be drawn (Dollar et al. 2001: 427). Other studies have reached similar conclusions by analysing the gendered results of public attitudes/values surveys and correlating the data from such surveys to women's presence in government and levels of corruption (again measured against an accepted corruption index) (Swamy et al. 2001). These kinds of study have been critiqued not only in terms of the methodologies and methods utilised to reach such conclusions (Sung 2003) but also on the grounds that they are predicated on ideological assumptions about women's 'essential nature' which in the past posed barriers to women's entry into politics (Goetz 2007).

While there are no available studies on the link between women's increased presence in political decision-making structures and political corruption in France, there are some French data (compared with

Germany, Italy and the USA) on perceptions of corruption and women's role in anti-corruption actions. One such study was undertaken by the Women's Forum for the Economy and Society (Ricol 2007) on the basis that:

> When I had to manage the fallout from the Enron scandal on behalf of the accountancy profession worldwide, I got the feeling of there being a serious crisis in confidence, a moral failure, a kind of schizophrenic attitude which said that people who were normally honest at home were dishonest in the workplace. In examining the consequences of this crisis, I was able to observe that each time a woman held an important position within the company, precisely as in the case of Enron, the company was better protected or that it ran fewer risks. I wanted to back up my empirical observation with an international study. (Ricol 2007: 2)

One could use the data from a study such as this in association with other similar studies and empirical data on corruption in French political institutions in order to test the claims made by parity campaigners about the positive effects of parity reform on corruption and hence on the advancement of democracy. However, as Goetz points out there are several dangers attached to doing this:

> Like any instrumentalist argument, the 'women are less corrupt than men' justification for bringing women into politics and public institutions is not just vulnerable to exposure as a myth; it puts women's engagement in the public arena on the wrong foot. Women are seen as instruments to achieve a broader development goal, not welcomed to public office as a matter of their democratic and employment rights. The new stress on women's gender as a useful instrument for good governance is another example of the dangers of using the notion of 'women' as a single category in social analysis and in development policy. Critical social differences between women disappear before the presumed fact of the probity and virtues inherent to their gender. (Goetz 2007: 88)

Goetz rightly recognises that 'politics is the very worst place to ignore differences between women' because 'arrangements for the inclusion of women in politics that are insensitive to differences of race, class, and ethnicity between women will see elite women capturing public office' (ibid.).

Hence, in doing further research on parity reform and good governance versus corruption, it would possibly be more useful to explore the impact of existing corrupt practices on women who enter political institutions and to ask what kind of gendered processes and power relationships are at work when corrupt exchanges occur. We could also ask what government can do for women who find themselves caught up in such processes and relationships in order to promote democracy rather than what women can do for good political practice by virtue of their presumed uprightness in the face of corruption.

Conclusion

There is a now a vast literature in French and English on the subject of parity reform in France. A few texts have been referred to in this chapter in order to give the reader some pointers for further exploration of this subject. This chapter has attempted to give a brief though useful background to the introduction of equal representation between men and women in French elected assemblies and has assembled as up-to-date figures as possible in relation to the presence of women in political institutions. Additionally it has highlighted questions or themes of particular interest to the authors. Questions about what parity campaigners meant when they spoke of the completion of democracy and about whether or not their aims are being met in that respect are worth pursuing further. Hence, the problematic of gender, politics and corruption is of relevance and raises a set of subquestions. Similarly, reflections on how the worst effects of occupational resegregation can be avoided at local political decision-making levels are also important and will provide directions for future research in this area.

Notes

1. Issue 15(4) of *Nouvelles Questions Féministes*, edited by Christine Delphy, contains articles by Françoise Gaspard, Alain Liepietz and Eliane Viennot, arguing in favour of parity.
2. Issue 16(2) of *Nouvelles Questions Féministes*, edited by Delphy, contains articles by Michèle Le Doeuff, Eleni Varikas and Josette Trat, arguing against parity.
3. Similar arguments were put forward by proponents of the Islamic headscarf ban in France; see Chapter 6.
4. PR was applicable to all *départements* (which also constitute senatorial constituencies) returning three or more senators of which there were 56. This changed in 2003 when a new law made PR applicable to *départements* returning four or more senators (Sénat 2008). As there are only 28 such *départements*, the overall effect after 2003 was to slow down the progression of gender parity in the Senate.

5. As parties prefer nominating women as stand-ins rather than as actual candidates at cantonal elections, the hope is that more women will gain general council seats vacated under the conditions stipulated by the law.
6. Gender segregation in the labour market is conceptualised in terms of the location of men and women in different occupations, organisations and industries with women typically concentrated in those that are poorly remunerated. Resegregation occurs when an occupation becomes devalued in real or perceived terms through the process of feminisation.
7. The liberal democratic state in France has been touched by myriad political scandals and corruption through the centuries. Paul Jankowski (2007) argues that while the scandals of the post-1945 era may be less dramatic (compared with the Dreyfus Affair or the Panama scandal for example), what distinguishes political corruption today is its endemic nature at all levels of the polity, hence the decreased capacity of politicians to be outraged by it, and public resignation in the face of it.

3
Abortion

This chapter focuses on implementation or the extent to which women in France have been able to exercise the right to abortion introduced by the Loi Veil in 1975. This law, although a compromise, was relatively liberal, allowing a woman who declared herself to be in a situation of distress to have an abortion within the first ten weeks of pregnancy. The problem, however, was exercising this right. The cost of an abortion was not reimbursed by the state. Conscience clauses allowed doctors to refuse to perform abortions and did not oblige them to refer the woman to another doctor, leading to severe lack of provision in parts of the country. Minors needed parental consent, and there were residence conditions, intended to prevent 'abortion tourism'. Minor amendments were made to the Loi Veil, including the reimbursement of costs in 1982, the decriminalisation of the act of performing an abortion on oneself in 1993, and the creation of the new offence of obstructing abortion in the same year. It was under the Jospin government, however, that concerns about access prompted a more thorough review of abortion law. A report by Professor Israel Nisand, submitted to the Minister for Employment and Solidarity, Martine Aubry in 1999, highlighted the difficulties faced by many women trying to obtain an abortion in France, and a bill presented by Aubry the following year aimed to resolve these problems. The successful passage of the bill through Parliament resulted in the 2001 law on abortion and contraception, which is discussed in detail later in this chapter.

Historical context

Abortion was made a criminal act by Article 317 of the Penal Code of 1810, but the law was rarely enforced and during the nineteenth century, the question of how to care for unwanted children was of more public concern than the illegality of abortion. Growing anxiety about population decline following the First World War stimulated public debate and prompted legal reform. The state regulation of abortion was justified in terms of population and the national interest, rather than religious or moral reasons (Stetson 1987: 56). Laws introduced in 1920 and 1923 made it illegal to induce an abortion by any means or to provide any information on contraception or abortion. Penalties were particularly harsh for members of the medical profession (Allison 1994: 224). The 1923 reform was intended to make these provisions easier to implement, by downgrading abortion from a serious to a less serious offence, thereby removing the requirement of trial by popular jury. The pronatalists behind this reform hoped that judges would take a harsher view than juries, and this was indeed the case, although there was no accompanying rise in the birth rate (Mossuz-Lavau 2002: 88). In 1939, penalties were increased for members of the medical profession caught performing abortions and for repeat offenders. In 1941, abortion became a crime against the state (Mossuz-Lavau 2002: 90).

At the Liberation, the laws passed under Vichy were repealed. A series of incentives to procreate were introduced by the state, taking the form of financial assistance and state approval. In 1945, De Gaulle asked young couples to provide him with 'millions of beautiful babies' (Allison 1994: 223–4). In 1955, abortion was legalised on medical grounds if the pregnancy endangered the life of the mother, but remained illegal in all other circumstances. Illegal abortions continued to take place, and the number of convictions fell (Mossuz-Lavau 2002: 93). A family planning movement began to emerge, with the creation of the Mouvement pour la Maternité Heureuse in 1956, becoming the MFPF in 1960. This was to play an important role in subsequent debates about contraception and abortion.

In 1967, the legalisation of contraception in strictly delineated circumstances (Loi no. 67-1176 du 28 décembre 1967 relative à la régulation des naissances) paved the way for demands to be made for the legalisation of abortion by raising the question of what should be done when contraception fails. The failure rate was high, and there were other problems: contraceptives were not free of charge; they were only available on prescription from pharmacies; minors needed the permission of their parent or guardian; and advertising was banned unless it was directed at doctors or pharmacists.[1] Women with the financial means to travel to England for a safe and legal abortion did so, but backstreet abortions were common and were a danger to the health and lives of a disproportionate number of working-class women who could not afford to travel.

The first of a series of bills proposing the legalisation of abortion in certain circumstances was tabled in the National Assembly in June 1967. The changing social and political climate meant that these proposals were increasingly favourably received, and public acceptance of more liberal abortion laws was fuelled by a series of actions by feminists, doctors and predominantly left-wing politicians. The new women's liberation movement which emerged in 1970 was united in its demand for free and legal contraception and abortion, despite deep divisions on other issues (Jenson 1996: 90). It played an important role in the creation of a climate which would be more favourable to the legalisation of abortion. In 1971, a declaration published in the weekly news magazine, *Le Nouvel observateur* and signed by 343 women, many of them prominent public figures, challenged the state to prosecute them or to admit that the current law was no longer workable. The association Choisir was formed in order to defend any who were prosecuted, but none were, adding further support to the argument that the law was unenforceable and crystallising support for liberalisation. Public support was growing, particularly on the left, and this was reinforced by the Bobigny trials. Feminist lawyer, Gisèle Halimi, founder and president of Choisir, acted for the defence of a teenage girl, who had had an abortion after having been raped, and of her mother and her mother's friend who had assisted her. Halimi used the trial to make a case for legislative reform, calling as witnesses a series of high profile figures who spoke in their defence. The case was won, along with much public sympathy. The witnesses, all of whom supported the right to choose, criticised the glaring inequalities between those who could afford to go abroad or to private clinics and those who could not; they exposed the conditions in which illegal abortions took place; and they rejected the argument that the embryo in the first few weeks of pregnancy is a human being (Mossuz-Lavau 2002: 103). These arguments were echoed by the 331 doctors who signed a petition published in 1973 declaring that they had performed illegal abortions and calling for the repeal of the 1920 law. They criticised the hypocrisy of a state which penalised abortion, but turned a blind eye to those who were able to travel overseas. They also condemned the dangers of backstreet abortions.

Feminists mobilised in favour of a woman's right to choose, using the slogan 'un enfant si je veux, quand je veux' ('a child if I want, when I want'). The Mouvement de Libération de l'Avortement et de la Contraception (MLAC) formed in 1973, and brought together a wide range of groups and activists. It organised mass demonstrations in favour of free and legal contraception and abortion; mobilised feminists, doctors and their supporters; and provided illegal abortions.

There was opposition, however. The small conservative association, the Ordre des Médecins, formed under Vichy in order to repress abortion (Allison 1994: 224), was opposed to any liberalisation of the laws which would shift responsibility for decision-making on to doctors, force them to perform abortions, or permit abortions for reasons of personal convenience rather than medical necessity or extreme social need (Mossuz-Lavau 2002: 119). The main arguments against abortion were voiced by the Catholic Church and the organisation Laissez-les vivre, both of which argued that life begins at conception and that abortion is murder. Laissez-les vivre, which was founded in 1970 in order to obstruct all attempts to reform the 1920 law, contended that abortion contravenes the right to life guaranteed in the French Constitution; that abortion is a threat to the survival of the nation; and that it has dangerous consequences for the health and future reproductive capacity of the individual woman.

Given the heated public debate, political action was unavoidable. In 1973, a number of bills were tabled and began their troubled route through the legislative process. A government bill reached the National Assembly in June 1973. It stated that the 1920 law was ineffective, archaic and unjust and proposed legalisation in certain cases. It defined abortion as a medical act and made two medical consultations compulsory. A detailed parliamentary inquiry revealed fundamental splits around the issue, which stalled the bill's progress, but the potentially long-term paralysis was ended in May 1974 by the election to the presidency of Giscard d'Estaing, following the sudden and unexpected death of Georges Pompidou. Giscard saw himself as a political moderniser, and his election had a dramatic effect on the agenda. He created a department for the status of women under Françoise Giroud and gave the Minister for Public Health, Simone Veil, the task of finding a way of making the legalisation of abortion attractive to Parliament (Mossuz-Lavau 2002: 129–30). Veil did this by framing it as an issue of public health. The bill aimed to update the abortion law and address its shortcomings, including the unjust impact of the law. It aimed to reduce the number of deaths and serious injuries to women incurred by backstreet abortions. It set out the conditions under which abortion would be available, and stressed that it would be a last resort (Allison 1994: 229–30). However, the passage of the bill was not easy: debates were heated, hostile personal attacks were directed at the minister, and the National Assembly in which she defended her bill on 26 November 1974 was made up of 481 men and only 9 women.

The Loi Veil permitted abortion during the first ten weeks of pregnancy when the woman declared herself in a state of distress. Doctors were required to inform the patient of the risks and to have her confirm her decision one week after the initial request. Doctors could exercise a conscience clause, and foreigners had to meet residence requirements (Mossuz-Lavau 2002: 13).

In an unprecedented move, the bill was passed for a fixed five-year term and had to be re-examined and passed permanently in 1979. Consequently, the debates were reopened. A demonstration in October brought 20,000–30,000 feminists onto the streets of Paris in defence of the right to legal abortion. The Ordre des Médecins admitted the health benefits which had resulted from the introduction of the Loi Veil. Despite right-wing opposition in Parliament, the new law was passed in December 1979 (Mossuz-Lavau 2002: 135). It contained new provisions intended to reduce recourse to abortion and others intended to make access easier. For example, on the one hand, doctors had to provide more information about the health risks and the available alternatives. On the other hand, measures were introduced to try to ensure that women did not exceed the time limit when their doctor invoked the conscience clause, and that abortion services were made available even when the doctor in charge of a particular unit refused to perform abortions personally (Mossuz-Lavau 2002: 136). However, there was still a shortage of service providers, and the costs of abortion were not reimbursed by the state. When the Socialist Party came to power in 1981, this was one of the first issues on the agenda of the new Minister for Women's Rights, Yvette Roudy. A law passed in December 1982 ensured abortions were paid for by the state. Roudy also launched a public information campaign and insisted that all public hospitals provide abortion services (Mossuz-Lavau 2002: 138).

During the parliamentary debates 1973–9, there was a pronounced left–right split. Members of the right and centre opposed to abortion put forward four main arguments. The first was the need to respect life. The second was that abortion was a sign of moral decline that signalled the end of civilisation. M. Bizet (UDR) for example, exclaimed during a parliamentary debate in 1973: 'Tomorrow, you will be asking us to legalise the marriage of homosexuals' (quoted in Mossuz-Lavau 2002: 141). The third was that abortion contributed to the serious problem of population decline. Finally, it was argued that abortion would quickly become normalised and a substitute for contraception. This was the main argument against liberalisation between 1979 and 1982 (Mossuz-Lavau 2002: 146).

Right-wing and centre supporters of liberalisation argued that the child is not viable before ten weeks; that respect for life should extend to the (sometimes suicidal) woman; that population decline and abortion are not necessarily closely linked; and that there was an urgent need to address the serious problem of illegal abortions. This was the argument that was stressed in particular by Jean Taittinger and Simone Veil and largely ignored by right-wing and centre opponents of liberalisation. Illegal abortions were estimated at around 1,000 per day, at least one of which was fatal. They argued that if women were desperate enough to abort regardless of the risk, then it might as well be as safe as possible (Mossuz-Lavau 2002: 147).

In contrast, the left argued that women had the right to control their own body and the right to choose if and when to have a child. They wanted the removal of the 'distress' condition, of the preliminary interview, and of the requirement that minors have parental consent. The PS favoured a time limit of 14 weeks; the PCF 12 weeks (Mossuz-Lavau 2002: 148).

The Loi Veil was welcome, but not perfect. One of its major short-comings was that the cost of abortions was not covered by the state. This was rectified by the Loi Roudy (31 December 1982), and although feminists continued to express concerns about problems accessing abortion, especially within the short time limit of only ten weeks, it was not a major focus for them during the 1980s. The MFPF, by then a self-declared feminist organisation, worked hard to give advice and information to women and girls, but, until the 1990s, there was no sense that the right to abortion was under threat.

Abortion came back onto the feminist agenda in the early 1990s in response to the increasingly violent attacks on abortion clinics, the Catholic Church's repeated insistence on the right to life, and attempts to have the foetus recognised in law as a person with human rights. Catholic fundamentalist activists began to attack abortion clinics towards the end of the 1980s and by 1992, these attacks had become so problematic that a new offence of obstructing abortion was created by the Loi Neiertz (1993). This law also decriminalised the act of carrying out an abortion on oneself (27 January 1993).

In January 1995, 10,000 people demonstrated in the streets of Paris at the call of fundamentalist associations and the far right, demanding the repeal of the Loi Veil. In response, feminists organised a 40,000-strong demonstration in defence of abortion and contraception. At the forefront of French feminist action was CADAC (Coordination des Associations pour le Droit à l'Avortement et à la Contraception) which had formed in 1990 in response to the growing threat to women's reproductive rights. Despite the existence since 1993 of the Loi Neiertz prohibiting the obstruction of abortion, the courts continued to take a lenient view of anti-abortion attacks, and in 1995 the new government proposed granting amnesty to a number of convicted anti-abortion commandos.

CADAC brought together various feminist associations, including the MFPF and women's sections or committees from the main trade unions and political parties. It was responsible for a number of high-profile campaigns and lobbied intensively to urge court action against violent anti-abortion groups, to guarantee free contraception for young women, and to acquire publicly funded status for abortion clinics. These actions raised awareness of the precariousness of rights taken for granted by many young women and also drew attention to the difficulties experienced by many, in particular young and migrant women, when they attempted to exercise these rights. Although the Loi Veil was seen by feminists as an important victory for women's rights, access to free and legal abortion and contraception was nevertheless patchy, and the inadequacy of the resources available which restricted the proper implementation of the law was subject to criticism by feminists, family planning associations and health professionals. Some groups of women were particularly harshly affected by the lack of resources: those who could not afford private clinics, when public ones were too far away or had long waiting lists; and those who could not afford to travel abroad should the difficulty accessing abortion in France result in their exceeding the time limit. Young women and girls often fell into this category, and many of them were already in the difficult situation of needing to provide evidence of parental consent before they could have an abortion, but feeling unable to approach their parents for this. When the left returned to government in 1997, abortion was once again firmly on the political agenda.

One of the major criticisms of the 1975 law was that it was not supported by adequate resources. In 1999, these criticisms were confirmed by a report commissioned by the government and submitted to the Minister for Employment and Solidarity, Martine Aubry, by Professor Israel Nisand. This report catalogued obstacles to abortion, for example, the requirement that in order to obtain an abortion in France, a woman must have been resident in the country for at least three months. This condition was included in the Loi Veil because of the fear of 'abortion tourism', but resulted in discrimination against immigrant women. It was removed in June 2000. The Nisand report prompted Aubry to begin a broad consultation with health professionals, teachers, practitioners, family planning associations, activists and pro-family groups. This consultation resulted in the plan presented by Aubry in July 1999, which stressed the importance of improving knowledge about and access to effective contraceptive methods; reducing the need for abortion, which should be seen as a last resort; and respecting women's rights, by ensuring proper access to abortion (Bousquet 2000: 17). In 2000, Aubry presented a bill to the National Assembly which aimed to improve access to abortion and to emergency contraception.

Despite its good performance on a range of health indicators, France nevertheless has a high teenage pregnancy rate. Schools minister, Ségolène Royal, announced in the summer of 1999 that school nurses would be able to administer the morning-after pill, Norlevo, which had been available over the counter in pharmacies since 1 June 1999, to pupils in distress. Guidelines appeared in *Le Bulletin officiel de l'Education national* in January 2000. Pro-family and anti-abortion groups opposed this and appealed to the Conseil d'Etat, which annulled Royal's decision, on the grounds that it contradicted the 1967 law on contraception, and this subsequently became the focus of campaigns for change. The issue was finally resolved by a law on public health passed in 2000, which permitted school nurses to administer emergency contraception, as well as making it free of charge in pharmacies for minors. There was also a national information campaign on contraception launched in 2000 (Mossuz-Lavau 2002: 393–5).

The international context

In common with prostitution, abortion has been an issue which has divided policy-makers internationally and regionally and there has therefore been a tendency to see it repeatedly pushed back into the national arena. Even at the national level, politicians do not like to engage with the abortion issue. It is emotive, often associated with morality, and not easily conducive to compromise. In Britain, where MPs voted on reducing the time limit for legal abortion from 24 to 20 weeks in May 2008, there was a free vote (Sparrow 2008). Other avoidance tactics include trying to keep it off the political agenda, for example, by passing responsibility to the medical profession (Outshoorn 1996: 156). At the international level, the opposition of the Vatican and conservative US administrations since the 1980s, the EU's insistence that abortion policy remain an issue for member states, and the complexity of reproductive rights in a world where forced abortion and sterilisation are more pressing concerns for many women, have all mitigated against global or regional consensus. However, certain factors are challenging this.

The first is the emerging global consensus on reproduction and sexual health which became visible at the International Conference on Population and Development (ICPD) in 1994 and has been reinforced not only by reaffirmations of the commitments made there, but also by the development of an international human rights agenda. The claim made by feminists during the 1990s that women's rights are human rights (Bunch 1990) and the introduction in the UN in 2002 of a special *rapporteur* for health, giving the right to health the same status as other human rights, both contributed to reinforcing the idea that women everywhere have the right to reproductive and sexual health. Although this stops short of declaring a universal right to abortion, it provides a framework within which claims for safe and legal abortions can be made.

The ICPD marked a shift in population policy from a concern with population reduction to a concern with reproductive health and the empowerment of women. The agenda was wide-ranging, but the most heated debates were around abortion, largely as a result of the Vatican's opposition to it and its attempts to build a coalition with Islamic and other Catholic countries. This coalition lost momentum as preparations for the conference progressed, and by the end of the conference, a Programme of Action had been agreed by all 179 states, with the Vatican entering formal reservations on those parts which dealt with reproductive issues (McIntosh and Finkle 1995: 248). Although the Programme of Action is not legally binding on the 179 states which accepted it, it exerts moral and political pressure, and can be referred to by NGOs and other actors in domestic policy debates.

The Cairo conference was important in that it became the forum for a recognition of the worldwide reality of abortion, whether it was legal or not. Although the Programme of Action did not call for the legalisation of abortion, it endorsed the concepts of reproductive and sexual health and the services necessary to support them. It advocated the provision of high quality family planning services, stressed the importance of reducing the need for abortion, and stated that, where abortion is legal, it should be safe (Cohen and Richards 1994: 275).

During the preparations for the Cairo conference, the US, under newly elected President Bill Clinton, was supportive of safe, legal and voluntary abortion for all women. This was a reversal of the Reagan and Bush governments' abortion policy which included the denial of US funding for any NGO which practised or advocated abortions, regardless of how they were paid for: 'the global gag rule' or 'Mexico City Policy' (McIntosh and Finkle 1995: 244). However, the US position weakened as the conference approached for domestic political reasons, Bill Clinton not being in a position to risk losing the votes of US Catholics (McIntosh and Finkle 1995: 247). The global gag rule was reintroduced by President George W. Bush in 2001 (International Planned Parenthood Federation 2008a), but overthrown by President Barack Obama in January 2009 (Stein and Shear 2009).

The Fourth UN Conference on Women took place in Beijing in 1995, just one year after the ICPD. Its Platform for Action reaffirmed the ICPD Programme of Action and called upon governments to 'review laws containing punitive measures against women who have undergone illegal abortions'. At the Special Session of the UN General Assembly to evaluate progress of the ICPD in 1999, governments adopted by consensus specific recommended actions to make abortion safe and more available (Hessini 2005: 91).

The UN's Human Rights Committee (HRC), Committee on Economic, Social and Cultural Rights (CESCR), Committee on the Elimination of Discrimination Against Women (CEDAW) and Committee on the Rights of the Child (CRC) have all increased the attention paid to human rights in relation to abortion (Hessini 2005: 91).

In 2002, the UN established a Special Rapporteur for Health to report on the realisation of the right to health and to make recommendations on the steps needed to promote and protect this right. The right to health is accorded the same status as other human rights. The 2004 report of the Special Rapporteur stresses the obligations of states 'to address the factors that lead to unsafe abortions, to produce access to safe, accessible services where abortions are legal and remove punitive measures against women who have undergone abortions' (Hessini 2005: 92). Also in 2004, all of the original 179 governments which signed the ICPD Programme of Action reaffirmed their commitment to it.

Another factor pushing towards a minimal global acceptance of access to safe and legal abortions in certain cases (especially when the pregnancy results from rape or incest or represents a serious threat to the life of the woman) is the recognition of the links between women's human rights and this minimal access. Despite its neutrality on abortion since its creation in 1963, Amnesty International abandoned this position in 2007 on the grounds that it could not ignore the consequences of rape, especially within situations of conflict. This has been a major focus of its international campaign Stop Violence Against Women (Allen 2007). Kate Gilmore, Executive Deputy Secretary General of Amnesty International, said: 'Amnesty International's position is not for abortion as a right but for women's human rights to be free of fear, threat and coercion as they manage all consequences of rape and other grave human rights violations' (Amnesty International 2007). Prompting calls from the Vatican for Catholics to withdraw their support from the NGO, Amnesty International has declared its support for the decriminalisation of abortion, access to healthcare when complications arise from abortion, and women's access to abortion when their health or human rights are in danger.

At the European level, freedom of movement between EU member states means that citizens of a state where abortion is illegal (in late 2007 this was Ireland, Malta and Poland, following Portugal's legalisation of abortion during the first ten weeks in July 2007) can, if they can afford it, travel freely to a member state where it is not. However, an EU-wide abortion policy is not on the horizon. Before it accepted the Maastricht Treaty, Ireland insisted on an assurance that its national abortion ban would not be overturned. In 2007, Poland refused to agree to the Reform Treaty at the Intergovernmental Conference in Lisbon until it was reassured that the distribution of voting rights would not threaten its ability to object to any future EU-wide legalisation of abortion (Fong 2007), and Ireland's rejection in a referendum in June 2008 of the Lisbon Treaty was partly explained by commentators at the time by fears that developments in the EU would decrease national decision-making in this area, amongst others (Henry McDonald, 'Irish Voters Reject EU Treaty'; Allegra Stratton, guardian.co.uk, 13 June 2008, accessed 25 June 2008).

The European Parliament has passed several resolutions since the ICPD, including one that calls on member states to 'legalise induced abortion under certain conditions, at least in cases of forced pregnancy and rape, and where the health or life of the woman is endangered, on the principle that it must be the woman herself who takes the final decision' (European Parliament, Texts Adopted by Parliament, Final Edition: 9 March 1999, Women's Health. A4-0029/1999, Resolution on the report from the Commission to the Council, the European Parliament, the Economic and Social Committee and the Committee of the Regions on the state of women's health in the European Community (COM(97)0224 – C4-0333/97) (accessed 24 June 2008)). In a landmark case on 8 July 2004, the European Court of Human Rights refused to recognise a foetus as a human being under the European Convention for the Protection of Human Rights and Fundamental Freedoms (Hessini 2005: 92).

A 2008 Council of Europe resolution states that, 'abortion should not be banned within reasonable gestational limits . . . The lawfulness of abortion does not have an effect on a woman's need for an abortion, but only on her access to a safe abortion . . . The Assembly affirms the right of all human beings, in particular women, to respect for their physical integrity and to freedom to control their own bodies. In this context, the ultimate decision on whether or not to have an abortion should be a matter for the woman concerned, who should have the means of exercising this right in an effective way' (Council of Europe Parliamentary Assembly, Resolution 1607, Access to safe and legal abortion in Europe, http://assembly.coe.int/Documents/AdoptedText/ta08/ERES1607.htm, accessed 28 May 2008).

These resolutions are non-binding and have no direct effect on member states or on EU policy. They can, however, be used as references by NGOs and other campaigners, and contribute to the framework within which French abortion policy debates are situated.

The Aubry bill 2000

The reforms proposed in the Aubry bill were presented as pragmatic and reasonable responses to specific problems. In the introduction, Aubry set out a number of problems that she aimed to address: the high number of abortions that take place in France; the high number of unwanted teenage pregnancies; and the high number of women who travel abroad to have an abortion because they have exceeded the ten-week time limit. She stressed that the government had already introduced measures to improve the provision of abortion in public hospitals and to increase access to new abortion techniques, including pharmaceutical, as opposed to surgical, abortion. It had also launched a wide public information campaign on contraception. Aubry argued that it was now time to update the Neuwirth and Veil laws, improving access to abortion by extending the time limit for voluntary termination from ten to twelve weeks and by modifying the requirement for parental consent for minors; ensuring free and confidential access to contraception for minors; and improving access to good contraceptive methods (Aubry 2000: 3–5).

Parliamentary committees

The bill was discussed at length by parliamentary committees, each of which produced a detailed report which was then used to inform debates in the National Assembly and the Senate. Preliminary reports were prepared by the Delegation for Women's Rights in both the Assembly (Bousquet 2000) and the Senate (Terrade 2001), and by the Assembly's Committee for Cultural, Family and Social Affairs (Lignières-Cassou 2000). The National Assembly's Delegation for Women's Rights had already conducted a year-long inquiry into contraception and abortion, intending to make it the subject of its annual report in 2000.

Instead, it used the information collected, including the transcripts of hearings of a large number of expert witnesses, to produce a report on the bill (Bousquet 2000). The reports by the Senate's Delegation for Women's Rights (Terrade 2001) and by the National Assembly's Committee for Cultural, Family and Social Affairs (Lignières-Cassou 2000), drew on these findings, especially as the *rapporteure* for this Committee, Martine Lignières-Cassou, was also the president of the National Assembly's Delegation for Women's Rights.

France has a relatively high number of abortions in relation to other European countries, despite its consistently good international ranking on other health indicators. The comparison is frequently made with the Netherlands, to which many French women travel to obtain abortions after the legal limit. The abortion rate in the Netherlands is 6.5 per thousand. In France, it is 15.4 per thousand. The relation between abortions and births in the Netherlands is 1:9. In France, it is 1:3. The Netherlands has very liberal abortion legislation, and a time limit of 22 weeks (Terrade 2001: 18). All three reports attribute the high abortion rate in France to inadequate access to appropriate contraception and to the information necessary to use it effectively. Terrade points out, for example, that, despite the Loi Roudy introducing state funding for contraception, this does not apply to all forms. In particular, third generation mini-pills, which suit many women better than earlier versions, are not reimbursed by the state (Terrade 2001: 21).

The authors of all the reports call for better information on contraception and sex education for all school pupils in order to reduce demand for abortions, particularly amongst teenagers. Bousquet states that there are 10,000 unwanted teenage pregnancies every year in France, ending in abortion for 7,000 of them (Bousquet 2000: 6). Reducing unwanted pregnancies is highlighted as a key policy objective.

All three reports stress the need for sufficient resources to make abortions available to all those who need them, regardless of their financial means and without the current regional disparities. Bousquet states that uneven and insufficient provision has the harshest effect on women with the least access to information and the fewest financial resources and that travel abroad is an unacceptable response to the unmet demand for abortions in France (Bousquet 2000: 9). Lignières-Cassou calls for improved provision of abortions by public hospitals, and Terrade argues that the right to abortion is obstructed by anti-abortion activists, the conscience clause, which can destroy local provision, and the lack of new practitioners to replace pro-choice activists who are reaching retirement age. This area of healthcare remains undervalued and underpaid.

In addition, Bousquet suggests legalising sterilisation as a form of contraception (Bousquet 2000: 32). Although this was not strictly illegal in France, Article 222-9 of the Penal Code prohibiting violence leading to permanent mutilation or disability and Article 16-3 of the Civil Code which permits interference with the integrity of the human body only in the case of medical necessity for the person concerned, were normally interpreted as prohibiting sterilisation, and the sterilisation rate in France is therefore much lower than in comparable countries, such as Great Britain (25 per cent) and Canada (45 per cent). As a result of the delegation's suggestion, an amendment was added by the National Assembly (Terrade 2001: 25).

Terrade calls for the removal of the compulsory second consultation a week after the first, arguing that this infantilises women. The Loi Veil required women to have two medical and social consultations eight days apart. Aubry's bill removed the compulsory nature of the social consultation. Terrade argues that women should be correctly informed as they make their decision, but this should be in their capacity as adult women, exercising a right enshrined in law in a respectful and equal relation with their doctor. The bill proposes that the medical consultation should provide objective and neutral medical information (Terrade 2001: 39). Terrade argues that it should no longer have a legally enshrined aim to discourage abortion.

Terrade's report, which was accepted by the delegation by a majority of only one, is notable for the way in which it explicitly situates abortion and contraception as hard-won rights which lie at the heart of women's emancipation. Terrade states that the ability to control their own reproduction frees women from patriarchy, and that constant vigilance is required to ensure that women retain this right and can exercise it effectively. However, having said this, she argues that women would always prefer not to have to exercise their right to abortion, that this is a last resort, and that everything must be done to reduce the need for it (Terrade 2001: 7). Lignières-Cassou's more measured report states that the Neuwirth and Veil laws were, in their time, brave texts representing considerable progress for women's reproductive rights. They nevertheless need bringing up to date because of medical progress and changes in social attitudes. This process can take place in a calmer social climate than that which surrounded the original laws (Lignières-Cassou 2000: 1). She argues that the vast majority of abortions are due to contraceptive failure, and that the decision to abort is never taken lightly and is not viewed as an alternative form of contraception (Lignières-Cassou 2000: 8). She introduces the aims of the government's policy as firstly reducing demand for abortion, by launching contraception publicity and awareness raising campaigns. The second aim is to improve the provision of abortions by public hospitals, since large disparities exist between the speed and quality of provision according to region and time of year. The third area in which government is active is in improving the Neuwirth and Veil laws.

The only mention of religious opposition to abortion is in Terrade's report where she states that the delegation will not be entering into this debate, despite the fact that religious convictions 'explain for many the passion that the issue arouses' (Terrade 2001: 8). The relation between religion and French abortion policy is an interesting one, which remains to be investigated. France, as a secular state with a Catholic social and cultural heritage and exceptionally high levels of atheism, rarely fits into typologies constructed by comparativists studying the influence of religion on state policy. This is as true for abortion policy as it is for other issue areas. Minkenberg, for example, found that:

> France is a special and particularly revealing case. It deviates from those cases of separation in southern Europe and in Ireland in that the French tradition of *laicité* and the high levels of secularisation in terms of conventional measures of church-going and religiosity have resulted in a cultural paradigm which severely restricts the room for manoeuvre for the Catholic Church. It is only now that the traditional hostility towards the Catholic Church and religion in general is giving way to a new appraisal of the role of religion in French public life which may lead to a new social contract between the churches and the lay public. (Minkenberg 2003: 213–14)

Framing abortion in the parliamentary debates (2000–2001)

The climate in which abortion and contraception came onto the political agenda in 2000 was much calmer than that surrounding the Neuwirth and Veil laws. In 2000, there was broad acceptance of the principle of legal abortions during the early stage of pregnancy. Notable exceptions to this consensus were speeches by Philippe de Villiers and Christine Boutin who, along with the Archbishop of Paris, called for better support for pregnant women in order to reduce demand for abortion (*Le Monde*, 27 November 2000, p. 10). Right-wing parties instituted a free vote, although made it clear that they opposed the contents of the bill. One of their objections was to the proposed loosening of the requirements for parental consent for minors on the grounds that this would undermine the family.

Although the principle of abortion was not challenged by the mainstream parties, this does not mean that they agree on the underlying justification. If many on the left perceive abortion as a right, on the centre-right it is constructed as a social necessity in order to reduce distress and the health risks of backstreet abortions. Many of the contributions from the right, particularly in the Senate, portrayed women who turn to abortion as pitiful and helpless, and at the same time, liable to abuse any opportunities offered by the law. For example, Jean-François Mattei claimed that extending the time limit to twelve weeks would encourage women to leave their decision until this later date. The availability of antenatal test results before the proposed time limit would lead them to selectively abort foetuses of the 'wrong' sex or with unwanted imperfections.

The women who contributed to the debates as ministers (Aubry, Guigou), as authors of the various reports (Terrade, Bousquet and Lignières-Cassou) and as backbenchers (Roudy), spoke of abortion and contraception as a right won by women's struggles. Elisabeth Guigou, Minister for Employment and Solidarity, presenting the bill in the National Assembly (Assemblée nationale 2000) stated that the main priority of the government's action in proposing this bill was to reduce the number of unwanted pregnancies by assuring better access to contraception. She stressed that the motivating force behind the bill was concern with public health, and that it was a question of taking into account the difficulties of deprived populations and introducing measures to enable them to access a right which has already been won but whcih they have had trouble exercising (Assemblée nationale 2000: 09498).

The extension of the time limit for voluntary terminations from ten to twelve weeks proved to be the most contentious element of the bill. The reports of the two Delegations for Women's Rights supported the move, as did that of the National Assembly's Committee for Cultural, Family and Social Affairs. The National Assembly passed this measure. Opposition came from the Senate, and was based on three reasons. The first was an attempt by Jean-François Mattei to demonstrate that the extension would not help 2,000–3,000 of the 5,000 women who currently travel abroad each year. He argued that this would be the first step on a slippery slope of ever longer extensions. Mattei's proposal was to leave the ten-week limit in place, but open up the possibility for medical, rather than voluntary, terminations after this time. Decisions would be made on a case by case basis by panels of medical and psychological personnel

(Assemblée nationale 2000: 09510). The Senate's Delegation for Women's Rights rejected his suggestion on the grounds that it removes the decision from women (Terrade 2001; 34).

In contrast to Mattei's position, the Ordre des Médecins argued that the increase in the time limit would help women in distress who are currently forced to travel abroad, and therefore supported Aubry's proposal (La Délégation aux Droits des Femmes et à l'Egalité des Chances entre les Hommes et les Femmes 2000a). In response to the slippery slope argument, Jacques Milliez, head of obstetrics and gynaecology at the Saint-Antoine hospital in Paris, in evidence to the National Assembly's Delegation for Women's Rights stated that women only seek late abortions when they have no alternative. He argued that there is always a serious reason, and that this needs to be taken into account (La Délégation aux Droits des Femmes et à l'Egalité des Chances entre les Hommes et les Femmes 2000b): if they exceed the legal limit, it is because they are badly informed about access to abortion or because they have been slowed down by attempts to dissuade them; in the case of adolescents, it is because they do not realise they are pregnant or have not come to terms with it; and this is not their fault. He claims that there is a lack of sex education at school; that teenagers often lack an adult in whom they can confide; and that some attempt suicide or hide their pregnancy and give birth in the school toilets (La Délégation de l'Assemblée Nationale aux Droits des Femmes et à l'Egalité des Chances entre les Hommes et les Femmes 2000b). In his evidence, Milliez stated that doctors sometimes agree to perform abortions on women who have exceeded the time limit. In a testimony reminiscent of those made by doctors in the early 1970s in support of the legalisation of abortion, Milliez stated: 'Personally, I do what I believe to be my duty as a doctor. Between ten and twelve weeks, abortion is almost always justified, and I agree to do it. I am not the only one, believe me. Some things are left unsaid. This is not necessarily a bad thing, and has something in common with adult euthanasia, for example. These are areas that are not spoken about and acts that are performed through tacit agreement' (La Délégation de l'Assemblée Nationale aux Droits des Femmes et à l'Egalité des Chances entre les Hommes et les Femmes 2000b). He states that there are two alternatives available to doctors faced with women who have exceeded the time limit and want an abortion: they can advise women to continue with the pregnancy, give birth anonymously, and give the child up for adoption; or they can send them abroad. The first, he states, is inhuman in the case of women at the beginning of their pregnancy. The second is unacceptable in that it discriminates between those who can afford to travel and those who cannot. For these reasons, Milliez gives his full support to the proposed extension from ten to twelve weeks (La Délégation de l'Assemblée Nationale aux Droits des Femmes et à l'Egalité des Chances entre les Hommes et les Femmes 2000b).

The second reason for opposing the proposed extension drew on the evidence of many medical experts to argue that there is a major difference in the substance of the foetus and the method needed to remove it between ten and twelve weeks. The evidence on this is mixed and contradictory. Many of the medical experts interviewed by the various committees claimed that the nature of the medical procedure changes after ten weeks, requiring extra training and facilities. Many other experts contradicted this, however, arguing that there is little change in the foetus or in the technique required, as demonstrated in other countries, but also in France in the case of medical abortions performed beyond the legal limit for voluntary terminations. Given the contradictory nature of the expert evidence heard, it was very difficult for the parliamentary committees to reach a conclusion on this point, but Terrade argues that the answer to the question of whether or not to extend the time limit must be yes, in order to remove the discrimination between those who can afford to travel abroad and those who cannot, as well as the discrimination between those whose doctors can get around the law, and those who cannot (Terrade 2001: 33).

The third reason put forward by those who opposed the extension was the risk of selection given better ultrasound results after ten weeks. Mattei conceded that the National Consultative Committee on Ethics (CCNE) was right in its decision that there was no threat of eugenics in the sense of a 'an institutionalised collective practice, that aims to encourage certain characteristics and eliminate others'. However, he claims that, with abortion at twelve weeks, it will not be the distress of the woman or the presence of a particularly severe foetal malformation which is the deciding factor; instead, it will simply be a question of whether or not the foetus meets their requirements and this is unacceptable (Assemblée nationale 2000: 09510). The CCNE found that opposing the extension of the time limit on the grounds of the availability of more information about the foetus would seem 'excessive and in a way prejudicial to the dignity of women and couples' and that 'it would be an insult to them and would put them in the position of the accused to think that pregnancy is experienced in such an opportunistic way that the decision to continue or terminate it should rest solely on this knowledge' (Terrade 2001: 34). The delegation concluded that the risk of eugenics cannot be used as a reason to oppose the extension of the time limit.

The 2001 law on contraception and abortion

The 2001 law was an incremental reform of the Loi Veil. It was the subject of less public controversy than the Loi Veil, and the basic principle of early abortion in certain circumstances was not contested, although right-wing opposition in the Senate was solid enough for the bill not to be passed in that chamber.

The bill was passed by the National Assembly on 5 December 2000, the left voting for and the right, with a handful of exceptions including Roselyne Bachelot (RPR), voting against. The Senate, in its first reading on 28 March 2001, removed the extension of the time limit from ten to twelve weeks. The second reading in the National Assembly led to a seven-hour debate, before the bill was passed, with a number of points removed by the Senate reintroduced. A 'commission mixte paritaire' sat on 4 April, but could not agree. The final reading took place in the National Assembly.

The 2001 abortion and contraception law (2001) extends the time limit for legal abortion from ten to twelve weeks (Article 1). It makes it possible for pharmaceutical abortions to take place under GP supervision (Article 3). Counselling continues to be available before and after the abortion, but is no longer compulsory for adults. Pre-abortion counselling is compulsory for minors and, for those who do not wish to reveal the abortion to their parents or guardians, it includes discussion of the choice of an adult referent. The doctor should try to persuade the minor to seek parental consent, but if she does not want to, or if the consent is not given, the abortion can still take place on request of the concerned party only. In this case, she will be accompanied by the adult of her choice. After the abortion, a second consultation will take place, with the main aim being to give contraceptive advice (Articles 5 and 7). The conscience clause is retained for individual doctors, but a doctor wishing to exercise this right must tell the woman concerned immediately and refer her to colleagues who do carry out abortions (Article 8). Article 11 sets out the conditions and procedures for medical abortions which can be carried out at any time in the pregnancy, including after twelve weeks. Article 17 states that obstructing abortion is punishable by two years in prison and by a 200,000F fine, whether the obstruction is physical or 'involves exerting moral or psychological pressure, threats or any act of intimidation towards medical and non-medical personnel working in these institutions, women who have come to have an abortion or those accompanying them'. Article 26 states that sterilisation can be performed on fully informed and consenting adults after a period of reflection of four months.

The implementation of the 2001 law

Feminists were pleased with the law, but concerned with its implementation. There was a long delay before the 'décrets d'application' appeared, and questions remain over the adequate provision of resources. The first impact assessment was published eight months after the law was passed, as part of the National Assembly's Delegation for Women's Rights Annual Report for 2001 (Lignières-Cassou 2001). Authored by Martine Lignières-Cassou, this report finds continuing problems with the implementation of the extension of the legal time limit and of the removal of the requirement for parental consent. Concerns about the technical difficulty of performing abortions between ten and twelve weeks had been voiced on many occasions during the parliamentary debates, and had not disappeared by the time of the report. Doctors were found to be hesitant about performing 'late' abortions and did not feel that they had been adequately trained. Some expert witnesses allayed these fears, however, reporting that doctors were returning from training in Spain and the Netherlands reassured that the procedure was not that difficult (Lignières-Cassou 2001: 110). Lignières-Cassou states that, while training is clearly necessary, it is also important to stop over-dramatising an operation which is carried out in neighbouring countries, apparently without any particular problems (Lignières-Cassou 2001: 111). Parental consent has remained the norm, but the 2001 law allows alternatives in certain situations. The inquiry found variations and uncertainties about the application of this clause, especially on the part of anaesthetists (Lignières-Cassou 2001: 117), and later reports in *Le Monde* found that, in the context of public concerns with medical liability, anaesthetists are still reluctant to anaesthetise minors with no parental consent (Krémer 2002: 10).

The report found regional variations in hospital provision, despite the attempts by the 2001 law to address this by requiring doctors exercising their right to refuse to perform abortions for reasons of personal conscience to refer women quickly to appropriate colleagues and by insisting that public hospitals provide abortion services, regardless of the personal convictions of the director, who can no longer exercise the conscience clause on behalf of the whole hospital. Regional disparities were also found in the delays experienced by women both before the first appointment and before the abortion itself, delays which can lead to them exceeding the time limit. There is still a requirement for a period of reflection of one week between the first appointment and the abortion, although this can, in principle, be reduced in urgent cases. These regional disparities have resulted in an increase in 'regional tourism', although data from Dutch clinics suggest that this has been accompanied by a decline in the number of women travelling abroad to obtain abortions beyond the ten-week limit (Lignières-Cassou 2001: 115).

By 2003, a report submitted to the Minister for Health found that the number of women forced to travel abroad had fallen, that doctors were more willing to perform abortions up to twelve weeks and felt more competent to do so, and that there had been no increase in the number of doctors invoking the conscience clause since 2001. On the other hand, it found regional disparities in the provision of abortions between ten and twelve weeks and long waiting lists. It called on the minister to sign the decrees necessary to permit pharmaceutical abortions with GP supervision, freeing up space in abortion clinics (Mathieu 2003). This did not happen until 2004 (Blanchard 2004: 5). By 2005, only 260 agreements had been signed with GPs allowing them to provide pharmaceutical abortions, although this number was expected to increase as GPs are informed and trained. In 2003, 38 per cent of abortions were pharmaceutical, compared with 21 per cent in 2001 and 20 per cent in 1998 (République française 2006: 62).

Despite these indicators of gradual change, however, critics are still cautious about the effective implementation of abortion policy. In March 2006, *Le Monde* reported concerns about the budget allocations for abortion, the retirement of doctors, the long waiting lists, the illegal refusal of hospitals to recognise the partner of a minor as their adult referent, and their refusal to carry out abortions on minors free of charge. Françoise Laurant, president of Le Planning Familial stated, 'The battle is not won. Access to abortion is still a problem. Budgetary restrictions are hitting departments that provide abortions and it is difficult to replace the activist personnel who are now retiring. Not to mention the excessively long waiting lists and the hospitals that, completely illegally, refuse to treat minors free of charge or to accept permission from their boyfriend' (Chemin 2006a: 23).

Conclusion

Framed as a public health issue (1975) or as a pragmatic response to a series of specific problems (2001), abortion was first legalised, then made more accessible to those women experiencing particular difficulties obtaining an abortion in France within the short legal time limit. Ensuring that debates took place within these frames and were concerned only with pinning down the technical details avoided the danger of debating the more fundamental split between those who advocate the right to life and those who advocate the right to choose.

Abortion policy is not just a series of pragmatic responses to the problems caused by contraceptive failure and lack of adequate information. Anti-abortionists have been protesting publicly against the legalisation of abortion since it appeared on the agenda in the early 1970s. During the late 1980s and early 1990s, anti-abortionist groups and individuals had become so obstructive that a new offence was created in the Loi Neiertz of 1993. Other more insidious attempts have been made to introduce into the law the legal status of the foetus as a person with human rights. The recognition of the right to life of the foetus in cases such as miscarriage caused by medical error or by dangerous driving could establish this as a principle. The Garraud amendment, named after the UMP deputy Jean-Paul Garraud and passed into law on 27 November 2003, created the offence of involuntary termination of a pregnancy. Many lawyers argue that this does not grant a legal status to the foetus and does not challenge abortion. The Minister for Justice, Dominique Perben, for example, argued that it simply offers protection to pregnant women; Minister for Health, Jean-François Mattei, declared that, 'This in no way interferes with the current right to abortion' (Benkimoun et al. 2003: 8).

Others, however, see the Garraud amendment introducing the possibility of recognising the legal status of the foetus as a person as the beginning of an attack on abortion and on women's right to make decisions concerning their own bodies. The national secretary of the PCF, Marie-George Buffet, the president of the MFPF, Françoise Laurant, and feminist lawyer, Gisèle Halimi, were amongst those who expressed these concerns, with Halimi stating that this vote is indicative of the influence of the ideas of the extreme right and Catholic fundamentalists (Blanchard 2003). Catherine Génisson (PS) expressed concerns about the 'worrying social and political context in which this vote took place in the National Assembly, with anti-abortionists demonstrating in front of the Planning Familial' (Benkimoun et al. 2003). Jean-Marie Le Guen (PS) stated that anti-abortionists are trying to introduce into the law measures that would allow them to begin legal proceedings and mask their intentions through appeals to compassion around specific cases (Roger 2003: 11).

It is moves such as these which threaten the principle of abortion. The crux of the matter for the anti-abortion lobby is to succeed in enshrining in law the right to life of the unborn child. Anti-abortionists remain active, for example SOS Tout Petit, which has links with the Front National (*Le Monde*, 29 November 2003 p. 11). In its acquittal of militant anti-abortionist Xavier Dor in 1999, the Paris Court of Appeal found that the Loi Neiertz, prohibiting the disruption of abortion clinics, was an infringement of the right to demonstrate (Surduts 2000: 4). Le Pen's election promises in the 2002 presidential election included banning abortion as well as reintroducing the death penalty, introducing the principle of national preference into the Constitution and using referenda to sidestep current checks and balances (Krémer and Phelippeau 2002: 4). However, his daughter, in charge of Le Pen's 2007 election campaign, has been trying to 'modernise' the party and has stated that in the case of an electoral victory for the FN, a referendum would be held on the Loi Veil (Le Pen 2007).

Abortion is currently perceived as an issue for national policy-making, although there have been attempts to initiate international and European policy, and the freedom of movement within the European Union has had an impact on the ability of individual member states to restrict access to abortion for their citizens. The ability to travel to obtain an abortion is not the same as the right to sexual and reproductive health. It discriminates against those who do not have the resources necessary to obtain a safe abortion, whether this is the financial means to travel or the information necessary to make an effective decision. The 2001 law was an improvement for women in France, but the protection of the right to safe and legal abortion is a continuous struggle undertaken by women's rights advocates in France as elsewhere.

Note

1. From 1974, prescription contraceptives were reimbursed by the state, the ban on sale to minors without parental consent was lifted, and family planning centres were permitted to give free contraceptives to minors confidentially and on prescription. AIDS campaigns led to the lifting in 1991 of the ban on the advertising of condoms and the removal of the need for prescriptions for condoms (Terrade 2001).

4
Prostitution

Prostitution has been high on the French political agenda since the late 1990s, but the way in which it has been framed as a policy issue has undergone a radical change since the elections of 2002. Under the Jospin (1997–2002) government, prostitution debates were polarised: abolitionists, who formed a powerful coalition with access to policy-makers, in particular state feminists, perceived prostitutes as victims who needed to be saved; sex workers' rights advocates called for better living and working conditions for those in prostitution. Relations between the two sides were hostile. In 2002, however, the newly elected right-wing government reframed prostitution as a law and order issue, including it in the security discourse, which dominated its election manifesto. This chapter traces these debates, asking how the various actors involved have framed prostitution as a political issue, how prostitutes have been constructed within these frames, and what implications this has for the women concerned. It argues that the consequences of the new law are harsh, in particular for migrant women, who can be deported for the newly created serious offence of passive soliciting.

Prostitution debates prior to 1997

Prostitution was prohibited by royal decree in 1254, but later tolerated in specific areas and, from 1796, prostitutes in Paris were registered with the newly created (1778) vice squad. The state regulation of prostitution and state control of prostitutes, through registration and compulsory medical examinations, characterised French prostitution policy throughout the nineteenth and twentieth centuries. A report on public health published in 1837 stated that prostitutes are as inevitable a part of the city as sewers, factories and rubbish dumps and should be contained in secure premises and closely monitored. State-regulated brothels, ranging from the luxurious to the sordid, flourished until their closure by the Loi Marthe Richard in 1946. By this time, there were 1,500 officially recognised brothels in France, 177 of them in Paris (Derycke 2001).

It was 1960, however, before France became officially abolitionist, with the ratification of the 1949 UN Convention on the Suppression of the Traffic in Persons and of the Exploitation of the Prostitution of Others. Police files on prostitutes were no longer maintained and military brothels were finally closed. The foundations of state abolitionism were laid in a series of policy measures in the early 1960s, but for most of the following thirty years, implementation varied locally, and prostitution rarely appeared on the political agenda. The exceptions were a brief mobilisation of prostitutes' rights groups against police harassment in 1975 and debates surrounding a suggestion in 1990 by the former Minister for Health (1986–8), Michèle Barzach (RPR), that state brothels be reopened in order to reduce the risks to public health associated with unregulated prostitution (Mazur 2004).

The mobilisation in 1975 of prostitutes' rights groups was a reaction to a series of arrests of prostitutes and pimps by the Lyon police following the trial of the head of the city's vice squad for corruption and pimping (Mazur 2004: 126). A collective was formed which occupied two churches, organised public meetings and sent representatives to speak to the president and members of the government (Mazur 2004: 127). This brought the claim for prostitutes' rights into the public arena for the first time. Prior to this, the main focus of government policy and support associations was to prevent women entering prostitution or to facilitate their exit. The prostitutes' rights movement demanded the recognition of the rights of women in prostitution both as workers and as people with private lives: they argued, for example, that it should not be assumed that their partners were necessarily their pimps and that they had the right to private relationships. In an attempt to resolve the issues raised by the collective, the Minister for Health, Simone Veil, appointed Guy Pinot, President of the Court of Appeal of Orléans, to conduct a public inquiry. The Pinot Report, submitted in 1976, has been described by Amy Mazur (2004: 128) as a 'symbolic government response to two months of direct action and protest by the prostitutes' movement'. Françoise Giroud refused to comment on the issue; no new policies were adopted as a direct result of the report; and the prostitutes' rights position which was reflected in the report quickly disappeared from policy statements.

Michèle Barzach's suggestion in 1990 that state brothels be reopened in order to reduce the spread of AIDS was not the first of its kind and received some public support (64 per cent in favour, according to a May 1990 opinion poll cited by Mazur 2004: 132). With two exceptions, however, politicians on the right and the left opposed the idea, most of them arguing that it would weaken women's rights. The Minister for Women's Rights, Michèle André, the PS, and the MFPF all argued that prostitution was a form of sexual slavery or of the oppression of women. André stated that 'women are not commodities' (Mazur 2004: 133). Barzach withdrew her proposal in December 1990, in the face of strong cross-party opposition to a return to the state regulation of prostitution.

Prostitution was also debated briefly as part of the major overhaul of the Penal Code, which came into effect in 1994. The main reforms with regard to prostitution were the introduction of harsh penalties for large-scale pimping and the protection of male clients and individual pimps. The parliamentary debates in 1992 did not refer to the gendered nature of prostitution. However, the implementation orders included the proposals made by the Ministry for Women's Rights in the 1980s and a definition of pimping which would prevent the police from arresting the partners of prostitutes (Mazur 2004: 139).

Prostitution debates 1997–2002

Prostitution rose up the political agenda in the late 1990s as the result of a number of factors: international and European measures focused in particular on trafficking, child prostitution and child pornography, and transnational organised crime; a growing awareness of the presence of East European and African prostitutes,[1] some of whom appeared very young; and the initiatives of women's policy agencies, which combined with powerful abolitionist lobbies to influence the policy agenda and stimulate public debate (Mazur 2002; Stetson and Mazur 1995). In 1999, the newly created Delegation for Women's Rights in the Senate decided to focus on prostitution as its first subject of inquiry. It produced a detailed and critical report on prostitution and public policy, arguing that France's official policy of abolitionism was inadequately implemented (Derycke 2001). Prostitution policy consisted of harsh penalties for those who profited from the earnings of prostitution alongside social protection measures for those who agreed to exit. Prostitution itself was a civil liberty, although soliciting was a minor offence. The Senate's Delegation for Women's Rights was particularly critical of the state's failure to ensure adequate social provisions for those who wanted to exit prostitution.

A series of international assertions of the French position on prostitution were made in the late 1990s, in the context of pressure by some countries and international organisations (notably the Netherlands (Outshoorn 2000) and the International Labour Organisation (Lim 1998)) to recognise prostitution as a legitimate occupation and prostitutes as sex workers. Foreign Minister, Hubert Védrine, reaffirmed the French commitment to abolitionism in various international negotiations on trafficking and child prostitution and pornography,[2] and Minister for Women's Rights, Nicole Péry, included prostitution in her department's high-profile campaign against violence towards women, naming it as a form of violence at the UN Beijing +5 Conference in New York in 2000. In these statements, France reaffirmed its commitment to the 1949 Convention which states that 'prostitution and the accompanying evil of the traffic in persons' are 'incompatible with the dignity and worth of the human person' and condemns any person who exploits the prostitution of another with or without their consent. In March 2001, Christine Lazerge, Vice President of the National Assembly, launched an inquiry into forms of modern slavery, much of which focused on prostitution. The ensuing bill was passed unanimously by the National Assembly in January 2002 but not read in the Senate before the end of the parliamentary session. It confirmed the view of prostitution as a form of violence and exploitation and of prostitutes as unconditional victims, who should be saved by the state (Vidalies 2002b). Such a position rejects the distinction between forced and voluntary prostitution that some vocal participants in international policy-making were trying to legitimise.

The distinction between free and forced prostitution was integrated into Dutch public policy debates as early as the mid-1980s (Outshoorn 2001) and is defended on the grounds that it will improve the living and working conditions of prostitutes and that it will strengthen the fight against transnational organised crime and in particular the trafficking of women and children. As well as embedding the distinction in national policies, the Netherlands has pushed for its inclusion in international treaties and conventions. The UN Declaration on the Elimination of Violence Against Women (1993), the Beijing Platform for Action (1995), the Council of Europe Recommendation 1325 (23 April 1997) on the traffic in women and forced prostitution in Council member states, and the European Parliament Resolution of 19 May 2000 all refer to 'forced' prostitution, thus implying that there can be a voluntary kind. The report by the International Labour Office in 1998 further reinforced the notion that voluntary prostitution should be considered a legitimate economic activity. Within France, the community health group Cabiria also supports the distinction between free and forced prostitution. They argue that prostitution is not an inherent violation of human rights, as abolitionists maintain, and that it is the working conditions of some prostitutes (non-consent, exploitation), which should be condemned, not the sale of sexual services itself. They state that 'it is not the activity as such, but the conditions in which the activity takes place, that make it a violation of human rights' (Cabiria 2000: 2).

The framing of all prostitution as an inherent act of violence and violation of human rights has a tendency to construct prostitutes as victims who need to be saved and reintegrated into society. This can deny them subjecthood and agency. At a high-profile conference at UNESCO in Paris in 2000, organised by the abolitionist NGO, Fondation Scelles, Phillippe Scelles, for example, declared, 'Prostitution is not an expression of women's freedom, but of their profound misery, the tragedy of destiny, a descent into hell' (Fondation Scelles 2000: 5–6). In *Le Livre noir*, prostitution is portrayed as 'the alienation and destruction of women, men and children reduced to the state of sexual objects, of commodities in a global market, an attack on the integrity and the dignity of the human being, a negation and violation of human rights, neither "inevitable" nor a "necessary evil"' (Coquart and Huet 2000: 5–6). In this view, the victims of prostitution are usually unaware of their own oppression and alienation. Derycke for example states, 'One day or another, all prostitutes aspire to a life away from prostitution, *whatever they may say*' (my emphasis) (Derycke 2001: 26).

AIDS prevention and community health groups are deeply critical of what they perceive as a moralistic and paternalistic attitude towards prostitutes, to whom all voice and agency is denied until they agree to be 'reintegrated' (Mathieu 2001: 24). They claim to give voice to prostitutes and to work in partnership with them to meet their needs. Cabiria takes this further, presenting prostitutes not only as agents, but as rational decision-makers. The group's annual report emphasises the agency of prostitutes, including migrants who choose to come and work in France:

> If the fact of prostituting may at first sight seem a submission to the system, from the perspective of the strategies of agents, one could consider that through prostitution these women make men pay directly and explicitly for what other women give freely or [charge for] indirectly in this same system of domination, thus gaining autonomy. (Cabiria 2000: 4)

Abolitionist discourse became so dominant during the Jospin government that its proponents could present it as non-ideological (Nor 2001) or above the abolition/regulation dichotomy (Derycke 2001).

Abolitionist organisations formed a powerful lobby with effective access to policy-makers and with the resources to fund conferences and publications. The UNESCO conference was supported by prominent public figures including a leading light on the Republican left, founder of the Mouvement des Citoyens party and presidential candidate, Jean-Pierre Chevènement, and philosopher and academic, Sylviane Agacinsky. The thirty-five signatories of a declaration in *Le Nouvel Observateur* that the body is not a commodity included prominent political figures François Hollande, Robert Hue and Dominique Voynet. Senator Dinah Derycke's report on prostitution for the Senate's Delegation for Women's Rights did not question the principle of abolition, but merely assessed the extent to which the state implemented this policy at the national and local level.

In direct opposition to the dominant state-sanctioned abolitionism, prostitutes' rights advocates, community health associations and some feminists called for the removal of the stigma attached to prostitution and for the recognition of the rights of sex workers. They argued that the state's blinkered commitment to abolitionism ignored the difficulties, dangers and the denial of rights faced by prostitutes in their daily lives and that their existence and needs must be recognised, that they should be seen as subjects and agents, not victims. The associations Act Up-Paris, PASTT, Cabiria and AIDES Paris-Ile-de-France condemned the UNESCO conference, which, they argued, further stigmatised sex workers and denied them the right to use their own bodies (Act Up-Paris, PASTT et al. 16 May 2000). They argued that the sale of sexual services should not be confused with slavery and trafficking, and demanded that the government concentrate on improving the working conditions of sex workers and their access to health and social services.

Vigorous debate took place, artificially and unproductively polarised around victims or sex workers; abolition or prostitutes' rights; violence or work.[3] Feminists and the left were split. These debates are replicated throughout the world, and are expressed in the existence and activities of transnational organisations as well as in the divisions that arise in international arenas, such as UN negotiations. What is specific about the French case, however, is that France presents itself as the epitome of abolitionism and at the forefront of the struggle against what it portrays as the Dutch-led drive towards decriminalisation.

By 2002, public debate on prostitution, whether in institutional politics, the media, the organisations that work with prostitutes or against prostitution, was starkly polarised. Relations between the two poles were hostile, there was little, if any, dialogue, and the policy solutions which seemed to follow from their arguments were incomplete: sex workers' rights advocates fought for better living and working conditions for those in prostitution, but did not challenge the circumstances which brought them there. Abolitionists were caught in the contradictions of the term 'abolitionism', which can refer to the abolition of the state regulation of prostitutes or to the abolition of prostitution itself. They could not endorse any legislation that addressed prostitutes specifically, because this was reminiscent of the regulationist regime they oppose. One of the problems this produced was that they could not find a solution to the question of taxation. Prostitutes and pimps are currently liable for tax on their earnings from prostitution, according to the principle that all income is taxable, regardless of its source. Prostitutes who appear to be working independently are placed in the same category as professionals and non-commercial service providers. Those who are clearly working for a pimp are taxed as wage earners. The tax office has considerable powers of investigation and can estimate taxable earnings if no tax return is received. This estimate rarely takes into account the proportion of these earnings which is paid to the pimp, and few prostitutes identify their pimp to the tax office for obvious reasons. Abolitionists object to the current situation on the grounds that it appears to legitimise prostitution, to suggest that it is an occupation, and to place the state in the position of profiting from the prostitution of another, which is an offence (Article 225-5 of the Penal Code). The official recognition of prostitution in taxation policy contradicts the state's abolitionist position. However, if prostitutes were exempt from tax liability, this would mean that there would be specific laws which applied to them, and this is also contrary to the principle of abolitionism. It might even encourage prostitution and would make pimping even more lucrative, since pimps would not be discovered by the tax office in the course of investigations into the tax liability of prostitutes (Derycke 2001: 35). The abolitionist goal of eradicating prostitution has as a direct and immediate consequence opposition to measures which would improve the health and safety of those in prostitution. The solution to unpleasant working conditions, they claim, is to leave prostitution, not to make it less unpleasant.

Sex workers' rights' advocates provide short-term services and solutions to everyday problems. Abolitionist organisations attempt to provide long-term solutions to prostitutes who seek an alternative. Although some individuals and organisations on the ground (for example the Amicale du Nid and the Bus des Femmes) were working together across these ideological differences to enable people in prostitution to access health, social and legal services, it seemed that the (false) abolition/regulation dichotomy was preventing any possibility of fighting for a real and immediate improvement in the living and working conditions of prostitutes, as part of a long-term strategy to remove the conditions which enable prostitution as an institution to exist. A broader, interagency, preventative approach, called for by Derycke and Marcovich (Marcovich 2002) amongst others, would require sustained political will if it were to be pursued. Any political will that may have existed prior to 2002 has been neutralised by the reframing of the 'problem' of prostitution as one of law and order. This severely curtails the possible policy responses.

Despite the irreconcilable dichotomies around which the debate was organised at this time, the central concern was what was best for prostitutes themselves. This is illustrated by the claims made by all parties that they spoke on behalf of/in the interests of/with prostitutes themselves, and that their opponents refused to give prostitutes voice and agency (Cabiria 2000; Coquart and Huet 2000; Fondation Scelles 2000; Louis 2001b; Mathieu 2001). Whether the ideal outcome was seen as their escape from prostitution or improved living and working conditions with access to full citizenship rights as prostitutes, this was the heart of the issue. There was never any question of penalising prostitutes, who were positioned either as victims or as workers. Nicolas Sarkozy's Domestic Security Bill, however, radically changed this, launching a war not on prostitution, but on prostitutes.

Even before Sarkozy had drafted his bill, mayors were beginning to respond to complaints by local residents about the presence of prostitutes in their neighbourhoods. In the summer of 2002, Françoise de Panafieu, UMP deputy for the 17th arrondissement in Paris, led a high-profile campaign against the way in which prostitution lowers the tone of her neighbourhood and upsets its residents. There was particular concern about keeping prostitution out of the sight of children (and in particular, away from school entrances), always phrased to suggest that it is the sight of prostitutes which is a threat to children's moral development, not the sight of the local male clients.

Mayors (on the right and the left) passed by-laws preventing prostitution in particular residential and business areas (initially in Strasbourg, Orléans, Aix-en-Provence and Metz). As the state's commitment to abolitionism prevented it from passing legislation aimed specifically at prostitutes, these mayors initially took pains to circumvent the restrictions by introducing traffic and parking by-laws to drive prostitution out of certain areas. This meant that prostitutes were forced to leave well-lit busy streets and move into car parks, lay-bys and wasteland, where they work in far less safe conditions. However, with the rise of law and order discourse, in particular since the run-up to the 2002 presidential elections, an increasing number of local authorities introduced more explicit by-laws aimed at preventing prostitution in designated areas.

The Domestic Security Bill

Despite the positive reception of the Derycke Report by Parliament, its conclusions were pushed into the background by a combination of factors: the senator who wrote it fell ill and retired; international and European measures demanded parliamentary debates on transnational organised crime, modern slavery and trafficking; and, in 2002, the presidential and parliamentary elections brought to power a right-wing president and parliamentary majority, at the end of a campaign focused almost exclusively on law and order. Prostitution suddenly found itself redefined as a law and order issue.

The Domestic Security Bill was tabled in October 2002 by the Minister for the Interior, Nicolas Sarkozy, and brought into force in March 2003 after successful readings in both houses of Parliament. The bill was presented by Sarkozy as a welcome response to a widespread feeling of insecurity which was dominating public concerns. It aimed to combat types of behaviour which were causing increasing concern and 'legitimate exasperation' amongst French citizens (Sarkozy 2002a). These types of behaviour are soliciting, exploitation of begging, aggressive begging, occupying someone else's land and assembling in the entrance or the stairwell of blocks of flats. According to the government, clamping down on these activities would improve the quality of life and especially the feeling of security of the poorest members of society who are most likely to become the victims of crime. According to their critics, these proposals constituted an attack on the poor (Ligue des Droits de l'Homme, Syndicat des Avocats de France et al. 2002).

The bill provoked petitions, demonstrations and calls for action by parties of the left, trade unions and associations concerned with human rights, poverty and social justice. They accused Sarkozy of exploiting the climate of insecurity and rejected the plans to criminalise beggars, prostitutes, travellers and young people, arguing that 'no one chooses to be a beggar or a prostitute, to live in neighbourhoods with no facilities and no public services' (Ligue des Droits de l'Homme, Syndicat des Avocats de France et al. 2002). Claude Boucher from the Bus des Femmes, a support service in Paris run by prostitutes and former prostitutes, insists that many women she meets work as prostitutes in order to preserve their dignity, since neither social security benefits nor the minimum wage are enough to live on. Treating them as criminals will make their lives more dangerous, she argues: 'This is a law against those who are excluded, against the most vulnerable' (Délégation de l'Assemblée Nationale aux Droits des Femmes et à l'Egalité des Chances entre les Hommes et les Femmes 2002).

Sarkozy, however, claimed that the poor support a tougher stance on crime, that law and order is the main concern of the general public, and that 80 per cent of people on the minimum wage approved of his bill. An Ipsos poll, cited by *Le Figaro*, demonstrated that the lower the income and education, the greater the support for the bill. Sarkozy claims that 'it is precisely for this forgotten France that the government has tabled this bill', and while his opponents argued that it was in place of a social policy, Sarkozy stated that 'Creating public security is the first step in an effective social policy' (*Le Monde*, 23 October 2002).

Three parts of the law are concerned specifically with prostitution: Article 18 which, firstly, criminalises soliciting and, secondly, makes it an offence for clients to pay for sex with a particularly vulnerable person; Article 28 which permits the removal of a visitor's permit from foreigners caught soliciting; and Article 29 which allows a foreign prostitute who brings charges against or who testifies against her pimp to remain in the country until the case has been heard, and, as a result of a government amendment during the debate in the Senate, to remain in the country permanently if the pimp or trafficker is convicted.

Criminalisation of soliciting

The Domestic Security Bill reclassified soliciting as a serious offence, incurring a prison sentence (six months in the original, two months as the result of a successful amendment during the parliamentary debates) as well as a more substantial fine. It also means that suspected offenders can be held in custody for up to forty-eight hours. And this is one of the main justifications for the reclassification, because it allows the police to obtain information from them during their time in custody (Fabre and Le Coeur 2002) – in other words, it is intended to contribute to the fight against the exploitation of prostitution.

Secondly, the law reintroduces the notion of 'passive soliciting', which was removed from the new Penal Code in 1994 (interestingly by a right-wing majority). Before 1994, there was a distinction between active and passive soliciting, with passive soliciting defined as loitering in a way that was likely to encourage vice. The new Penal Code retained only the notion of active soliciting. Sarkozy, arguing that it was inconvenient for the police to have to obtain evidence of active soliciting, proposed the insertion of a new article in the Penal Code (Article 225-10-1) creating a serious offence of soliciting by any means including 'dress or posture'. The reference to 'dress' caused an outcry and was removed by a government amendment during the Senate debate. The version that was passed by the Senate refers to 'a posture, even passive' (Sénat 2002a). Some newspapers argued that the introduction of passive soliciting as a major offence effectively makes street prostitution illegal (*Libération*, 23 October 2002; *Le Monde*, 23 October 2002). It opens up opportunities for police harassment, discrimination and arbitrary decision-making. Foreign nationals accused of soliciting, whether actively or passively, can be deported through administrative rather than judicial channels, whether they were legally present in the country or not. They may be given temporary leave to remain in the country and to work in exchange for denouncing their pimp or trafficker. This applies until the case has been heard, and in the event of a conviction, becomes permanent (Article 76).

Sarkozy justified the criminalisation of passive soliciting on the grounds that it protects prostitutes, and helps them to escape from the mafia networks which exploit them (*Le Monde*, 23 October 2002). Apart from being an unacceptable justification for arresting somebody, this is disingenuous, since Sarkozy knows that not all street prostitutes are mafia controlled. This demonstrates that prostitution is not the only issue targeted by this law. It is intimately connected with the control of immigration. Much of Sarkozy's discourse suggests, often explicitly, that the real targets of his bill were foreign prostitutes. They are portrayed as a homogeneous group, controlled by trafficking rings and victims of slavery, who, he argues, must therefore all be charged with passive soliciting, held in custody while the police obtain information about the trafficking rings, and then deported, in order to rescue them from their exploiters. There is no distinction between relative autonomy and lack of autonomy and no concern with the conditions under which foreign women enter the country and begin to work as prostitutes.

There have been many calls for measures aimed directly at trafficking rings, rather than claiming that arresting prostitutes will have significant impact on their activities. These calls have come from the Senate's Law Commission, the Delegation for Women's Rights in the Senate and the National Assembly, and opposition members of both houses. Some changes have been made in response: trafficking has now been defined as an offence and penalties set, although this was at least partly a response to international and European requirements. Also, when Sarkozy addressed the National Assembly on the first day of the debate on his bill, he announced that the means for combating trafficking rings were to be doubled.

Article 29 states that temporary permission to remain in the country can be given to a foreigner who brings charges or gives evidence against a pimp. A government amendment passed by the Senate extends this to permanent permission when it leads to a conviction. But critics ask why it should be conditional on testimony, when the person concerned is recognised as a victim of trafficking. There are still contradictions here, which derive from the different objectives of the people concerned. Sarkozy's aim was to remove foreign prostitutes from the country. In his preliminary statements in July 2002 (LOPSI), he made it clear that the targets of his prostitution policy were migrant women. But he has been forced to add some less punitive measures and to increase the possibilities for reintegration into French society for some victims of trafficking under certain conditions.

In April 2006, PCF Senator, Nicole Borvo, tabled a private member's bill which aimed to undo what she perceived as the harmful effects of Sarkozy's law (2006). Very much in the spirit of the Derycke Report, the bill is based on the view that prostitution takes place within a framework of domination and is a form of violence. It calls for an end to the exploitation and commodification of the human body and rejects the distinction between free and forced prostitution. It criticises the Domestic Security Law for constructing prostitution as a law and order issue and claims that it has been ineffective in addressing the organised crime responsible for trafficking. It argues that the criminalisation of passive soliciting has not reduced prostitution, but has changed the status of prostitutes from victims to criminals. Again reminiscent of the recommendations of the Derycke Report, Borvo's bill calls for coherent government policy on prostitution, which stresses prevention and support for prostitutes, combined with harsh measures aimed at those who profit from it. Like most private members' bills, it did not make it on to the parliamentary agenda, but does suggest an alternative frame which could re-emerge at some point.

Constructing prostitutes in policy debates

Under the Jospin government, the dominant representation of prostitutes in national policy debates was as victims who needed to be saved and reintegrated into society. This view was held by state feminists, government ministers, members of Parliament, and the heterogeneous and powerful abolitionist lobby. It dominated the Derycke Report on public policy and prostitution (Derycke 2001), the report on prostitution which was part of the work of the National Commission on Violence towards Women (Marcovich 2002), and related debates which took place within the government's extensive enquiries into modern forms of slavery (Vidalies 2002b). Consultation on prostitution and related policy provided an opportunity for civil society organisations to enter policy debates, for example, by giving evidence to parliamentary committees, such as the Law Commission and the Women's Rights Delegations in each chamber, and, although some of those who gave evidence constructed prostitutes as workers denied access to decent living and working conditions, they formed the minority.

At the same time, at the municipal level, prostitutes (but not clients) were constructed as a source of public nuisance who needed to be confined to certain locations. As was mentioned above, Françoise de Panafieu, UMP deputy for the 17th arrondissement in Paris, campaigned against the effects of street prostitution in her neighbourhood. Responding to pressure by local residents' groups, mayors on both the right and the left introduced by-laws that, implicitly at first, then more explicitly, banned prostitution in certain areas. Nicolas Sarkozy built on this public nuisance discourse when he became Minister of the Interior in 2002. He combined it with elements of the discourse around insecurity which had dominated the presidential and parliamentary elections and which he used to justify his Domestic Security Bill. He represented prostitutes as a danger to citizens' sense of security, but also as victims who needed to be saved, and as potentially useful witnesses in trafficking cases. The coherence of these apparently contradictory representations depended on his almost exclusive concern with foreign women in prostitution, a category he homogenised and opposed to the unproblematic 'traditional' (French) prostitutes who work in clearly delineated parts of town and whom he rather warmly represents as part of the national cultural heritage.

In his presentation of the bill, Sarkozy argued that the problem that needed addressing was not 'classic prostitution', but the presence of the 'poor foreign girls', victims of violent traffickers and pimps, who cause problems for the local residents. The solution he proposed was to rescue them from their traffickers and return them to their homes, and he argued that the only way this could be done was by making soliciting an arrestable offence, so that the victims of trafficking can be arrested and returned to their families: 'Far be it from me to suggest punishing these poor girls: the offence that we are creating must come to their aid … I hope that these women will have a better future than facing degrading encounters night after night' (Sarkozy 2002b). He states that 'taking them home' is a humanitarian duty (Sarkozy 2002b).

The inability to speak French has become an important marker of Otherness in the construction of the foreign prostitute/victim of trafficking. Sarkozy portrays this as a major obstacle (and in his more recent (2006) immigration laws, a minimum requirement for the non-deportation of children born in France to foreign parents). The inability to speak French exacerbates prostitutes' status as victims and justifies their rescue: 'They become prisoners of a criminal gang because they are in a country – ours – whose language they do not speak, where they do not know anyone and where they are controlled by their pimps. If soliciting is recognised as a serious offence, the police will be able to take these girls home' (Sarkozy 2002b), returning them, as his critics have pointed out, to the very conditions which prompted their departure in the first place (Borillo, Fassin et al. 2002).

Both the abolitionist construction of the problem of prostitution that dominated the discourse of the Jospin government and Sarkozy's reframing of the issue as one of security and immigration deny agency to the women concerned. This is not to say that there are no abolitionists who recognise the subjecthood of women in prostitution and their individual actions within the structural constraints of patriarchy and capitalism (for example, Claudie Lesselier (Lesselier 2005)), but Senator Dinah Derycke's claim that 'All prostitutes hope to leave prostitution one day or another, no matter what they might say' (Derycke 2001: 26), suggests that even when prostitutes do intervene in public debates, their words are not accorded any validity. Even when they are not physically excluded from conferences and meetings, as they were from the UNESCO conference in Paris in May 2000 (Fondation Scelles 2000) their discourse can be undermined by the view that they cannot understand their exploitation or that they are the mouthpieces of their pimps. Abolitionist groups such as Le Mouvement du Nid and Fondation Scelles represent prostitutes as absolute victims, plunged into despair, solitude and desperation (Lemettre 2002).

A disparate minority accords them some measure of subjecthood, although those who campaign for sex workers' rights, such as the associations Cabiria and the Bus des Femmes, struggle in the face of an overwhelming domination of policy debates by abolitionists. The research project funded by the Paris city council and conducted by Janine Mossuz-Lavau and Elisabeth Handman has made a significant contribution to giving voice to sex workers within public and policy debates and aims to fill the silence broken only by the occasional autobiography by a former prostitute or a prostitutes' rights activist (Handman and Mossuz-Lavau 2005).

The internet also offers some opportunity for sex workers to express their opinions: on the feminist website Les Pénélopes, on the site of the community health group Cabiria, and on the newer site of the recently formed group Les Putes (Whores), for example. Cabiria publishes regular research reports and has links with organisations in other European countries, including research links as part of the EU-funded DAPHNE programme. In terms of access to the national media and to policy-makers, however, those who represent prostitutes as subjects and agents are not those who are working with them on the ground. Instead, they are a small number of intellectuals who take a liberal individual rights approach to prostitution, making it a question of choice and, in some cases, self-expression (E. Badinter 2002, 2003b; Borillo 2002; Iacub, Millet et al. 2002).

Although the abolitionist construction of prostitutes as victims makes the criminalisation of prostitutes unthinkable, it denies them all agency and voice and refuses to respond to their immediate needs and interests, on the grounds that improving their living and working conditions would make their exit less urgent and essential.

The client

Until recently, French policy-makers ignored the clients of prostitutes above the age of consent, which is fifteen. The Derycke Report drew attention to the way in which the client 'benefits from a sort of consensual indulgence on the part of society' (Derycke 2001: 24) and argued that he could no longer be ignored. The report found that clients are ordinary men from all parts of society, and it argued that they should be made to take responsibility for their actions, whether this was through criminalisation or education (Derycke 2001: 44). The introduction in Sweden of a law criminalising the client of prostitution drew attention to the way in which French policy had been silent in this respect. Could the problem of prostitution be resolved by focusing on demand rather than, or as well as, supply?

The first parliamentary debate on clients of prostitution came about indirectly, when, in November 2001, a government amendment was added to a bill on parental authority, proposing the criminalisation of clients of prostitutes under the age of eighteen. The main concern was 15–18-year-olds who are above the age of consent and therefore were not covered by the law on underage sex. The amendment proposed the creation of a new offence in the criminal law, which would apply not only when the act was committed in France, but when it was committed in another country by a person with French nationality or normally resident in France. The final version, passed into law on 4 March 2002, imposes a sentence of three years in prison and a fine of 45,000 euros for soliciting, accepting or obtaining, in exchange for payment or the promise of payment, sexual relations from a minor who participates in prostitution, even occasionally. Article 225-12-2 increases the penalties to five years in prison and a 75,000 euros fine when there are aggravating factors (Rozier 2002: 22–3).

The trigger for the amendment, which bore little relation to the bill to which it was attached, seemed to be the presence of underage prostitutes on the streets of Paris. The salient characteristics of the minors who were to be protected by the law which were highlighted by the then Minister for Justice were that they were foreign, brought into France by traffickers, and unable to speak French (Lebranchu 2001). The increase since the late 1990s in the number of underage prostitutes on the streets of Paris (estimated by UNICEF at the time at 8,000) had already led the Bus des Femmes to stop distributing condoms to under-18s as a symbolic protest against the inertia of the state (Borvo 2001). Lebranchu argued that, 'even if the pimp is the most at fault, we must, in the words of the Paris public prosecutor, "destroy the market"' (Lebranchu 2001). This focus on removing demand in order to reduce the number of underage prostitutes on the streets is in contrast to the responses proposed to adult prostitution, arguably because there is a consensus that child prostitution is wrong and must be stopped. It was left-wing women who spoke in favour of the amendment: Nicole Borvo, Dinah Derycke, Marylise Lebranchu and Ségolène Royal. Ségolène Royal, Minister for the Family, Children and the Disabled, claimed that, 'The associations that help them escape this slavery are clear: child prostitution exists because clients exist ... We are therefore committed to finding a way of dissuading clients and pimps, because, without clients, there will be no pimps' (Royal 2002). Lebranchu argued that harsh penalisation of clients would dissuade pimps from putting under-18s on the street, just as the imposition of ten-year sentences for sexual assault of under-15s in exchange for payment has dissuaded them from putting children of this age on the street (Lebranchu 2001).

There was no consensus amongst members of Parliament on the criminalisation of the clients of underage prostitutes as opposed to the prohibition of underage prostitution. Prohibition was advocated by Robert Badinter, former Minister for Justice and PS senator, in order to take into account 'the not just pitiable, but tragic, condition of children, mostly foreign, in prostitution' (R. Badinter 2002). Michel Dreyfus-Schmidt suggested that prohibition of underage prostitution would enable the police to arrest underage prostitutes, who might then gain access to opportunities for rehabilitation (Dreyfus-Schmidt 2001).

The Domestic Security Law extended the penalties introduced in 2002 for clients of underage prostitutes to clients of prostitutes with a 'particular vulnerability', apparent or known to the client, as the result of illness, physical or mental disability, or pregnancy (Sénat 2002a). The PS called for the removal of this Article, which, they argued, discriminated against disabled or pregnant women in prostitution (Mahéas 2002). Johanne Vernier, lawyer and member of Le Gisti, argues that, if the 'particular vulnerability' does not affect the individual's decision-making capacity, then she should be free to prostitute herself, since prostitution is not illegal. If her decision-making capacity is affected, then she is already protected by laws on rape and sexual assault (Vernier 2005b).

The criminalisation of all clients of prostitution was also discussed within the debates on passive soliciting in the Senate in November 2002. Nicole Borvo, for example, stated that, 'If there are lots of prostitutes and if prostitution can be lucrative for some, it is because there are lots of clients!' (Borvo 2002). 'The clients must be made to take responsibility for their actions. The debate on criminalisation is open.' However, in the face of concerns that penalising the clients would push prostitutes underground and exacerbate their problems, Borvo recommended instead public information campaigns to raise awareness of prostitution and trafficking (Borvo 2002).

Bernard Lemettre, president of the Mouvement du Nid, was also hesitant about penalisation, calling instead for a better understanding of clients and how society constructs them. He portrays the client as a lonely individual who does not really understand what he has done wrong. After hearing his evidence to the committee, Danièle Bousquet, a member of the Women's Rights Delegation, commented, 'I share your view that criminalisation is not the only possible response because the client, in the current context, does not understand how it is that he has done something abominable' (Lemettre 2002).

Claudine Legardinier, a journalist associated with Le Nid and present in the same hearing, was much less indulgent, arguing that society is increasingly requiring men to take responsibility for their actions, but not with regards to prostitution: 'As soon as clients have got their money out, they have the right to do anything – and especially the right not to ask themselves any questions about the journey that has brought the young woman to where she is today. They buy – excuse the expression – the right not to give a damn' (Legardinier 2002). Legardinier calls for a range of measures, including education and a re-examination of masculinity, intended to reduce demand and to make men recognise their role and their responsibilities.

Laura Duchêne (PCF and a member of the network 'Pour un monde sans exploitation sexuelle') states that feminists were initially in favour of the criminalisation of clients, but evidence from associations on the ground led them to believe that France is not ready for this. She argues that it would obscure other problems and would be counter-productive, increasing the marginalisation of prostitutes, hindering their access to care and exposing them to more violence (Duchêne 2002: 13). She argues that what is currently needed in France is better sex education in schools, a debate within the political parties, and public information campaigns (Duchêne 2002: 13). Le Nid and Fondation Scelles have both launched education and information campaigns. In August 2005, Fondation Scelles launched an awareness-raising campaign around clients of prostitution, attempting to convey the message that criminal networks function because of demand (Fondation Scelles 2005).

Policy debates on the client are recent and concern only clients of street prostitution. This coincides with a reported move by middle-class men away from street prostitution to more discreet forms where the client is better protected from any problems with the law and is more anonymous (Simon 2002; Welzer-Lang 2003: 6). The first major academic study of clients, conducted by sociologist Said Bouamama, found that street prostitution is still the most popular form, particularly for clients with less money (Bouamama 2004: 30), but that other forms are developing quickly: 39.7 per cent of participants in the study were clients of more than one type of prostitution (Bouamama 2004: 138). PS deputy Alain Vidalies labelled society's reaction to the public nuisance caused by street prostitution hypocritical, given the way that other forms of commercial sex are ignored (Vidalies 2002b). Nicole Borvo's 2006 bill criticises the current impunity for those who profit from 'hidden' forms of prostitution in bars and saunas (2006).

Impact

In principle, at least, the law before 2002 criminalised only the exploitation of prostitution and imposed harsh penalties for those who profited from it, whether they were landlords, hotel owners or pimps. Prostitutes were constructed as victims of prostitution, and, although active soliciting was considered a minor offence, prostitution itself was not illegal. Critics of the Domestic Security Law argued that criminalising prostitutes would shift the power relations between prostitutes, clients and pimps, and that this would make the lives of prostitutes more difficult. They objected to the change in emphasis from targeting pimps to targeting prostitutes, and argued that it was the introduction of passive soliciting that most affected the relation between prostitutes and clients. In the parliamentary debates on the Domestic Security Bill, Jacques Mahéas (PS) argued that criminalising passive soliciting would push prostitution underground, making it more dangerous for prostitutes and disadvantaging them in relation to clients, pimps and the police (Mahéas 2002). Studies of the impact of the law suggest that he was right.

Evidence of the impact of the Domestic Security Law can be gathered from the police, support groups and journalistic reports which began to appear within months of the introduction of the law. The evidence suggests that clients have nothing to fear from the new measures, and there are many reports of them becoming more violent and demanding unprotected sex more frequently. *L'Humanité* (29 June 2005) quotes a 'traditional prostitute' in her sixties, who claims that, 'Violence has increased ... We are often asked for unprotected sex. And when a prostitute, because of police harassment, has not been able to work for three days, sometimes she resigns herself to agreeing. This law, in fact, has simply reinforced the power of the police and of clients over women' (Mouloud 2005).

Deteriorating relations between prostitutes and the police mean that prostitutes are no longer protected from violent clients, and the clients know this. *Libération* quotes a prostitute who says, 'Before, when we saw a police car, we felt reassured. The clients knew that we had good relations with them. Now, as soon as we see the officers, we hide. The clients have understood that we are no longer protected, and they do what they want' (Grosjean 2003).

Prostitutes have moved from more public to more isolated areas and work much later in the night in an attempt to avoid arrest. This not only increases the risk of violence, but makes it more difficult for the support associations to maintain contact with them (Handman and Mossuz-Lavau 2005: 34). Police harassment is widely reported by prostitutes and support associations (Grosjean 2003). Some prostitutes have organised in an attempt to deal with it, building up funds to pay fines and staging protests. Act Up (Act Up 2005) reports that African prostitutes from the Bois de Vincennes created a collective in March 2005 in an attempt to defend themselves against police harassment. One member of the collective states that the women are sometimes held for 72 hours, are repeatedly fined, and report being badly treated by the police (Act Up 2005). Traffickers have put more women on the streets to compensate for the possibility of deportations (Grosjean 2003). They keep tighter control over the women and use more violence towards them. Claude Boucher of the Bus des Femmes claims that traffickers show no fear of the authorities. Their victims, on the other hand, are scared of the police, the courts, clients and passers-by (Grosjean 2003).

The measures introduced by the Domestic Security Law were intended to target foreigners. Head of the BRP (Brigade de Répression du Proxénétisme – vice squad), Daniel Rigourd, told the Women's Rights Delegation in November 2002, 'Let's not beat about the bush, it is foreign prostitution that is targeted, prostitution controlled by mafia-type organisations' (Rigourd 2002). The distinction between 'traditional' and 'foreign' prostitutes was reinforced by the Ministry for the Interior, the police and the media. It divided prostitutes and tempered organised opposition to the bill, which was more likely to involve 'French' prostitutes than those who risked deportation. A report in *Le Monde* on a demonstration by sex workers against Sarkozy's proposals stated that, 'The young undocumented foreign women held by criminal networks are not part of this demonstration. There is even evidence of a certain amount of animosity towards them on the part of the so-called "traditional prostitutes": "They are dirty workers; they leave condoms on the ground. It is because of them that we have to put up with Sarkozy's bill" stated a young woman who works in rue Saint-Denis' (Fabre and Krémer 2002). Claude Boucher, of the Bus des Femmes, also claims that, 'Traditional prostitutes and these slaves are completely different. Traditional prostitutes did not come into prostitution because it was their dream job, but that doesn't make them victims. If they have made this difficult choice, it is in order to escape the indignity of poverty' (Boucher 2002).

Although in the months immediately following the introduction of the Domestic Security Law, the police arrested mostly foreign prostitutes, by 2004, they were arresting 'traditionals' too (Handman and Mossuz-Lavau 2005: 36). *L'Humanité* (21 February 2006) reported the occupation of an employment agency by 'traditionals' from the Bois de Vincennes, protesting against police harassment which prevents them from working. They stated that the police give them on-the-spot fines because the public prosecutors will not pursue the cases. Judges, too, appear to be reluctant to impose large fines and prison sentences for what they see as a social problem (Mouloud 2005). Some judges refuse to apply the law on passive soliciting and release the accused immediately. Others only impose fines, but these fines are heavy enough (350–1,000 euros) to send the women straight back onto the streets to raise the money. Sometimes their vans are confiscated, and sometimes they receive prison sentences, which may or may not be suspended. Some judges ignore previous convictions and give suspended sentences every time (Handman and Mossuz-Lavau 2005: 36).

The Lyon-based NGO, Cabiria, states that some prostitutes had already been making racist comments about migrant women, but tensions within the community have exacerbated, transforming turf wars into hatred for foreigners (Monnet 2003). Associations report that traditional prostitutes are suffering from the competition of trafficked women, from the fall in prices brought about by their presence and by the shift in bargaining power between prostitutes and clients. Some have lost their homes and go to the associations to beg for help. Government promises of alternative employment for those who choose to exit have amounted to nothing more than a few hours of cleaning a week (Grosjean 2003). The head of the vice squad, Daniel Rigourd, claims that there are few French prostitutes still on the streets in Paris. In Rue Saint-Denis, there are 350 prostitutes, 'real French-French women', aged 40–70 (Rigourd 2002). Most French prostitutes have moved off the street, where competition is fierce, into apartments (Rigourd 2002), escort agencies and bars.

Some temporary residence permits have been issued, but only a small number in relation to the number of arrests. According to the Central Office for the Repression of Trafficking in Persons (OCRTEH), 104 temporary residence permits were issued between March 2003 and September 2004 to prostitutes who have denounced their pimps. Those who have no papers and do not denounce their pimps are deported through administrative, not judicial, channels (Handman and Mossuz-Lavau 2005: 37). *L'Humanité* reports that 'The law, which was intended to help dismantle criminal networks and free foreign prostitutes from their grasp, has turned out to be a new deportation machine. Since the end of 2003, more than 300 women from Eastern Europe have been deported' (Mouloud 2005). In Paris, between 1 April 2003 and 1 May 2004, 3,192 prostitutes were detained in custody but only 158 gave evidence. Vernier argues that:

> Either the majority of people in prostitution are not victims of traffickers or pimps, or the conditions in which they are asked to denounce them are unfavourable. Prostitutes on the street have therefore become the prime target of criminal law in order to fight against pimping and trafficking. But punishing all prostitutes in order to reach

> this goal assumes that they are all victims. On the one hand, penalising prostitutes who do not have a pimp or trafficker is a kind of 'collateral damage' in the war on pimping and trafficking. On the other hand, prostitutes who are victims of pimps and traffickers are penalised in their own interest. (Vernier 2005a: 137)

The government claims that the Domestic Security Law has reduced the public nuisance caused by some forms of prostitution and had an impact on trafficking. Charges for soliciting have certainly increased, and Sarkozy claims that, in 2004, 47 international prostitution rings were dismantled, compared with 39 in 2003 (Sarkozy 2005). The opposition claims that, although visible prostitution can be shown to have declined since the introduction of the Domestic Security Law:

> all the associations on the ground agree that prostitution has not decreased. As we feared, the law and order approach simply moved it to less exposed areas, making it more dangerous and less visible, leaving prostitutes exposed to violence on the part of clients and increased health risks. At the same time, the humanitarian part, including support for victims, does not seem to be living up to its promises in terms of places in accommodation, and access to training. (Mahéas 2005)

A joint report published in February 2007 by the human rights organisation, the Ligue des Droits de l'Homme, and two trade unions for members of the legal profession, the Syndicat de la Magistrature and the Syndicat des Avocats de France, concludes that the law does not fight against pimping but against prostitutes, and has not affected organised crime. The authors state that there are few convictions, but the number of arrests is increasing, because it is an easy way for the police to meet their targets. Prostitutes are 'handcuffed, insulted and searched before being held in custody. Transsexuals are the most likely to be strip searched, humiliated and treated like freaks. It is not unusual for custody to last much longer than the investigation requires' (Ligue des Droits de l'Homme, Syndicat de la Magistrature et al. 2007).

Conclusion

This chapter has shown that the dominant frame of prostitution as a policy issue has undergone major changes. Between 1960 and the late 1990s, the problem was profiting from the prostitution of another. Women in prostitution were constructed as victims, and state policy was intended to save them from their misery and rehabilitate them. In the late 1990s, this frame, endorsed by abolitionist associations and government ministers, was joined by a state feminist construction of prostitution as a form of violence towards women. This tipped the balance in favour of the definition of abolitionism which, in this context, means the eradication of prostitution, rather than the removal of all regulations targeted at prostitutes. The inclusion of prostitution in the 2002 Domestic Security Law reframed it as a law and order issue, and this has had direct consequences for women in prostitution, as this chapter demonstrates. The challenge for prostitution policy advocates who are concerned with the well-being of women in prostitution is to find a frame which resonates with that of their target, whether their target is the French government, or policy-makers at the local, European or international level.

Notes

1. Foreign prostitutes are estimated by the Office Central pour la Répression des Trafics d'Etres Humains (OCRTEH) to account for two thirds of the 15–20,000 prostitutes currently working in France, *Le Monde*, 11 July 2002.
2. Such as the additional protocol to the Convention on Children's Rights on the sale and prostitution of children and on child pornography, passed by the UN on 25 May 2000 and signed by 69 states, including all the member states of the EU, and the Convention on Transnational Organised Crime with the additional protocol on trafficking, negotiated in Vienna and signed in December 2000 in Palermo.
3. For abolitionist arguments see, for example Coquart and Huet (2000); Nor (2001); UNESCO (2000). For prostitutes' rights arguments see Boucher (2002); Cabiria (2000); Mathieu (2001).

5
Domestic Violence

Domestic violence is now firmly on the French public and political agenda. It has been declared a national priority by governments of the left and the right since 2001, and was the subject of a new legislative act in 2006. This chapter aims to explain how domestic violence arrived on the French political agenda and how the problem of domestic violence has been constructed in policy debates. It takes into account the actions of feminist activists, the influence of the international context, the national social and political context, and the actions of government, including ministers for women's rights. It also asks how we can account for the current cross-party consensus on the condemnation of domestic violence, and whether this is anything other than symbolic, given the concerns about the implementation of the legislative tools and about the impact of existing policy which have been expressed by the Council of Europe Human Rights Commissioner and by Amnesty International, amongst others. It concludes that until implementation improves, legal provisions will continue to be necessary but insufficient in the fight to combat violence towards women.

Historical context

The arrival of domestic violence on the political agenda is a relatively recent development. Until 1975, French law excused the murder by a man of his wife if he caught her committing adultery in the marital home. Until 1980, there was no legal definition of rape. It was not until 1994 that the law took into account the relationship between the perpetrator and victim in certain acts of violence and considered it an aggravating factor. The following sections set out the factors which contributed to bringing about these changes and which provide the historical background to the more recent debates which resulted in the 2006 law.

French feminist activism

The status of domestic violence as an issue for public debate and policy action is arguably one of the greatest achievements of the second-wave feminist movement. Feminist action was to a large extent responsible for breaking the silence around domestic violence, revealing its widespread nature, and gathering information through direct contact with victims which could then be used to build knowledge and propose solutions. The first priority in the early 1970s, however, was to provide support for victims. Numerous associations were formed, including SOS-Femmes Alternatives in 1975, and these provided information, support and legal advice, telephone helplines, and, from 1978, a number of refuges. The various associations joined together in a national federation, Solidarité Femmes (FNSF), in 1987. In addition to providing support for victims, the associations aimed to raise public awareness, facilitate debate and research, and influence public policy. Information obtained from the helplines and refuges contributed to knowledge about male violence towards women. Analyses of the data collected by the Collectif Féministe contre le Viol, for example, suggested that perpetrators came from all parts of society and that 40 per cent of rapists were known to their victims (Allwood 1998: 109). The national helpline of the FNSF is a valuable source of quantitative and qualitative data.

Violence towards women is one of the clearest examples of feminists engaging actively with the state in order to achieve changes in the way the issue is framed, the way the law is worded and interpreted, and the way victims and perpetrators are represented. Feminists have used the knowledge gained from contact with victims to raise public awareness and to make demands for state action. They have fought for legislative reform; monitored the interpretation and implementation of legal instruments; and called for better treatment of victims within the legal system and by the police. They have also highlighted the underlying assumptions about gender relations and male and female roles on which court decisions and police behaviour are often based.

Relations between feminists and the state have been affected by changes in government. The 1997–2002 Jospin government was particularly receptive to feminist ideas about violence towards women. The 2004 bills, which resulted in the 2006 Domestic Violence Act, discussed later in this chapter, were presented by private members of Parliament from the PS and Communist Party, and were not government sponsored.

International activism and initiatives

French national policy on domestic violence has developed within a broad international context, which includes grassroots activism by feminists and other social movement organisations; top-down measures emanating from the UN, the Council of Europe and institutions of the EU; and the influence of legislative reform in neighbouring countries, in particular Spain.[1]

During the 1970s, feminists in many countries demonstrated against violence towards women, created refuges and helplines and, in some cases, demanded legislative reform. Transnational networks were quickly established and were reinforced by events such as the first International Tribunal on Crimes against Women in Brussels in March 1976. Although in the 1970s radical feminists (as opposed to socialist or liberal feminists), who were most likely to be engaged in action against male violence, were least likely to see the solution as lying in reform by the patriarchal state, change was becoming apparent by the mid-1980s. United Nations conventions, declarations and conferences have provided key openings for feminist discourse on violence to enter political debate; opportunities for transnational networking to take place; and instruments which can be used to exert pressure on national governments and local authorities.

In contrast to prostitution and abortion, which have been kept off international agendas by fundamental disagreements between and within states, violence towards women has gained a prominent place on the international agenda, and this has influenced debates, demands and policies in France. In 1985, women's rights NGOs forced violence onto the agenda of the Third UN Conference on Women in Nairobi. During the early 1990s, women's NGOs launched and reinforced the idea that women's rights are human rights (Bunch 1990). Major human rights NGOs, including Amnesty International and Human Rights Watch, supported this initiative, and following the Human Rights Conference in Vienna in 1993 and the recognition of all forms of violence against women as a human rights violation, the UN General Assembly adopted the Declaration on the Elimination of All Forms of Violence Against Women and appointed Radhika Coomaraswamy as a Special Rapporteur on Violence Against Women (Joachim 2002: 11). These UN initiatives provided opportunities for women's NGOs to demand state action. The rise of human rights discourse and the broad acceptance of the claim that women's rights are human rights meant that it was relatively easy to create a universal condemnation of violence towards women as a violation of their human rights, and this brings with it state obligations to protect women from such violations. The Beijing Declaration and the more detailed Platform for Action set out states' obligations in the area of violence towards women, including the requirement to collect and submit data. The French national survey on violence towards women (ENVEFF), discussed later in this chapter, was a response to this, and was one of sixteen large-scale surveys published by Council of Europe member states between 1995 and 2006 (United Nations General Assembly 2006: 68).

The Beijing +5 Conference in New York in 2000 was intended to review progress on the implementation of the Platform for Action. Amnesty International reports having been 'dismayed at the rollback of progress made on women's human rights' and refers to 'the unfavourable political climate for women's rights which has continued to prevail' (2005: 4). In March 2003, the UN Commission on the Status of Women, which is responsible for the implementation of the Beijing Platform for Action, failed for the first time in its 47-year history to reach agreement on all the recommendations before it. A group of states, including the US, blocked recommendations on violence against women (Amnesty International 2005).

In a wide-ranging report on women published in 2006, the UN reiterated its condemnation of all violence towards women, which it declares 'a pervasive violation of human rights and a major impediment to achieving gender equality' (United Nations General Assembly 2006: 9). It stresses the binding obligation of states to protect women from violence, hold perpetrators accountable, and provide justice and remedies to victims (United Nations General Assembly 2006: 9). The report calls for implementation of the internationally agreed measures; the proper collection of data; and the creation and maintenance of a political and social environment where violence against women is not tolerated. France was one of the main financial contributors to this report (République française 2006: 41).

Categorising violence towards women as a violation of human rights makes it clear that states are under a binding obligation to prevent, eradicate and punish this violence. When violence is framed as a human rights issue, states can be held accountable at the international and regional level (United Nations General Assembly 2006: 17–18). Furthermore, state responsibility is not limited to responding to acts of violence against women, but extends to identifying patterns of inequality that could result in violence and taking steps to overcome them (United

Nations General Assembly 2006: 75). The UN has produced a detailed list of recommendations for action at the national level aimed at eliminating violence towards women. They include achieving gender equality and protecting women's human rights. The various UN declarations, conventions and reports provide leverage for NGOs when making demands upon individual states and act as a measure against which state action or inaction can be assessed.

Council of Europe

The Council of Europe adopted a Recommendation on the protection of women against violence in 2002 (Rec. 2002(5)), and in 2005, the Action Plan adopted by the Heads of State and Government of the Council of Europe at the Warsaw Summit included the organisation of a pan-European campaign to combat violence against women, including domestic violence (Parliamentary Assembly of the Council of Europe 2006). In 2006, the Directorate General of Human Rights published a report on the implementation and follow-up of Rec. 2002(5) (Council of Europe 2006).

This report found that the police and criminal justice system was essential but not sufficient to ensure the protection of women against violence (Council of Europe 2006). Most European states do not have specific legislation on domestic violence, but apply general provisions of criminal law, in some cases specifying that violence is considered as serious within the family as outside. In some member states, including France, violence is more severely sanctioned when it is committed against a spouse or partner. In Sweden and, since 2004, Spain, specific legislation has been adopted on violence against women, shifting the focus from the family to gender (Council of Europe 2006: 19–20).

The Council of Europe found that there is an overall trend towards legislation that punishes domestic violence more severely than in the past, but that the proportion of cases prosecuted is not systematically monitored, and victims are not adequately protected in their roles as witnesses. It stated that harsher penalties may make public prosecutors more reluctant to initiate criminal proceedings (Council of Europe 2006: 20). It found high attrition rates and a failure to coordinate across different parts of the criminal and civil law and policing (Council of Europe 2006: 39).

The Parliamentary Assembly of the Council of Europe issued a resolution in 2006, deploring 'the upsurge in domestic violence against women in Europe, a problem . . . resulting in serious violations of human rights'. It called on national parliaments to take a range of actions with the aim of eliminating domestic violence including the introduction of legislation where necessary and the effective implementation of already existing laws, along with public information and prevention campaigns (Parliamentary Assembly of the Council of Europe 2006). It also invited the European Parliament to join its condemnation of domestic violence as an unacceptable violation of human rights and to raise the awareness of public authorities and the general public in the EU of the need to combat domestic violence against women (Parliamentary Assembly of the Council of Europe 2006).

EU

Before 1992, violence towards women was not considered to fall within the policy remit of the European Communities. However, the inclusion of Justice and Home Affairs in the European Union, created by the Maastricht Treaty (1992), and the emphasis on human rights and gender equality in the Amsterdam Treaty (1997), transformed the European arena into a potential source of policy on violence and a potential target for those attempting to influence decision-making in this area. In 1997, the European Women's Lobby established a Policy Action Centre on Violence against Women as well as a European Observatory on Violence against Women. Together, these provide data, policy proposals and comparative information from the member states (Joachim 2002: 13).

Within the EU, the Women's Rights Committee of the European Parliament has been particularly active on violence towards women, issuing a number of resolutions which refer to UN documents. It had difficulty gaining support from the other institutions until the mid-1990s when a report by Swedish MEP Marianne Eriksson framed violence towards women not only in terms of women's human rights and non-discrimination, but also in terms of the values and norms of the member states and in terms of the costs of gender violence and the savings for a state providing assistance to victims (Joachim 2002: 14–15). In 1995, the year of the Beijing Conference, Sweden, Finland and Austria joined the EU, the number of women commissioners rose to an unprecedented five, and Santer agreed to establish a new 'Commissioners' Group on Equal Opportunities'. There were five female Commissioners, one of whom, Anita Gradin, former Minister for Equality in Sweden, emerged as a leader and institutional entrepreneur on the issue of violence against women (Joachim 2002: 15).

The European Economic and Social Committee, a consultative body within the institutional structure of the European Union, produced an 'own-initiative opinion' in July 2005 on Domestic Violence against Women, which it adopted in plenary session in March 2006. The opinion frames domestic violence as a human rights issue, and places strong emphasis on prevention, along with law enforcement and support. In its conclusions and recommendations, it states that:

> Domestic violence by men against women, whether physical or psychological, is one of the gravest violations of human rights: the right to life and to physical and psychological integrity. Since the roots of such violence lie in the unequal balance of power between the sexes that still characterises our society, it affects women at all levels of society. As a result, the overall development of a democratic society is held back. That is why one of the most important functions of a European policy based on respect for fundamental human rights is to prevent such acts and to establish effective educational, preventive, law enforcement and support procedures. (European Economic and Social Committee 2006: 89)

The opinion also states that, 'The safety and equal treatment of women, which are inherent fundamental human rights, must be basic conditions and minimum requirements for all countries that are, or wish to become, EU members' (2006: 89). It therefore calls on the Commission to undertake an EU-wide study on the prevalence of domestic violence against women, its impact on individuals and society, and its financial costs. It states that each member state should draw up a national action plan for combating domestic violence against women in the light of the planned pan-European strategy.

In 2006, the Commission produced 'A Roadmap for Equality Between Women and Men 2006–2010', which outlines six priority areas for EU action, including the eradication of all forms of gender-based violence (Commission of the European Communities 2006). The Commission states:

> The EU is committed to combating all forms of violence. Women are the main victims of gender-based violence. This is a breach of the fundamental right to life, safety, freedom, dignity, and physical and emotional integrity. Violation of these rights cannot be tolerated or excused on any ground. Prevention is essential and requires education and knowledge, the development of networking and partnership, and the exchange of good practices. (Commission of the European Communities 2006: 7)

As part of the Commission's avowed commitment to combating all forms of gender-based violence, the Roadmap specifies the need for urgent action on 'customary or traditional harmful attitudes and practices, including female genital mutilation, early and forced marriages and honour crimes' and devotes a separate article to trafficking. However, there is no specific reference to domestic violence.

The main role of the EU in relation to violence towards women has been to encourage member states to take action and to share best practice. The Draft Reform Treaty, passed by the Intergovernmental Conference in Lisbon on 18 October 2007 contains the following declaration: 'in its general efforts to eliminate inequalities between women and men, the Union will aim in its different policies to combat all kinds of domestic violence. The Member States should take all necessary measures to prevent and punish these criminal acts and to support and protect the victims' (Presidency of the Intergovernmental Conference 2007).

Government initiatives, women ministers

Government initiatives and, in particular, the actions of women in government have played a role in shaping domestic violence policy. They have also revealed tensions between feminist activist associations and women in the political elite, tensions which were a major contributory factor in the perceived decline in feminist activism in the 1980s, portrayed in the media as the 'death of feminism'. It was not until the 2000s that a more positive image of feminism emerged, and this was partly because of media approbation of young feminist groups, such as Ni Putes Ni Soumises (NPNS), which campaigned against violence towards women in areas of high migrant population. It will be shown later in this chapter that one of the outcomes of high media attention to this particular issue was that it deflected attention from domestic violence in the non-migrant population, the high levels of which had just been demonstrated in the first large-scale national survey of this issue, ENVEFF.

Violence emerged on the agenda of the French political elite during the preparations for the UN Conference on Women in Nairobi in 1985, and as a result of a combination of pressure from grassroots feminist activists, international expectations and the actions of women in government. The first national public information campaign against domestic violence took place in 1989, on the initiative of the then Minister for Women's Rights, Michèle André. State subsidies for associations providing support for victims of violence (AVFT, Collectif Féministe contre le Viol and Fédération Nationale Solidarité Femmes (FNSF)) were made available at the same time, and departmental action committees were formed in order to coordinate local government, statutory agencies and the voluntary sector. The impact of the departmental action committees varied widely, and in a report published in 2000, the Ministry for Women's Rights recognised that, eleven years after their introduction, there were still departments in which they had not yet been established (Secrétariat d'Etat aux Droits des Femmes et à la Formation Professionnelle 2000: 67–8).

Feminists were critical of the inadequate resources committed to the public information campaign and to the refuges and helplines which had to deal with the increased demands that resulted from it. The minister responsible was quoted as saying, 'The aim of the campaign was to improve knowledge of the law, not for women to leave their husbands and the marital home with their children and go instead to a refuge' (Louis 1990: 143).

The limited nature of French policy on violence towards women in the 1990s can be seen in the national reports that France was required to produce in preparation for the Beijing Conference in 1995 and the Beijing+5 Conference in 2000. The authors of the 1994 report identified violence towards women as one of four priority areas, along with women's participation in politics, the role of women in economic and professional life, and women and social cohesion (Aubin and Gisserot 1994). However, it occupies only four of the report's 105 pages. The report states that violence towards women has become more visible as a result of pressure by feminist-inspired associations, which have raised the awareness of local authorities and relevant professionals. It describes the public information campaigns; the establishment of departmental action committees; and the measures taken to improve the treatment of victims by the police and medical profession. It admits, however, that most support for victims is provided by the associations, in particular the Collectif Féministe contre le Viol and FNSF. It outlines legislation introduced in 1992 on domestic violence and sexual harassment, and case law recognising rape in marriage (Aubin and Gisserot 1994: 75–6). It states that statistics are only available on reported violence, and increases within them reflect attitudes to reporting, rather than prevalence. It highlights the lack of knowledge and understanding of the problem, for example, the number of repeated incidents cannot be known from the data (Aubin and Gisserot 1994: 76).

The two pages of the report about combating violence towards women consist of very broad statements about what should be done. There is a call for good research-based understanding of violence in order to prevent it; for a broad policy addressing the whole spectrum of violence towards women, bringing together the different institutions and associations concerned; for better services for victims; and for training for the relevant personnel (Aubin and Gisserot 1994: 95).

Five years later, a follow-up report was required for the Beijing+5 review of progress on the Platform for Action. The French report reiterates the lack of knowledge. It states that data are unavailable, that the issue is difficult to define, and that most cases go unreported, but adds that a survey has been commissioned to address this (ENVEFF) (Secrétariat d'Etat aux Droits des Femmes et à la Formation Professionnelle 2000: 61). It describes measures introduced since the previous report, including a 1996 circular on departmental action committees and an increase in state financial support for services for victims, benefiting twenty reception and support services (Secrétariat d'Etat aux Droits des Femmes et à la Formation Professionnelle 2000: 65). Tellingly, however, the conclusion to the section on violence towards women in the Beijing+5 report focuses heavily on prostitution.

Since the first initiatives by Michèle André in 1989, ministers for women's rights, under pressure from associations and activists, have played a role in putting domestic violence on the agenda and keeping it there. In 2001, Socialist Secrétaire d'Etat aux Droits des Femmes, Nicole Péry, declared violence towards women one of her four priorities, along with parity in politics, equality at work and reform of the laws on contraception and abortion. Prior to this, she had been involved in a number of interministerial actions, including a circular on domestic violence from 8 March 1999, co-signed with the Minister for Work and Solidarity, the Minister for Justice, the Minister for the Interior and the Minister for Defence. This circular reinforced the partnership between the various grassroots actors, the state and the courts, and in particular between the ministries concerned. It called on public prosecutors to ask investigative judges to introduce security measures guaranteeing victim protection, especially by evicting the violent partner from the family home and preventing any kind of contact with the victim (Direction des Affaires Criminelles et des Grâces 2004: 19).

The Minister for Justice and the Minister for Women's Rights in 1999 commissioned an interministerial study of the law and court practices in France in both civil and criminal law and a comparison with other European countries. In March 2000, Nicole Péry and the Minister for Housing signed a circular on housing for women in serious difficulties, which stated that prefects must ensure that women victims of domestic violence forced to leave their homes are given priority for social housing.

In partnership with the Minister for Work and Solidarity, Péry created the ARAF – Aide à la Reprise d'Activité des Femmes – a one-off contribution to childcare costs for women returning to work or training. She also established the Commission Nationale contre les Violences Envers les Femmes, in order to coordinate the work of local partnerships between the state, statutory agencies and NGOs. There has been training for legal professionals and for the police, run by the Délégations aux Droits des Femmes and specialised associations (Secrétariat d'Etat aux Droits des Femmes et à la Formation Professionnelle 2000: 67–8), and a circular of 22 October 2001 introduced clinical psychologists experienced in working with victims of violence into accident and emergency services (La Ministre de l'Emploi et de la Solidarité et al. 2001: 43–4).

Following the 2002 elections, the new right-wing Minister for Parity and Equality at Work, Nicole Ameline, maintained the high-profile status of domestic violence as a policy issue. In a cabinet meeting in 2003, Ameline stated that 'family violence' is a major problem, threatening the health, the rights and the responsibilities of 'the person'. It causes illness, medical consultations and hospitalisation; consumption of drugs and pharmaceuticals; time off work; and ruined lives. 'It therefore results in an increase in social, economic, and professional inequalities' (Ameline 2003). She states that in order to prevent such harmful effects, it is essential that social workers, doctors, associations, the police and the legal system take all necessary action to stop 'family violence' as soon as they become aware of it. If there is one domain in which zero tolerance is appropriate, she states, it is this one. Prosecutors should be able to act rapidly, the violent partner should be removed from the home without delay, and prosecution should take place quickly, accompanied by injunctions to protect 'the spouse or the children who are victims of violence'.

Throughout this statement, gender-neutral language is used to refer to the perpetrator and the victim, and references to 'family violence' replace Péry's emphasis on violence towards women. This changes, however, when Ameline refers to domestic violence affecting immigrant women:

> When it comes to domestic violence, more than any other kind, immigrant women are the victims because their status in this country is linked to their spouse and because their lack of financial autonomy, their isolation and the socio-cultural specificities of their country of origin prevent them from resisting and escaping. Moreover, the social control of the estate or local area which weighs on women of immigrant origin, and even more so on young girls, is an obstacle to their

autonomy. This is what the women say when they speak about their experience in the outskirts of Paris and cities elsewhere in the country when they denounce the double oppression that they experience on a daily basis: that of their fathers, brothers and all the men in the neighbourhood who treat them like children for life and that of the society which confines them to ghetto neighbourhoods. (Ameline 2003)

The Ministry for Justice was responsible for chairing a multidisciplinary working group on domestic violence, created by the Conseil National d'Aide aux Victimes (CNAV) in October 2004. This was part of the government's attempt to address the prevention of domestic violence and to pay more attention to victims' needs. It consists of two subgroups, the first of which is concerned with the provision of services for victims of domestic violence, mainly by civil society organisations, and works within the Service de l'Accès au Droit et à la Justice et de la Politique de la Ville. The second is concerned with criminal justice and domestic violence policy. Led by the Direction des Affaires Criminelles et des Grâces, it brings together judges, public prosecutors, defence lawyers and the central administration of the Ministry for Justice, representatives of the Ministries for the Interior, Defence and Parity and Equality at Work, members of the Ile de France regional Delegation for Women's Rights and Equality, lawyers, doctors and representatives from NGOs. This subgroup produced a set of guidelines on domestic violence aimed at the legal profession and all other relevant professionals (Branger 2005: 55). The publication of these guidelines forms part of the Minister for Justice's commitments as outlined by Nicole Ameline in her charter for equality between women and men (8 March 2004) (Direction des Affaires Criminelles et des Grâces 2004: 13). The 2004 guidelines refer to the 2001 Henrion Report which found that domestic violence results in the death of three women every fortnight, accounts for 20 per cent of medical emergencies, and occurs in all socio-professional categories and all age groups. The guidelines state that domestic violence is specific in that it takes place between couples bound by strong emotional ties and has repercussions for the whole family, especially children. They were intended to highlight best practice and standardise the implementation of the legal instruments currently interpreted in different ways in different parts of the country (Direction des Affaires Criminelles et des Grâces 2004: 15).

Ameline stated in 2004 that preventing domestic violence was now a priority area for state action, and that domestic violence should be recognised as a serious crime. She advocated placing responsibility firmly with the violent partner, evicting him from the home, and enabling women to rebuild their lives. The divorce law of 26 May 2004 introduces the possibility of evicting the violent partner from the marital home. Article 22 states that, 'when violence by one of the spouses endangers the other spouse or one or more of the children, the judge can give a ruling on the separate residence of the spouses, specifying which of the two will remain in the marital home'. The law states that, unless there are exceptional circumstances, this will normally be the non-violent partner (République française 2006: 66). In November 2004, the day after a bill was tabled in the Senate by the opposition Socialist and Green groups, Ameline announced a ten-point plan to combat violence towards women. The ten measures are:

- improved access to accommodation for victims of domestic violence;
- financial support for victims, who would have access to single parent allowance, minimum income, or young person's allowance, as appropriate;
- unemployment benefit for those who resign because of domestic violence;
- harsher penalties and better procedures for evicting the violent partner;
- more violence and health networks in legal medicine units, bringing together social workers, doctors and legal services;
- an increase of one million euros in funding for associations;
- a national information campaign and training for police officers and legal professionals;
- a national crime observatory to study violence towards women;
- prevention work in schools;
- cooperation in Europe and the world (Couret 2004).

Amnesty International suggests that it would have been better if Ameline's ten measures had led to coordinated cross-ministerial action, rather than assigning responsibility to the underfunded and understaffed women's rights services. It stresses that it is not possible for a single government department to implement this plan, especially following the reshuffle of 2005, as a result of which Ameline's staff of twenty was reduced to four under Catherine Vautrin (Amnesty International Section Française 2006: 42).

A public information message intended to raise awareness of domestic violence was aired by the main public and private television channels in March 2005 (Perben 2005). By 2005, victim support offices had been opened, fifteen social workers had been assigned to police stations, and designated domestic violence units created, notably in Strasbourg (Branger 2005: 49). A study carried out by the Minister for the Interior in 2005, based on police data from 2003–4, focused on violent death within the couple. It found that in mainland France, on average, one woman dies every four days as a result of domestic violence. Half of them had already reported violence. One man dies every sixteen days and in half of these cases, he has committed acts of violence towards the partner who then kills him (République française 2006: 65).

In January 2006, the Minister for the Interior, Nicolas Sarkozy, issued a circular aimed at improving the prevention of domestic violence and care for victims. It stated that emergency calls for domestic violence incidents will be treated as a priority, and the police were instructed to arrest perpetrators immediately when they are caught in the act, place them in custody and inform the public prosecutor. The victim can remain in the family home and will be encouraged to make a formal complaint. In the case of serious acts of violence, charges can be made independently of the victim's action. Sarkozy announced a pilot scheme involving placing psychologists in police stations (Smolar 2006). At the time of the issue of this circular, the Senate had already passed the second reading the bill on domestic violence, which became the Domestic Violence Act 2006.

The national context

Private members' bills were tabled in November and December 2004 in the National Assembly by Lachaud (UDF–UMP), and in the Senate by Boivo (PCF) and Courteau (PS–Verts). The latter two made it onto the Senate's agenda and resulted in the Domestic Violence Act 2006. A number of contextual factors are of particular interest in establishing the climate in which this bill was presented and debated.

In 2000, the large-scale national survey on violence towards women, ENVEFF, which had been commissioned in 1997 by the Minister for Women's Rights, Nicole Péry, as part of France's Beijing commitments, produced its first results. Prior to ENVEFF, there was information from national crime statistics and from associations which provide support for women who have experienced domestic violence, but there was no information on the extent of violence in the general population, much of which is known to be unreported. The primary aim of ENVEFF, which was carried out on 6,970 women aged 20–59, was to provide this information.

The preliminary findings were well received in 2000, but three years later, and before the publication of the book containing the full results, there was a surge of criticism by a number of public intellectuals, including the philosopher and media feminist, Elisabeth Badinter (Chetcuti and Jaspard 2007: 10). In her book *Fausse Route* (2003), Badinter criticised the survey for constructing women as victims. She accuses feminists of over-extending the concept of violence, creating a continuum that includes rape, verbal, moral and visual harassment, pornography and prostitution (Fabre and Weill 2003). Hervé Le Bras and Marcela Iacub (2003) criticised ENVEFF for constructing a continuum of violence and reigniting the battle of the sexes (see also Badinter and Iacub 2003). Badinter, Le Bras and Iacub criticise the growing criminalisation of amorous relations. They argue that, instead of laying the blame on men, we should be fostering women's autonomy.

This was the latest round in a long-running battle on gender issues conducted in the media by public intellectuals. It revisited themes established in the late 1980s and early 1990s and featuring prominently in the debates around sexual harassment, parity, the PACS (Pacte Civil de Solidarité – allowing same-sex civil unions) and prostitution. It constructs an opposition between harmonious, consensual gender relations in France and aggressive, non-consensual gender relations in the US, and argues that in France, sexuality is a private, not a political issue (Fassin 2007: 288; Scott 2005).

The full results of ENVEFF were published in June 2003. In common with similar research projects in countries all over the world, this study showed that violence towards women occurs in all social classes and is most likely to be perpetrated by a husband or partner. Interestingly, media attention to violence in the *banlieues* increased substantially around this time (Delphy 2004; Mabrouk and Berkani 2003: 56), suggesting, misleadingly, that violence towards women is concentrated in immigrant communities, and deflecting attention from domestic violence by white, middle-class men. The emergence in February 2003 of a group calling itself Ni Putes Ni Soumises (NPNS) highlighted this aspect of violence towards women. NPNS organised a Marche des Femmes des Cités to draw attention to violence in the *banlieues*. A 17-year-old girl who lived in a housing estate outside Paris had been burnt alive in October 2002, and her death became the focus for a number of local and national petitions and demonstrations, culminating in a 30,000-strong demonstration in Paris on 8 March 2003, International Women's Day (Falconnat 2004).

Critics of ENVEFF were temporarily silenced by the sudden and unexpected death in August 2003 of actor Marie Trintignant as a result of domestic violence (Fassin 2007: 294). Her partner was Bertrand Cantat, singer in the group Noir Désir (*Le Monde*, 9 August 2003). The message emphasised by much of the media coverage was that fame and wealth were no protection against a form of violence that affected women from all parts of society.

The mobilisation of women of migrant origin against violence towards women, the publication of the results of ENVEFF, and the death of Marie Trintignant reinforced the agenda status of violence towards women, but did not create it. Thirty years of feminist activism, an influential international context, and the actions of women in government have all played a role in domestic violence policy. The next section of this chapter will examine the content of the domestic violence bills tabled in 2004, the parliamentary reports on them, and the implementation of the ensuing Act.

The Domestic Violence Act (4 April 2006)

The Domestic Violence Act was passed by a right-wing majority and was the outcome of two private members' bills, rather than a government-backed initiative. The bills were tabled by Senators Roland Courteau (PS) and Nicole Borvo (PCF). Aggravating circumstances now apply in the case of murder, rape or sexual aggression within a married, cohabiting or PACS couple or when perpetrated by a former partner. For other types of violence, aggravating circumstances which already existed for married and cohabiting couples are extended to PACS couples and former partners. The Act also raises the age for marriage for women from 15 to 18 (Article 1). Article 11 recognises the act of rape, regardless of the relationship between the perpetrator and the victim, and explicitly includes rape within marriage. The presumption of consent to sex by a spouse applies only in the absence of evidence to the contrary. In the case of violence towards a partner, the perpetrator must leave the couple's home and, if necessary, undertake treatment. This applies to current and former partners. Article 13 requires the government to report to Parliament every two years on domestic violence policy.

The bills

Roland Courteau's bill on combating violence against women, especially within couples, by prevention, repression and support for victims, was presented to the Senate in November 2004. It defines the issue as one of public health and respect for the person. It states that zero tolerance can only be imposed by a global approach of repression, prevention and aid for victims. It proposes the imprisonment of repeat offenders and introduces explicit mention of rape within the couple, including

PACS couples. It also extends aggravating circumstances to PACS couples. Preventative measures focus on education in schools and through the media. Victim support requires training for all professionals including doctors. The bill also explicitly permits judges to issue exclusion orders and to oblige perpetrators to follow treatment.

Nicole Borvo's bill on combating violence within the couple was presented in the Senate in December 2004. Violence towards women was framed within this bill as an issue of health and public safety. The bill emphasises aid, protection and financial support for victims, and treatment for the perpetrator. It encourages relevant professionals to engage actively in the prevention, identification and protection of women victims of domestic violence, and calls for interagency approaches. It extends the application of aggravating circumstances introduced by law no. 92-683, 22 July 1992 to PACS partners and requires the removal from the home of the violent partner, not the victim. Referring to the Henrion Report of 2001, which demonstrates the damaging effects of domestic violence on its victims, it states that victims should be protected and compensated. It emphasises that, in accordance with international obligations, it is the state's responsibility to prevent violence, to punish perpetrators and to compensate victims.

The measures proposed in the bills were greeted with consensual approval at the committee stage and during the formal debates in both houses of Parliament. Although there was general consensus both in the Senate and in the National Assembly that domestic violence was an issue requiring state intervention, committees and individuals differed in their understanding of the problem as one requiring primarily criminal justice responses or primarily prevention, victim support and treatment programmes for violent offenders. It is the balance between the two that colours policy approaches at any particular time.

Parliamentary reports

Branger's report for the Senate's Women's Rights Delegation stressed the need for a more coherent response to domestic violence, motivated by strong political will. It approved of the principle of aggravating sanctions for violence against a partner, PACS partner or ex-partner; the recognition of rape within relationships; and increasing support for victims. It also recommended raising the marriage age for women from 15 to 18 in order to reduce forced marriage, prohibiting criminal mediation in cases of domestic violence, extending the eviction of a violent partner from the couple's home to PACS partners and cohabitees, and extending aggravating circumstances to PACS partners and former partners. It called for better statistical data, an update on ENVEFF, studies on the influence of pornography, prostitution and alcohol, and studies of the financial and social cost of domestic violence. It called for better coordination between the various agencies and professionals involved in domestic violence and better recognition of the role of doctors (Branger 2005: 43). Finally, it called for the coordination of a network of support for victims, increasing the presence of support associations in police stations, improving training for all the personnel concerned and introducing discussion groups for violent men (Branger 2005: 87–8).

The Senate's Law Commission produced a report in March 2005, authored by Henri de Richemont (Richemont 2005) and drawing explicitly on Branger's report for the Women's Rights Delegation. It recommends the addition to the Penal Code and Criminal Procedure Code of the extension of aggravating circumstances to PACS partners; the aggravation of sanctions for violence committed against former partners, cohabitees and PACS partners; the application of aggravating circumstances to murder committed within the couple; the explicit criminalisation of rape within the couple; and the specific obligation of the criminal justice system to remove the perpetrator of domestic violence from the couple's home (Richemont 2005: 5–6). Richemont points out, however, that legal sanctions, although necessary, are not sufficient; sanctions which already exist are not systematically implemented for reasons which include the reluctance of victims to initiate proceedings, their lack of legal understanding and inconsistent decision-making on the part of public prosecutors. He, like Branger, is also critical of criminal mediation which is inappropriate in cases of domestic violence where the perpetrator often refuses to recognise his violent acts and where the victim is frequently unable to express herself freely (Richemont 2005: 13).

The Senate's Law Commission found that the criminal aspect is only part of the policy response, but can act as a dissuasive measure and can provide effective protection for victims. But criminal law in this area still has gaps, and the bills can fill them (Richemont 2005: 19). The Commission accepted many aspects of the bill's proposals, but not all. Firstly, public awareness raising is indeed an essential element in the fight against domestic violence, but is not an issue for legislation. Secondly, the proposed aid for victims seems to be satisfied by measures already in place, and there needs to be a more detailed assessment of their financial impact. Finally, creating an offence of 'habitual violence' and of 'psychological violence' poses certain problems (Richemont 2005: 20).

The final report was produced by the *députée*, Chantal Brunel, and was a response to the text passed by the Senate in its first reading (Brunel 2005). Brunel approved of the extension of aggravating circumstances for all domestic violence and for violence by PACS partners and ex-partners. She called, however, for additional measures enabling better prevention of violence towards women of immigrant origin such as forced marriage and polygamy. Measures aimed at women of immigrant origin include raising the age of marriage from 15 to 18, the justification being that, as adults, women will be in a better position to resist family pressure (although it is questionable whether this will make a difference, given that the measure affects only civil marriage, not customary marriage). A new offence is included in the bill – depriving another of proof of identity or residence or visitor's permits by any kind of intimate partner (including former partners) (Brunel 2005: 8).

Brunel called for further measures, including systematic checks that women living in France – of all nationalities – consent to their marriage before it is legally recognised in France. She stated that for all marriages abroad, there should be separate interviews of the spouses to establish consent (Brunel 2005: 9). She approved of the explicit recognition of rape within the couple and the explicit inclusion of the possibility of issuing an exclusion order for those released on parole keeping them from the victim's home.

Brunel also found the current text heavy on penalties, paying too little attention to prevention and support (Brunel 2005: 6). She called for the extension of successful pilot schemes such as those run in Paris, where psychiatrists, psychologists and nurses have worked together with the public prosecutor's office to deal with violent men, and in Nimes, where a centre for violent partners, linked to the criminal court, has been established.

The Act was uncontroversial and combined repressive, preventative and victim support measures. It recognised domestic violence within current and former married, cohabiting and PACS couples.

Implementation

In 2006, the French section of Amnesty International published a study of the state's response to violence towards women. It revealed women's difficulties accessing the legal system, their lack of knowledge of their rights, and the inadequacy of support for victims from the police, social workers and the legal profession. It found that the legal provisions for combating domestic violence are adequate, but that implementation varies across the country.

Amnesty International found that the police, medical and legal professionals who implement domestic violence policy are not always adequately trained, resourced or informed. There is inadequate awareness of the practical, comprehensive, but non-binding guidelines produced by the Minister for Justice in 2004 and distributed to all public prosecutors' offices (Amnesty International Section Française 2006: 59–60). Despite improvements in the way reports of domestic violence are treated in police stations, there are still cases where the police discourage victims from making a formal complaint, especially when there is no supporting medical evidence. Underreporting remains a major problem (Amnesty International Section Française 2006: 59–60). Amnesty calls on the state to honour its commitments under the Beijing Platform for Action and provide adequate training for all relevant professionals (Amnesty International Section Française 2006: 88–9). It calls for improvements in the implementation across the country of victim protection, rapid intervention and the removal of the violent partner from the couple's home. It calls for better funding for associations and state agencies and the provision of appropriate police resources and emergency accommodation (Amnesty International Section Française 2006: 95). Finally, Amnesty restates the need for comprehensive data on all aspects of domestic violence and for regular campaigns to raise public awareness of women's rights and domestic violence issues (Amnesty International Section Française 2006: 96).

Gil-Robles reached similar conclusions, in his report for the Council of Europe on human rights in France (Gil-Robles 2006). Problems which are reported to persist, despite legislative measures and political attention to domestic violence, include women who have left the family home with their children being obliged to give the father the children's address; the reduction in public funding for victim support associations; and difficulties finding housing, particularly social housing, which is in short supply. Gil-Robles stated that:

> while the French authorities claim that domestic violence is a priority issue, the actual situation in which victims find themselves is extremely rarely taken into consideration. More effort should therefore be directed towards implementing the existing provisions more effectively . . . All stakeholders, police officers and judges, the ones coming into most direct contact with domestic violence, also need to be made more aware of the issues involved. (Gil-Robles 2006: 92)

Associations continue to play a central role in victim support, and the possibility of being housed is crucial to victims. However, they suffer from financial problems and are often dependent on volunteers. The associations providing most of the victim support receive funding from the state, but this is rarely considered sufficient, is not permanent, and constructs a relationship of dependency. They also suffer from uncertainty about the renewal of state funding, which can be detrimental to the functioning of the association (Branger 2005: 62).

The presentation of domestic violence in policy debates

At the international and European level, a number of studies have focused on the cost of violence towards women in order to demonstrate that this is a public not a private issue. These studies can also help to support the case for resources to be made available for prevention. The costs include not only the direct costs of services, but also the indirect cost of lost employment and productivity, and the less readily quantifiable cost of human pain and suffering (United Nations General Assembly 2006: 50). The Council of Europe report on the implementation of Rec. 2002(5) states that:

> Gender-based violence has consequences for both the wider society and the individual victim. It causes pain, fear and distress, reduces the capacity of victimized women to contribute productively to the family, the economy and public life, and drains the resources of social services, the justice system, health care agencies, and of employers – costs that must be seen both in terms of human suffering and of economic loss. In a broader view, it lowers the overall educational attainment, mobility and innovative potential of a significant proportion of the population: the women who are victimized, the children growing up witnessing the violence, and even the perpetrators who resort to destructive acts are restricted in their potential. A society that tolerates seemingly private violence will be a crippled competitor in the knowledge- and creativity-based economy of the future. Analyses of the costs of violence thus highlight the gains which could result from its reduction and elimination. The high costs of violence underline that gender-based violence is a social, a public and no longer a private problem, and that it urgently needs to be addressed, as society as a whole, governments, individuals, organizations, and businesses pay for it. (Council of Europe 2006: 8)

In France, the Henrion Report in 2001, ENVEFF in 2003, and Nicole Borvo's bill in 2004 all highlighted the public health aspects of domestic violence, and the direct and indirect costs to individuals and society as a whole. On the initiative of the Service des Droits des Femmes et de l'Egalité a study of the economic costs of domestic violence in France was carried out by researchers at the Centre for Economic Social and Business Research at the Lille Catholic Institute. The results were published in 2007 by the Documentation française (Marissal and Chevally 2007).

Research on violence towards women which emerged from frontline contact with its victims via helplines and refuges gradually led to a shift away from seeking explanations based on the characteristics of victims (it found that the only thing they had in common was a violent partner) to trying to establish whether violent men were pathological or deviant. The evidence suggested that violent men were perfectly ordinary. Researchers concluded that it is gender power relations which allow this violence to take place, and that if it is to be stopped, these will have to be changed. This approach was visible in some policy statements and in demands for increased education and prevention by activists. For example, Branger stated that current efforts to tackle violence towards women are situated in a broader context of efforts to promote equality (Branger 2005: 6). Feminist movements highlighted 'male domination' as the main explanation for domestic violence, which, on this view, is an expression of gender power relations that favour men. Similarly, Roger Henrion, in his report for the Ministry of Health in 2001, stated that domestic violence differs from conflicts between spouses or partners by the unequal nature of the violence perpetrated by the man who wants to dominate, subordinate and humiliate his wife or partner (Branger 2005: 8).

However, Chetcuti and Jaspard (2007) note a return to explanations based on individual pathology, rather than systemic gender inequalities. A report on the perpetrators of domestic violence, commissioned by the Minister for Parity, Catherine Vautrin and carried out by the psychiatrist Roland Coutanceau, for example, made a number of recommendations for the treatment of violent men (Coutanceau 2006). Violent behaviour is increasingly attributed to individual factors, at the expense of feminist socio-political explanations. Claims that there is a parallel between violence towards women and violence towards men are part of this trend (Chetcuti and Jaspard 2007: 11). The psychopathological model sees violence as the result of deviant behaviour on the part of individuals whose personal history is disturbed. This approach designates an 'Other', a deviant or delinquent, who can be punished or medically treated. The feminist approach presents a socio-political analysis which is explicitly critical of the social order (Chetcuti and Jaspard 2007: 12).

Since 2002, violence has increasingly fallen within the remit of the ministers of health and justice, or even the interior, which is, according to Jaspard, a step backwards in the sense that the socio-political aspects of the issue are being ignored in favour of public health and security (Chetcuti and Jaspard 2007: 12–13). The post of women's rights minister has disappeared and been replaced by a ministerial delegation for social cohesion and parity:

> While feminist analysis defines violence towards women as a social problem, linked to the hierarchical relations between the sexes, the new institutional context hardly seems conducive to the development of this approach. The socio-political dimension of the phenomenon is at dire risk of being obliterated and violence towards women seems to be seen exclusively as a problem of public health, justice or domestic security. (Jaspard 2007: 37–8)

Conclusion

There was little government concern about domestic violence throughout the 1980s and 1990s, despite the activism of grassroots feminist organisations and, later, the initiatives of some individuals in government. The main pressure for action began to build in the mid-1990s, with the requirement that the French government produce a report for the 1995 UN Conference on Women in Beijing, and the policy environment of the 1997–2002 Jospin government was conducive to positive initiatives in this area as on other women's rights issues. Grassroots feminist activism and research had, by this time, built up a substantial body of knowledge based on quantitative and qualitative data, and this was drawn upon in parliamentary inquiries and committee work, building recognition of certain feminists as expert witnesses.

Public condemnation of domestic violence has increased, and there has been broad cross-party consensus on this, accompanied by a symbolic commitment to bringing about change. However, in 2005, a study of all homicides recorded in France in 2003–4 showed that during this period, one woman died every four days as a result of domestic violence. Half of them had reported previous acts of violence before the one that caused their death (Chemin 2006b). In 2006, according to government figures, 137 women died as a result of domestic violence, 330,000 women claimed to be living with a partner who had beaten them during 2005 and 2006, and only 8.8 per cent of the victims of domestic violence had made an official complaint (Létard 2007). Until implementation improves, legal provisions will continue to be necessary but insufficient in the fight to combat violence against women.

The tension between criminal justice and preventative responses to domestic violence has always been present and reflects different understandings of the problem. Criminal justice responses tend to correlate with individualised or pathological understandings of the causes of domestic violence, whereas preventative responses, such as gender equality education in schools and attempts to eradicate gender inequalities in society more broadly, tend to be advocated by those with a more systemic understanding of the causes of gender violence.

Since 2002, there has been a growing 'securitarisation' of domestic violence policy, with an increased emphasis on criminal justice responses. Sarkozy favours harsh sanctions for perpetrators and increased protection for victims. From 2002 there was a decline in gendered approaches to domestic violence, with Ameline's references to 'family conflict' replacing Péry's 'violence against women', for example, although the government's 2007 plan resumed a discourse of violence towards women and situated women firmly as victims in need of protection (Létard 2007).

The 'women's rights are human rights' frame which dominated the discourse of the UN and of international NGOs in the 1990s is less visible in French policy debates, and the commitments under the Beijing Platform for Action to eradicate gender inequalities which cause gender violence have been replaced by individualised criminal justice approaches to prevention and protection.

Note

1. A series of measures introduced between 1999 and 2003 culminated in the Organic Act 1/2004 of 28 December on 'Integrated Protection Measures against Gender Violence'. As a result, Spain has the widest-ranging domestic violence legislation in Europe, and campaigners in France refer to it as a model.

6
The Islamic Headscarf (*hijab*)

Controversy surrounding the wearing of the Islamic headscarf or *hijab*[1] in French state schools dates back to September 1989.[2] At the time, three schoolgirls of Maghrebi background were excluded from their local high school (Collège Gabriel Havez) in the town of Creil, by head teacher Ernest Chenière, for failing to remove their headscarves while on school premises. Chenière's argument for excluding the girls rested on the safeguarding of secular, Republican principles (*laïcité*)[3] in state schools, as set down by the Ferry Laws of 1881–2, and the drive to clamp down on exemptions claimed by certain pupils and their families on grounds of religion. For instance, the desire of Jewish families to observe the Sabbath meant that some children absented themselves from school on Saturday mornings while a number of Muslim schoolgirls asked to be excused from physical and sex education classes. Chenière's action, followed by the intervention of certain immigrant associations and Islamic bodies and the subsequent failure to reach a compromise, sparked off a polemical debate across France which split representatives of the state, civil society institutions, intellectuals, clerics and political activists into two camps: for or against the removal of the Islamic headscarf in school. Rather than mirroring established social cleavages or left–right ideological differences, the split over the headscarf at school cut across social groups, party political lines and religious affiliations.

The 'affaire du foulard', as it was termed by the media, broke out when it did for a number of reasons. First, voter disappointment at rising unemployment and social disadvantage, signalling the failure of the 1981 Socialist programme, was expressed by a marked shift to the right, giving the far-right Front National (FN) an unprecedented electoral break by 1986. The party obtained 10.95 per cent of the vote at the European elections of 1984 (Europe-Politique.EU 2008) and almost 10 per cent at the 1986 legislative elections (*Le Monde* 1986: 67). The results afforded the FN a presence in both the National Assembly (albeit for a short time only) and the European Parliament, converting it into a major organisational force behind the racism directed at populations of Muslim background amongst others. Second, hostility towards Muslims and the belief that they constituted a '[barbaric] enemy within' was reinforced by events which were taking place outside France. For example: the Rushdie affair in Britain set off Muslim protests worldwide and prompted the delivery of the *fatwa* against Salman Rushdie by Ayatollah Khomeini in February 1989, leading to the deterioration of relations between Muslims and Westerners; the birth of a powerful Islamist movement (Front Islamique du Salut) in Algeria led to the radicalisation of certain sections of the North African population in France and raised fears about possible internal challenges against the French state by Islamists; and finally, the first Palestinian *intifada* (1987–93) coupled with civil war in Lebanon (1975–92) hardened French Muslim opinion against the French and other Western governments.

The 'affaire du foulard' raised questions surrounding the meaning of secularity (*laïcité*); gender equality and women's rights; the place of Islam in a country where the Republican universal ideal of the abstract citizen conflicts with notions of difference whether based on class, gender, 'race', ethno-religious culture or any other markers of identity; and the integration of postwar immigrants from North Africa and the Middle East who were the main bearers of Islam in France. It cast a spotlight on the limits of tolerance in a society which prided itself historically on pluralism of political thought and practice and the protection of human rights and which had previously promoted itself as Europe's main rival to the USA as far as the long-term settlement of immigrants was concerned. The 'affaire du foulard' produced entrenched opposing positions over whether or not the headscarf and the distinct identity it expressed posed a threat to an undifferentiated French identity (and its attendant values) which could only be successfully forged within a secular education system (see, for example, Auge 1989; Badinter et al. 1989: 58–9; Bentbria 1989; Brunnerie-Kaufmann et al. 1989; Sebbar 1989).

Eventually, education minister, Lionel Jospin, referred the matter to the Conseil d'Etat, France's supreme administrative court. The Conseil d'Etat's decision proved a disappointment to opponents of the *hijab* as it ruled in favour of the schoolgirls' right to wear the headscarf in school as long as it did not signify an 'act of proselytism', offend the dignity or beliefs of other pupils and teachers, disrupt lessons in any way or cause breaches of health and safety regulations within the education system (Conseil d'Etat, 1989). This ruling was followed by a Ministry of Education circular (Education Nationale, Jeunesse et Sports 1989) to all schools and local education authorities explaining the decision. As the ruling was not based on generally applicable points of principle, schools were obliged to take a case-by-case approach to each headscarf dispute as it arose. The number of Muslim girls wearing headscarves increased in schools which interpreted the ruling pragmatically, whereas headscarves were hardly seen in schools which imposed a local ban, such as that at a high school in Montfermeil (north-eastern Paris) which was successfully challenged in 1992, in what came to be known as the case of 'Khérouaa et al.', or the ban imposed at the Collège Xavier Bichat, in Nantua (north-east of Lyon) which was eventually upheld by the Conseil d'Etat in 1994.

The majority of headscarf disputes were resolved through compromise at school or local education authority level or were referred to an administrative tribunal or passed further up to an administrative appeal court before a judgement was made. But a number of cases did reach the Conseil d'Etat between 1992 and 1994. In a handful (8 out of 49, of which the most cited is the Nantua case), the school authorities mounted a successful defence in favour of exclusions, ultimately gaining the Conseil d'Etat's support. In fact the Nantua case reignited the 1989 debates, stirring up public opinion against the headscarf to such an extent (*L'Express* 1994: 62–80; Schemla 1994), that the education minister, François Bayrou, issued a directive to head teachers at the start of the school year in 1994 asking them to ban any conspicuous religious symbols in school. In addition, a new office of mediator was created in order to deal with specific headscarf cases. Hanifa Chérifi, the first appointed mediator, dealt with 400 cases over the next four years (Quid.fr 2007).

Public and media interest in issues surrounding the headscarf remained on the back burner with the odd story of schoolgirl exclusions surfacing in the national press. However, heightened security concerns in a post-9/11 world over the presence of Muslims in France and the resultant tensions between majority society and Muslims led to the eruption of several disputes between pupils and education authorities, mainly in Lyon and Paris, over the right or otherwise to wear the headscarf at school. It is this second cycle of headscarf affairs (2002–4) culminating in legislation banning conspicuous religious symbols in school which forms the interest of this chapter. This chapter investigates the policy structures and processes in which the 2004 law was passed and has since been applied. It also examines the influence of various policy actors on the law's formulation through an examination of the main arguments for and against the headscarf and the principles underpinning these arguments. Some background knowledge of the political and social environment in which the debates took place is provided, as is a brief account of the events of the most recent headscarf affairs. But, to begin with, we outline the historical facts and factors which governed the emergence of *laïcité* and its connection with Republicanism and the state education system.

Historical background: religion, *laïcité* and education

A long history of religious war and anti-clericalism in France predates the Revolution of 1789, stemming from intense conflicts between Catholics and Protestants during the second half of the sixteenth century. The conflicts, exacerbated during successive economic crises, reflected deep political divisions between royal dynasties supported by opposing religious groups – namely, the Catholic House of Guise and the Huguenot House of Bourbon (Heller 1991; Holt 1995; Knecht 2000). The dominance of the Catholic Church in the sixteenth century wars of religion and subsequent conflicts meant that countering and eventually weakening its influence in the political arena became one of the main aims of the French Revolution. This was done though a series of measures between 1789 and 1795. Most importantly, the state invoked the authority of the people as opposed to that of God and also introduced a degree of state–church separation in matters of education, welfare and marriage. Strained relations between church and state persisted until 1801 when a truce, in the form of the Concordat, was reached between Napoleon Bonaparte and the Roman Catholic Church. The Concordat gave the French state significant control over the French Catholic Church through the appointment of bishops and archbishops and by obliging the clergy to swear a loyalty oath to the Republic. The 1801 Concordat regulated church-state relations until 1876 when a strongly Republican, anti-clerical political administration gained power. The Republicans' age-old mistrust of a monarchist Church, combined with the view that the latter continued to exert far too much control within the area of education, thus preventing the development of a modern (i.e. secular) system to rival that of Germany, meant that the 1801 Concordat was to become a dead letter. Between 1876 and the early twentieth century, anti-clericalism was expressed in the Ferry Laws (after Jules Ferry, Minister for Education from 1879 to 1883) and the resultant dissolution of large numbers of Catholic congregations and closure of hundreds of Church-run schools all seen to pose a political threat to the Republic. Conversely, the state education sector was bolstered by making primary education free and compulsory between the ages of 6 and 13 and through the introduction of civic and moral education in the place of religious instruction. This education would teach the values of French Republicanism, the rights and responsibilities of citizenship and truths held to be universal. Hence, in an open letter to teachers in the state primary education sector, Jules Ferry wrote:

> [the law of 28 March 1883] asserts the will to create a national education service in France, based on ideas of duty and law which legislators will unhesitatingly establish among the foremost truths that none can ignore. The public authorities are relying on you, teachers, to deliver this key stage of education ... What you will communicate to the school boy or girl is not your own wisdom but that of humankind ... there exists in each and every [primary] schoolteacher a natural supporter of moral and social progress. (Denmard 1981)

The anti-clericalist/pro-secularist actions described above eventually culminated in the 1905 law (Loi de Séparation des Eglises et de l'Etat) which formally ended the 1801 Concordat;[4] set down the terms for the legal separation of church and state;[5] and reinforced the principle of *laïcité* previously established by the 1881–2 Ferry Law banning religious teaching in schools. Hence the creation and consolidation of a formalised *laïque* state education system from the 1880s may be seen as an important step in the protection and perpetuation of the Republican regime. However, the problem of the place of religion in schools was not resolved as a result and has often proved to be a contentious issue from the late nineteenth century to the present day. More specifically, the 1905 law and its framing of *laïcité* and of the place of religious education in schools has been subjected to periodic challenges by Catholics.

The transformation of the state education sector into a secular space was strongly contested not only at the time of the 1905 law and during the early years of the twentieth century but also during the interwar period and at the beginning of Vichy rule, following the collapse of the Third Republic in 1940 (for a useful overview of the period 1880–1945, see Ognier 1994; Willaime 2007). So, for example, in the years following the 1905 Act, clergymen retaliated by refusing state school pupils the celebration of their first holy communion or by barring families of state school pupils from attending mass. Furthermore, in the interwar years, attempts made by the Radical-Socialist Cartel des Gauches government (1924–6) to enforce *laïcité* in Alsace and Lorraine were successfully countered through a formal denunciation of *laïcité* by the French Catholic Church in 1925; condemnation of French state schooling by papal encyclical in 1929; and through numerous street demonstrations and meetings organised by Catholics up and down the country. Finally, Catholics found some sympathy for religious education among Vichy government officials between 1940 and 1942. However, while the Vichy government failed to revive all those elements of the 1801 Concordat pertaining to religion and education, it did set the important precedent of granting state aid to private Catholic education – a move which was to have important political repercussions in the Fourth and Fifth Republics each time an attempt was made to reinstate any form of religion in state education and thus challenge *laïcité*.

The aforementioned precedent was invoked in various pieces of legislation during the postwar period. In 1951, the Marie and Barangé Acts, which provided for state grants to the most able and deserving children in state and private Catholic schools and for parental allocations for children attending state or Catholic schools, caused a deep left/right polarisation of public and political opinion. However, attempts by parties of the left to reverse these laws in 1956 were narrowly defeated. The objective of anti-secularists to reinstate religion in the state education sector was given a further boost in 1959 with the enactment of the Debré Law which arguably continued the process of chipping away at the monopoly of secularism within state schooling.

The Debré Law allowed private Catholic schools the opportunity to wholly or partly opt into the state system through acceptance of certain directives on curricula, timetabling of classes, financial accounting and operations, teachers' qualifications etc. Opt-ins could range from a minimal, provisional contract with the state, to a more comprehensive associative contract, to complete insertion into the state system. The Debré Law was denounced ferociously by the left and the Comité national d'action laïque as a contemptuous attempt by Gaullists to deprive working-class and secular-minded middle-class families of scarce educational resources and funding in order to enable private-sector Catholic schools to increase their pupil enrolment. A year after the law's successful passage through Parliament, over 10 million people had signed a petition against it (Hanley et al. 1984: 278), asking for its revocation, for an end to wasteful plural systems of schooling and for the principle of *laïcité* to be upheld. Although the Debré Law had provoked an enormous anti-clericalist reaction, by the end of the decade private schools (of which 90 per cent were Catholic) were educating 1.5 million pupils (Hanley et al. 1984: 277; Prost 1987: 230).

Public acceptance of the state financing of private-sector schools was recorded in numerous polls during the postwar period. For example, in

1946, 77 per cent of the public was against state subsidies to private schools on the basis that any help given to the private sector constituted an undermining of *laïcité* and meant fewer resources for the state sector. By 1951, this figure had decreased to 54 cent and in 1974 to 23 per cent (Prost 1987: 229). Majority opinion in France, it appeared, favoured the principle of freedom of choice in education (as guaranteed by the Constitution) above that of secularism. This goes some way towards explaining why the ambitious reform proposed by the Socialists, in the early 1980s, for 'a grand, integrated, secular state education service' (intended to restructure private sector schooling) failed so spectacularly, leading to the withdrawal of the education bill and resignation of Alain Savary, Minister for Education at the time. The majority of voters, millions of whom were moved to demonstrate in huge rallies around the country, saw Savary's proposed reform as nationalisation by stealth of private schools and an infringement of their constitutional rights. According to a number of writers on the subject (Baubérot 1994; Mayeur 1985; Prost 1987), the legislative ping-pong which had taken place since 1945 between those who wanted a unified, secular state system of education and those who believed in their right to a religious alternative, and which had culminated in the Savary reform debacle, was indicative of the fact that France had reached a stage where both secularists and their opponents, jealous of guarding their respective identities, had preferred compromise and acceptance of a plural system of education. Anti-secularists wished to preserve a certain religious identity within private-sector education while their opponents conceded that two systems were preferable to one system and the introduction of 'pluralism into the very bosom of the state school' (Prost 1987: 235). Paradoxically, however, the acceptance of a plural system of education may well have paved the way for the very situation that the defenders of *laïcité* had feared so much when they finally backtracked over the Savary reform in 1984. For, in 1989, the eruption of the first headscarf affair prefigured the possibility of pluralism within the heart of the state school system.

Headscarf affairs in the new millennium

Although the second cycle of headscarf affairs comprised numerous pupil–school disputes, two cases in particular hit the headlines and served as an initial catalyst for the mobilisation of public opinion in favour of a legal solution to the '*hijab* problem'. The first case occurred in Lyon, during the academic year 2002–3 at Lycée La Martinière Duchère where a majority of teachers took strike action following a

16-year-old girl's repeated refusal to remove her headscarf while continuing to attend school. Jean-Claude Santana, an economics teacher and branch secretary of the teachers' union SNES (Syndicat National des Enseignements de Second Degré), accused the pupil of breaking school rules not only by wearing a headscarf and claiming to do so for religious reasons, but also by apparently encouraging other girls, including her sister, to do the same (Bertrand 2004; Landrin 2004; Sanchez and Santana 2003). Santana's accusation and complaints led the school authorities to suspend her, although intervention by the local education authority (Académie de Lyon) and government (Education Nationale) mediator, Hanifa Chérifi, meant that she was readmitted in the spring term. The pupil's insistence on wearing her headscarf upon readmission coupled with the Lyon chief education officer's suggestion to involve a local mosque leader as mediator in the continuing dispute triggered the call for strike action by the teaching staff which in turn alerted the media and local politicians to events at the school. The dispute at La Martinière was never really settled locally. A war of attrition between a number of teachers and certain pupils simmered on even after teachers returned to work and only ended the following academic year when the law on conspicuous religious symbols was passed.

The second case involved two sisters, Lila and Alma, at the Lycée Wallon in the north-eastern Parisian suburb of Aubervilliers in 2003 (Lévy, 2003; Lévy et al. 2004; Nordmann 2004). Media interest in this case arose from the fact that the father of the two schoolgirls was of Jewish background, was married to a Kabyle woman and was an atheist lawyer who had acted on behalf of anti-racist organisations such as the MRAP (Mouvement contre le Racisme et pour l'Amitié entre les Peuples) and had helped prosecute Jean-Marie Le Pen over the latter's Holocaust denial statements. Laurent Lévy's firm support for the right of his daughters to wear the *hijab* in school and hence his seeming disregard for the principles of *laïcité* was deplored by the girls' teachers, intellectuals and others in the public eye. Furthermore, and more significantly, the fact that the girls' parents were clearly not responsible for their decision to wear the *hijab* led to the widespread assumption that they were being encouraged and manipulated by Islamic fundamentalists intent on destabilising French society. Their refusal, in the face of intense pressure, to remove the *hijab* in school eventually led to their exclusion and to a loud public debate over the girls' individual rights versus the safeguarding of Republican principles and French values. The case was dubbed 'this mini Dreyfus affair' by Alain Liepietz, MEP for the Greens and former Maoist militant (Liepietz 2003) as Lila, Alma and Laurent Lévy faced accusations of being used by anti-democratic forces and thereby of compromising public safety and the security of the French state.

The factors which contributed to the emergence of the first headscarf disputes between 1989 and 1994 were outlined earlier. Similar factors played a role in the early 2000s. There was widespread disillusionment with the established political parties and particularly the Socialists. Voter apathy and dissatisfaction were powerfully reflected in the results of the 2002 presidential elections when the far-right candidate, Jean-Marie Le Pen, polled the second highest number of votes after Jacques Chirac, beating the Socialist Lionel Jospin to the second round and placing the Front National among the big three parties for the first time since its creation. The new millennium did not signal an improvement in the high unemployment rates and poor prospects of upward social mobility among those in certain districts of Paris, Lyon and other large cities: that is, among young working-class populations and those from ethnic minority and immigrant communities many of whom are of Muslim background. The lack of material resources in these areas led to hostile relations between majority society and France's minority populations of immigrant origin. The latter were seen by the former as competitors in an unstable labour market and a drain on social welfare provision. On the other hand, if in the face of harsh socio-economic conditions minority groups did draw strength from traditional family and community networks and culture, they were accused of retreating from French society and becoming 'unintegratable'. In addition, rising crime rates in the late 1990s and early 2000s – France was one of three EU states to record the greatest increase in crime generally and violent crime in particular (Barclay et al. 2003: 2–4) – added to the discontent of voters. The association of unemployment, rising crime and what were seen as large influxes of 'foreigners' (often from Muslim-majority states), coupled with what Vincent Geisser has (contentiously) termed 'islamophobie à la française',[6] created the circumstances which provided Le Pen with vital electoral fodder in 2002 and which gave rise to the second cycle of the 'affaire du foulard'. However, combined with the cocktail of factors already mentioned, a critical external factor – the events of 9/11 and the repercussions which flowed from them – whipped up the tone and amplitude of the headscarf debates to fever pitch, dividing the opinion of various social actors including celebrity journalists, academics and intellectuals, politicians, mosque leaders, representatives of Muslim associations, high school pupils, their families and also so-called security experts who had not declared an interest in headscarves prior to September 2001 (for example, Alain Bauer, a self-styled public security consultant who appeared on the FR3 TV show *Culture et Dépendances*, on 22 October 2003).

The debates triggered by cases of Lycée La Martinière Duchère, the Lévy sisters and other less well-known ones eventually led Jacques Chirac (president since 1997) to commission an inquiry on the application of *laïcité* in public institutions, particularly state schools. In July 2003, a commission was established under the chairmanship of Bernard Stasi, a seasoned right-of-centre politician and Ombudsman of the French Republic between 1998 and 2004. The Stasi Commission's report (Stasi 2004) was submitted to Jacques Chirac in December 2003 and quickly led to the drawing up of a parliamentary bill which proposed a ban on conspicuous religious symbols in state schools and which was definitively adopted in March 2004 (Loi no. 2004-228 du 15 mars 2004 encadrant, en application du principe de laïcité, le port de signes ou de tenues manifestant une appartenance religieuse dans les écoles, collèges et lycées publics, *Journal Officiel*, 17 March 2004). The speed with which the bill was drawn up and passed has been attributed variously to Chirac and the Raffarin government's nerves over predicted heavy losses for the right in the results of the March 2004 regional elections.

Actors and arguments in the debates over the headscarf ban and the 2004 law

The debate over headscarves in French state schools which took place across the country was reproduced in reports and opinion pieces in the main newspapers and television channels. During 2003, one or more articles on the headscarf appeared in each of the three main dailies (*Le Monde*, *Libération* and *Le Figaro*) each day, totalling 1,284 articles that year (Tévanian 2005a: 15). An analysis of such reports and opinions indicates the type of social actors involved and how they lined up in the headscarf debate. In 2004, Tévanian carried out an analysis of both newspaper columns and television discussions. His analysis of 114 newspaper columns on the headscarf in *Le Monde* and *Libération*, (co)written by 155 authors, showed that the majority of social actors involved in debating the issue were academics (43 per cent), writers (novelists and essayists) (14 per cent), politicians (7 per cent) and journalists (8.5 per cent) (Tévanian 2005b). As far as television programmes were concerned (15 were analysed between April 2003 and September 2004), a similar profile emerged and the top four categories of social actors represented were: politicians (31 per cent), writers (20 per cent), journalists (16.5 per cent) and academics (15 per cent) (Tévanian 2005c).

What emerges clearly from Tévanian's analysis is that those social actors who were directly concerned by the headscarf affairs – headscarfed schoolgirls, their families, fellow pupils and teachers – were largely absent from the debates presented in the media. While head teachers, teachers and parents' group representatives accounted for 8 per cent of the social actors given a public voice, the pupil body and headscarf-wearing schoolgirls and young women in particular were ignored completely. Tévanian notes that if headscarfed women were given column inches or air space, they tended to be older, often represented Muslim organisations and frequently ended up defending themselves against charges of fundamentalism rather than being allowed to debate the issues on the table, on equal terms, with other social actors (Tévanian 2005a, 2005b). Moreover, the 'aristocracy' of social actors in this public debate, composed of politicians, journalists, writers and academics, overwhelmingly favoured the 'headscarf ban in schools' position while those with religious or minority community affiliations were more often than not invited to present the 'pro-headscarf in schools' arguments.

Consequently, more newspaper print space and television air time devoted to the headscarf debate was taken over by arguments in favour of a ban in schools; Tévanian found that 46 per cent of newspaper columns on the headscarf reflected a 'ban in schools' position as opposed to 38 per cent of space given to 'anti-ban' opinion and 16 per cent to unclear or neutral opinion (Tévanian 2005b). The bias towards the 'ban in schools' position was more pronounced – 55 per cent of the air time – in television discussions on the headscarf, with 37 per cent air time given to 'anti-ban' arguments and 8 per cent to those with unclear or neutral positions. Given the preponderance of politicians, journalists and intellectuals of one sort or another, it is not surprising that certain themes dominated the headscarf debate of 2002–4. Principal themes included secularism or *laïcité* in the public sphere versus private religion as symbolised by the headscarf; the protection of French democratic principles against Islamic fundamentalism and terrorism (the ex-Maoist philosopher, André Glucksmann had previously referred to the headscarf as 'a terrorist operation', claiming that the zealous schoolgirls who wore it knew that their headscarf was tainted with blood (Salom and Seksig 1999)); and the defence of women's rights and freedoms (undermined by the headscarf). These are examined below. On the other hand, questions about how schoolgirls affected by the ban coped with isolation from their friends or with the difficulties of following distance-learning courses, about how their classmates felt, or about the educational future of all those affected directly or indirectly by the ban met with deafening silence.

Laïcité/secularism and the pro-ban position

One of the main themes of the headscarf debates raised by both pro-ponents and opponents of the ban on headscarves in schools was that of *laïcité*, and indeed the law of March 2004 is constructed around this principle. It is argued that *laïcité*, although translated as secularism, has a more complex meaning than the latter. Secularism is widely defined and accepted as a (liberal) system of ethics where human improvement is sought not through reference to God and religion but through human, scientific logic and social organisation. The maintenance of such a system requires a strict separation between state and church so that state institutions and policy do not reflect any sectarian or religious ideals. However, the singularly French idea of *laïcité*, as opposed to the liberal conception of secularism, is shaped by the development of French Republicanism, itself the result of political reaction against the power of the Catholic Church. Thus *laïcité* is not understood simply as the separation between church and state but also in terms of state neutrality as expressed by the protection of the individual from any form of pressure exerted by religious groups and religion in the public sphere. This contrasts with the understanding of the role of the secular state in the US, for example, where state neutrality is demonstrated through the protection of the rights of American citizens to practise the religion of their choice. Moreover, it is argued that the French interpretation of state neutrality supports a more extensive notion of the public sphere and the public self. State schools are seen as a crucial part of the public sphere while their pupils, as trainee citizens, are required to restrain if not curb altogether expression of their religious beliefs (Laborde 2005: 307).

Thus, as Barbier asserts, the widely accepted if rather narrow definition of *laïcité* in France has been 'secularism-as-neutrality' and 'secularism-as-separation' (Barbier 2005: 129). However, this once largely uncontested definition has been variously (re)defined and (re)interpreted as a result of the headscarf affairs over the last twenty years and this is evidenced by the emergence of a very substantial literature on the subject during this period of time (for example, see the useful bibliography compiled by the Institut Européen en Sciences des Religions, 2008).

In debates over the headscarf, proponents of the ban have put forward three sets of interrelated arguments in relation to *laïcité* whereby its defence is advanced as a means of: upholding French Republican values, starting with civic education in state schools; preserving French democracy in a world witnessing the rise of what are considered fanatical ideologies; and integrating newcomers, particularly those from Muslim-majority cultures, in French society.

Laïcité, schools and Republican values

First, proponents of the headscarf ban have argued that *laïcité*, as a central component of French Republicanism, had to be accepted as conceived in the Ferry Laws of the early 1880s and the 1905 law separating church from state. *Laïcité*, they argue, is not up for negotiation depending on changes in political, economic or socio-cultural circumstances. *Laïcité* is a tool for the creation and continuation of a homogeneous or 'indivisible', national entity inspired by the majority conception of the public good rather than by the private interests, identities and loyalties of individuals. Furthermore, the job of creating this indivisible nation falls upon state schools and teachers as public servants. Thus:

> School is the most important site where our shared values are acquired and passed on. It is the most effective tool for planting the Republican ideal. It is the place where tomorrow's citizens are trained to question, to communicate and value freedom; where they are given the means to fulfil their potential and take control of their future; where each of us can broaden our horizons. (Chirac 2003)

This view enjoyed support across the political spectrum: from the right – François Bayrou (as UDF Secretary of State for Education in 1994), Jacques Chirac (as President of the Republic), François Fillon (as UMP Secretary of State for Employment in 2002) – to prominent Socialists such as Laurent Fabius, François Hollande, Jack Lang, Jean-Pierre Chevènement and Communist Party leader Marie-George Buffet.[7] It opposed the 'elastic' (*à géométrie variable*) conception of *laïcité* presented by the Conseil d'Etat in 1989 which drew on French law as well as international human rights conventions ratified by France (the European Convention on Human Rights and the UN's International Covenant on Civil and Political Rights):

> The wearing of [religious] symbols by pupils through which they intend to show their religious belonging is not in itself incompatible with the principle of *laïcité* in as much as it amounts to exercising [one's] freedom of expression and manifesting one's religious beliefs. (Conseil d'Etat 1989)

Pro-ban supporters argued that the Conseil d'Etat ruling of 1989, applied on a case-by-case basis, would eventually have had the effect of reducing *laïcité* to a consumerist concept where pupils would simply become users of educational services according to their different religious beliefs and needs rather than ensuring the future of the French Republic.

They also spurned arguments calling for 'Anglo-Saxon' conceptions of *laïcité* which include the recognition of difference (*'laïcité* de reconnaissance', see Roman 2006) or of diverse beliefs and perspectives (*'laïcité* délibérative', see Bauberot 2006). Again, in his speech of 17 December 2003, Jacques Chirac, speaking in favour of a law banning religious symbols, warned that France could not embrace any form of multiculturalism (*communautarisme*) in public institutions:

> Multiculturalism is not an option for France. It would be contrary to our history, our traditions and our culture. It would oppose our humanist principles, our faith in social advancement through sheer talent and merit and our values of equality and fraternity between all French people. (Chirac 2003)

The ultimate logic of these arguments was that the failure to introduce a ban on the headscarf (and other religious symbols) would eventually lead to the destabilisation of a thus far indivisible nation and the loss of French values such as solidarity, social justice, equality, tolerance and individual freedom.

Laïcité and the battle against religious extremism

Second, the defence of *laïcité* in public institutions, particularly in schools, was presented by many pro-ban supporters as a means of protecting French democracy against fanatical ideologies, namely Islamic fundamentalism – among them were President Chirac, the celebrity philosopher Bernard-Henri Lévy and Patrick Weil, research director at the CNRS (Centre National de la Recherche Scientifique). According to the pro-ban argument, the situation of Muslims in socially disadvantaged urban areas, where unemployment and racism were endemic, was such that rising numbers of youngsters were turning to Islam and certain extremist variants of the faith. In his speech of 17 December 2003, announcing support for a ban on religious symbols in schools, Jacques Chirac maintained:

> While it has brought new opportunities, globalisation causes concern as it destabilises individuals, forcing them to withdraw sometimes [from society]. At a time when the grand ideologies are crumbling, obscurantism and fanaticism are gaining ground in the world . . .

> At the same time, the continuation if not worsening of inequalities and the growing chasm between troubled [inner city] areas and the rest of the country contradict the principle of equal opportunities and threaten to tear apart our Republican pact. (Chirac 2003)

This view seemed to be echoed widely. A seventeen-country global attitudes survey carried out in 2005, by the Washington DC-based PEW research centre, found that 70 per cent of respondents in France felt that there was a growing sense of Islamic identity among Muslims in their country; 89 per cent believed this was a negative trend and 50 per cent believed that it was harmful because it would lead to violence (PEW 2005: 43–4). The argument ran as follows. Young women wearing the headscarf were easily identified and targeted as potential recruits by fundamentalist Islamists. Moreover, in accordance with their narrow interpretation of the *Qur'an*, fundamentalist groups were imposing the headscarf on non-wearers as a means of gaining and maintaining control over Muslims in Western societies. This control, it was argued, was accepted by young women either because they were too scared to refuse or because the option of wearing the headscarf and feeling protected was preferable to the isolation many experienced in increasingly hostile Western societies. The headscarf therefore has become a symbol of religious intolerance at best and terrorism at worst. Media stories and images of the Chechen 'black widow' terrorism and suicide bombings, reaching a height in 2004 against Russian targets (Campbell 2003), and of so-called honour killings of Muslim women in France (Henry 2007), added to the negative symbolism surrounding the headscarf. Proponents of the headscarf ban concluded that the prohibition of religious symbols in school would strike a blow against extremists and terrorism and in doing so strengthen the hand of secular-minded Muslims in France, thus adding to the stability of France.

Laïcité and the headscarf ban as a means of integration

Finally, an important argument presented in defence of an uncompromising interpretation and application of *laïcité* and against religious symbols in schools is that a headscarf ban would contribute to a more effective integration of immigrants and those of immigrant background in French society. France has long adopted what may be termed an 'assimilationist' model of integration despite recommendations from certain intellectuals to recognise cultural and religious particularities (Gaspard and Khosrokhavar 1995; Roman 1995, 1996, 1998; Wieviorka 2006). According to this model, the public expression of cultural or religious identity must be suppressed in the interests of social harmony. Thus the integration process necessarily works in only one direction where newcomers become French through learning the language, values, traditions, laws and history that make up France, in order to attain equality and socio-economic success.

The question of integrating Muslims within French society has been pushed to the fore since the late 1980s against a backdrop of explosions of discontent in inner-city neighbourhoods, the headscarf controversies and rising Islamist movements. Yet this question dates back to French colonialism in the Maghreb and particularly the 1848 reorganisation of northern Algeria into French *départements* which posed the challenge of granting French citizenship to Algerians and turning 'Muslims into Frenchmen'. Muslim Arabs ranked lowest in the league of those most likely to be 'civilised'/assimilated, hence deserving of full citizenship rights, after settlers of Christian-European descent and Algerian Jews. While laws in 1865 and 1870 defined the conditions and rights of full French citizenship for European settlers and Jews respectively, it was not until 1919 that naturalisation and full citizenship were extended to Arab Muslims although only to those 'meritorious' individuals who renounced their faith and all aspects of Sharia law to embrace French values.

In Algeria, as in other French colonies, young women were seen as key agents in the French 'civilising mission' and the modernising (i.e. frenchification) of Algerian men and Muslim society. Thus in the late 1880s certain senior civil servants in Algeria suggested that Frenchmen should marry Muslim-Arab women since 'it is through women that we can get hold of the soul of a people'. It was further suggested that to make Algerian women more modern (or attractive) they should be permitted to adopt French names and made to remove the veil and the 'repugnant' face tattoos common in rural Algeria (Judge Sabatier, province of Grande Kabylie, cited by Lazreg 1994: 49–50). These sentiments found an echo seventy years later at the height of the Generals' insurrection when a symbolic unveiling of Algerian women took place on 16 May 1958 as part of the French battle for hearts and minds, in order to demonstrate that Algerian women's support for France against the FLN (the national liberation movement) would deliver them from a backward, patriarchal (Muslim) culture into modernity (Gordon 1962: 56–8). Since veiled women were seen to represent authentic Muslim-Arab culture, gaining control over how they looked and what they wore symbolised effective domination over those colonised, their culture and their religion (Fanon 1967: 35–7).

Similar sentiments, albeit subconscious, may be detected in claims today that support for *laïcité*, through a headscarf ban, would ensure the effective integration of Muslims in French society. If, in today's world, the headscarf is symbolic of a 'clash of cultures' hampering the integration of Muslims in France, then the answer is to be rid of it. If the headscarf represents an Islamic challenge to the French state, then banning it appears to put the French state in a position of control. Joan Scott concludes:

> For a small piece of cloth, the veil is heavy with meanings for French republicans who are worried about schools and immigrants, freedom and terrorism … Banning the veil … became a substitute solution for a host of pressing economic and social issues: the law on headscarves seemed as if it would wipe away the challenges of integration posed for policymakers by former colonial subjects. (Scott 2007: 17–18)

Women's rights, freedoms and pro-ban positions

Pro-headscarf ban arguments which revolved around women's rights and freedoms were expressed by some feminists and a number of public figures, male politicians amongst them, not normally known to take a feminist position on social and political issues. These arguments fell into two categories: arguments which were influenced by radical, anti-patriarchy feminism and which tended to focus on women's sexual oppression and freedoms; and liberal feminist-inspired arguments which emphasised gender equality and linked women's rights with *laïcité*.

Rather than considering the headscarf as a religious symbol or expression of defiance, those who took a radical feminist stance on this particular issue saw the headscarf, first and foremost, as a symbol and instrument of women's oppression, particularly sexual oppression which prevents the wearer from exercising control over her own body. Hence, it was argued that the imposition of a headscarf ban in schools would amount to support for young Muslim women who wanted liberation and would, at the same time, combat the false consciousness demonstrated by those who actually chose to wear the headscarf. One of the staunchest advocates of this line was Fadela Amara, appointed Minister for Urban Affairs in the Fillon government in June 2007 but at the time spokeperson for the association Ni Putes Ni Soumises (NPNS). For Amara, the headscarf has become a means for Muslim extremists to 'confiscate' the female body and sexuality and hence impose social control:

> The moment these female bodies are confiscated … young women become totally incapable of holding on to their femininity … this

is demonstrated by the fact that they cannot dress as they want, cannot wear low-cut tops or tight jeans – anything that shows off the body is forbidden. That's why we see, for example, increasing numbers of young women in inner city housing estates dressed in over-sized clothes, covering up their body or where some Muslim women are concerned, wearing the headscarf … What's interesting today is that … they are called whores … you often hear young men say 'aside from my mother, they're all whores'. (Leitner 2004)

Amara's sentiments are echoed by a number of others including the political scientist Janine Mossuz-Lavau (*Le Monde*, 16 December 2003), who did not favour a ban by law, and philosopher Elisabeth Badinter, normally an unforgiving critic of radical feminism. Thus in 2003, Badinter argued:

You wear the kippah [Jewish skull cap] out of respect for God. You wear the headscarf so you're no longer an object of temptation for men, so you don't risk blame for sexually arousing a man. What it boils down to is that women are held responsible for men's potential sins. (quoted in Helft-Malz and Lévy 2003)

The celebrity journalist Christine Ockrent considered that much of the violence suffered by Muslim women (for example, honour killings) could be attributed to what she saw as abnormal (or non-Western) sexual relations and tensions within Islamic culture of which the headscarf was an indicator (Deltombe 2005: 70).

The liberal-inspired feminist argument against the headscarf was supported by a broader cross-section of the French commentariat including some who also used elements of the radical feminist argument in their fight against the headscarf (for example Badinter and Mossuz-Lavau) and key political figures in government and opposition parties. The liberal feminist line of reasoning against the headscarf was that it symbolised opposition to women's hard-won rights and to the principle of gender equality in the social, economic and political spheres. Hence, wearing the headscarf in school was unacceptable given that it was at school that pupils learned about equality and its relationship with public governance and citizenship. This line had been put forward since 1989. However, it was in 2003 that the idea that *laïcité* and gender constituted 'twin' principles of 'Republican feminism' was born. Badinter credits herself with making this connection. Hence, 'Defending *laïcité* means defending equality between the sexes. Nobody took account of this in 1989 … I was the one who, at the time, put forward the question of defending women in the following terms "Hold on firmly to *laïcité* because it's women that you're protecting"' (quoted in Helft-Malz and Lévy 2003).

Republican feminists opposed what they saw as 'victimism' and its logical outcome, positive discrimination. In the context of the headscarf affair this meant protecting *laïcité* by ridding schools of anti-democratic ideologies such as Islam, even if some of its believers included the most disadvantaged people in society and it meant that they were isolated in the process. Allowing the headscarf in schools was tantamount to special treatment based on religious difference. This position was held by a number of public figures among whom were Yvette Roudy (the former Minister for Women's Rights), Corinne Lepage (ex-minister in the Juppé government and co-founder with François Bayrou of the Mouvement Démocratique), Anne Zelensky, (chair of the Ligue du Droit des Femmes, see Vigerie and Zelensky 2003), Anne Vigerie of the Cercle d'Etude de Réformes Féministes (ibid.), the ProChoix collective (a 'feminist, *laïque*, anti-fascist and pro-abortion' information network established in defence of the 'right to choose', see ProChoix 2003: 87–191), the Association Femmes Solidaires (ex-Union des Femmes Françaises, linked to the French Communist Party) and the Coordination Féministe et Laïque (CFL 2005). It was also one adopted by many government ministers, such as Jacques Chirac (Chirac 2003) and by Bernard Stasi who claimed that '*laïcité* cannot be understood without direct reference to equality between the sexes' (Stasi 2004: 52).

Anti-headscarf ban arguments

The arguments of proponents of the headscarf ban have been countered variously by supporters of Muslim schoolgirls who wear the headscarf in state schools. Anti-headscarf ban arguments, summarised here, fall into four main categories.

Freedom of religion and the right to express one's beliefs

For many of those who oppose the 2004 law, the question of religious freedom is paramount and Article 18 of the UN Declaration of Human Rights, which forms the basis for religious freedom clauses in a number of international human rights instruments, is frequently cited. It states:

> Everyone has the right to freedom of thought, conscience and religion; this right includes freedom to change his religion or belief, and freedom, either alone or in community with others and in public or private, to manifest his religion or belief in teaching, practice, worship and observance. (UN 1948)

According to international human rights law, states may only restrict religious observance and practices if there are compelling reasons related to public safety or the infringement of others' rights or if legitimate educational functions (e.g. the maintenance of classroom discipline) are thwarted. It is argued that as conspicuous religious symbols such as the *hijab*, turban and kippah do not *per se* threaten public safety, infringe the rights of non-wearers or undermine educational instruction, then French law appears to contradict international law. France is a signatory to major international agreements such as the International Covenant on Civil and Political Rights (ICCPR) and the European Convention on Human Rights and as such is expected to honour the obligations imposed by such agreements. However, France has gained exemption from Article 27 of the ICCPR which states:

> In those States in which ethnic, religious or linguistic minorities exist, persons belonging to such minorities shall not be denied the right, in community with the other members of their group, to enjoy their culture, to profess and practice their own religion, or to use their own language. (Bossuyt 1987: 493)

The exemption was sought on grounds of incompatibility between ICCPR Article 27 and Article 2 of the French Constitution of 1958 but it is interesting to note that while this exemption was granted, France was reproached by the UN Human Rights Committee in 1997 for denying the existence of religious, ethnic and linguistic minorities and making the presumption that equal rights and freedoms for all before the law translated into equality and the safeguard of human rights *in actual fact*.

Moreover, where religious symbols are concerned, France's hand was strengthened in June 2004 by a European Court of Human Rights decision which ruled that state schools which ban Muslim headscarves do not violate the freedom of religion. The court's ruling, against an appeal by a Turkish student who was banned from Istanbul University's medical school because her headscarf violated the official dress code, was justified thus: 'The principle of secularism was surely one of the founding principles of the Turkish state' and 'Safeguarding this principle can be considered necessary for the protection of the democratic system in Turkey' (Johnstone 2004).

Despite this, opponents of the headscarf ban insist that the 2004 law on religious symbols in schools is wrong as it prohibits certain religious rites and in doing so condemns the religious content underpinning such rites. These arguments have been made not only by Muslim supporters of headscarfed schoolgirls but also by other faith leaders in France and abroad (including the Archbishop of Canterbury) and by politicians, such as the group of MEPs who tabled a 'written declaration' to the European Parliament in February 2005 calling on all MEPs to condemn the ban and promote freedom of religion across the EU.

Laïcité is not a fixed concept

The argument that *laïcité* is a concept that can and must evolve in line with socio-cultural and political change is based on the idea that it is purely a product of historical events and circumstances specific to France and which has then been elevated into a principle applicable over time and space. Moreover, its history is relatively short at just over a century. While *laïcité* has been useful in protecting the state and civil society institutions from past incursions by the Catholic Church, its protective role is overplayed today, specifically in relation to the Islamic headscarf, to the detriment of a democratic outcome for minority religions and for a minority population prevented from the right to education in state schools. The idea of applying a more flexible interpretation of *laïcité*, 'la *laïcité* ouverte', has been discussed by Jean Baubérot (2003, 2005) and many others (Bédouelle et al. 2003; Dubois 2001; Morineau 2000) as a means of obtaining practical solutions to the accommodation of religious and cultural difference generally and in relation to the wearing of the headscarf in state schools, more specifically. Furthermore, supporters of a more open understanding of *laïcité* argue that the French state has a history of accommodating the Catholic Church. For example, the state has tolerated special status for the Church in Alsace and Lorraine which were part of Germany in 1905 when the separation of church and state took place. The two provinces were allowed to keep the Concordat system (still in place today) when returned to France in 1918. More recently the state has also made space for Islam in respect of regulations governing the building of mosques and cemeteries and other religious practices related to food preparation and holy days.

Laïcité is a foil for racism and sexism

One of the pernicious aspects of the *laïcité*-at-all-costs argument, according to its opponents, is that of prejudice and the apparent willingness to establish discriminatory precedents. While its supporters claimed that the 2004 law was primarily an instrument used to uphold Republican principles, many saw it as proof of barely concealed anti-Arab/Muslim racism (or 'Islamophobia'). Despite the denials of its fans, the law was seen to target young Muslim women and figures relating to its application in the first year did in fact demonstrate that this group was disproportionately affected. Moreover, it was argued that exclusion from school was normally a last-resort measure applied in situations where serious pupil misbehaviour threatened actual violence or the disruption of teaching to the extent that it harmed other pupils and/or teachers physically or psychologically. But nowhere did the presence of the headscarf lead to such a scenario and hence the exclusion from school of young girls, often from communities already facing social exclusion and disempowerment and whose only action was a polite refusal to remove their headscarf, was deemed by many an extreme reaction which could only be founded on an age-old mistrust of people whose cultural and religious practices were not 'normal', i.e. French/European. Finally, by making an automatic link between the headscarf and Islamic fundamentalism, Muslims and Arabs in general were stigmatised as wreckers of French society and democratic values. Critics of the 2004 law who saw contained in it a defence of *laïcité* as a cover for racist attitudes were mainly on the left of the Socialist Party and included groups such as SOS-Racisme, the Mouvement contre le Racisme et pour l'Amitié entre les Peuples, the Alternative Libertaire collective, the Socialisme Par En Bas network, the majority of the Ligue Communiste Révolutionnaire and the Nouvelles Féministes collective.

*Women's rights arguments are undermined by the damage
caused to young Muslim women's future*

The political and media campaigns in favour of the 2004 law used familiar feminist arguments in its support (see above). Their broad line of reasoning was that the law would protect girls who were forced to wear the headscarf and who, in doing so, accepted the secondary status assigned to them by Islam. However, detractors (among them feminists such as Christine Delphy and Monique Crinon) of this line have pointed out that in their concern over the fate of those seen as young women controlled by powerful patriarchal forces within their communities, supporters of the 2004 law gloss over the fact that the law impacts most adversely on the very target of their concern. Not only does the law potentially promote a process that criminalises young women from a disadvantaged minority, but school exclusions mean that the same young women are denied an education which will prove their best chance of escaping oppression. Those who use a women's rights argument to support the 2004 law also stand accused of relativising male domination and its effects in French society (Delphy 2006).

The making of the 2004 law

While a number of wider social, economic and political factors (see above) accounted for the reignition of various headscarf affairs and debates in 2002–3, the trigger for a law banning the headscarf in schools was set off at a congress of the Union des Organisations Islamiques de France (UOIF) which took place on 15 March 2003 and to which Nicolas Sarkozy, then Minister for the Interior, had been invited to speak. Previously seen by the UOIF as a potential ally, Sarkozy was jeered off stage, in full view of journalists and their cameras, when he reminded the congress that women would have to remove their headscarf when posing for a national identity card or passport photo. Television images of those considered religious fanatics subjecting an official representative of the Republic to undignified treatment provoked a swift reaction from politicians of left and right. Echoing a sentiment shared by many politicians, UMP president Alain Juppé stated, 'Religious extremists are a threat to the Republic. We cannot accept people wearing conspicuous [religious] symbols. The law has to assume responsibility where the Islamic headscarf is concerned' (Boulangé 2004: 3). He was supported within the UMP camp by François Fillon (Secretary of State for Social Affairs at the time) and Jean-Louis Debré (National Assembly Leader), both pro-ban hardliners. At the Socialist Party's May 2003 Congress, Laurent Fabius argued in favour of a law banning all religious symbols to avoid accusations of discrimination against Islam, while Jack Lang defended the introduction of a parliamentary bill proposing a ban. In June, the National Assembly established a fact-finding mission on the question of religious symbols (Mission d'Information sur la Question du Port des Signes Religieux à l'Ecole) and in July the Stasi Commission, appointed by Jacques Chirac, began its work on the feasibility of a law.

The fact-finding mission on wearing religious symbols in school

This group of thirty was set up by Jean-Louis Debré, National Assembly Leader, under his own leadership and consisted of deputies from the UMP and from the Socialist Party. The group's mission was to assess the main issues involved in passing and applying a law banning religious symbols and make recommendations. It collected opinions and evidence from 120 individuals said to represent all parties involved in the debate, during the course of 26 meetings and 37 hearings and round-table events. In addition, an online discussion forum, launched on the National Assembly website, received over 2,200 postings from members of the public. It should be noted that the constitution of this mission was the first application of an amended rule voted by the National Assembly in March 2003 which allowed the Leader of the House to establish fact-finding missions on issues of national interest and which ostensibly allowed citizens to directly lobby their members of Parliament before the introduction of controversial legislation. Undoubtedly, Debré used the headscarf debate to experiment with this new type of parliamentary structure and it is debatable as to whether it added to or replicated the work of the Stasi Commission.

The group published its findings and recommendations in a report, a few days before the publication of the Stasi Report, in early December 2003 (Mission d'Information 2003). Its main conclusions were:

- that the battle to preserve *laïcité* could not be allowed to flag after the hard-fought struggles of the past to establish the principle in the Constitution;
- that the state school was the key arena in which a balance between *laïcité* and freedom of conscience should be struck in order to stem tensions arising from failed efforts at the integration of Muslims in French society;
- that far from symbolising religious belonging, the headscarf was a political instrument for the marking out of differences;
- and that it was necessary to stem the conflict between *laïcité* and religious extremism which was destabilising the Republic.

It was therefore recommended that a short and sharp legal measure, open to least interpretation, be introduced to prohibit visible religious symbols in school.

In addition to the fact-finding mission, two parliamentary bodies were also involved in the making of the 2004 law: the Commission on Cultural, Family and Social Affairs (Commission des Affaires Culturelles, Familiales et Sociales) and the Commission on Constitutional Law, Legislation and General Administration of the Republic (Commission des Lois Constitutionnelles, de la Législation et de l'Administration Générale de la République). Both commissions held hearings from various members of government and a round-table event on 'École et laïcité aujourd'hui'. The main contribution of the commissions was to add to the conclusions of the fact-finding mission through scrutiny and commentary on its report and to make a number of minor amendments to the parliamentary bill on the application of *laïcité* in state schools.

The Stasi Commission

The Stasi Commission (or Commission de Réflexion sur l'Application du Principe de Laïcité dans la République) comprised eighteen experts on 'race', immigration, faith and ethno-religious issues, alongside Bernard Stasi and Rémy Schwartz, a member of the Conseil d'Etat, acting as *rapporteur* to the Commission.[8] The Commission collected evidence in open hearings from 96 individuals from public life and in closed hearings from a further 64. In addition 220 school children (from France and from French *lycées* abroad) were invited to share their opinions and experiences of the headscarf with Commission members (Stasi 2004: 72–7).

The Commission's main conclusions are contained in its 77-page report (Stasi 2004), divided into four main sections. The introduction of the report specifies that *laïcité*, the cornerstone of French Republicanism, rests on three inextricable principles: freedom of conscience, equality of all faiths before the law and state neutrality vis-à-vis each religion. Part one of the report (2004: 10–18) restates the idea that *laïcité* is a universal, Republican principle. Hence any form of multiculturalism is denounced in favour of a 'common future' in which social diversity is respected and Republican unity strengthened. Part two (2004: 19–36), while comparing the French situation with that of other Western countries, considers *laïcité* in legal terms, stating that the principles of freedom of conscience and state neutrality can sometimes conflict with each other. Based on the evidence gathered from the Commission hearings, the third section (2004: 37–49) of the report examines the challenges faced by *laïcité*, prime amongst them religious extremism (namely Islam), feeding off socio-economic disadvantage among immigrant and ethnic minority populations, their consequent retreat into identity politics and the negative impact of this situation on integration and women's rights and freedoms. Part four and the conclusion of the report (2004: 50–69) contain twenty-five recommendations amongst which the adoption of a law on *laïcité* and the ban on conspicuous religious symbols in state schools were seized upon by the media and politicians to the exclusion of almost all else. Several of the Commission's members later expressed regret that other positive recommendations were not given publicity or followed up by government, for example those which called for: action against discrimination based on 'race' and religion and an end to urban ghettos; a *laïcité* charter to be followed in all public institutions; the recognition of the most important Jewish (Yom Kippur) and Muslim (Eid al-Adha) holy days as public holidays; the right to build places of religious worship, observe funeral rites and dietary customs; better instruction in schools about *laïcité* and religions practised in France; the teaching of minority languages such as Berber, Kurdish or Arabic; the establishment of a national school of Islamic studies; and the recruitment of chaplains from other faiths in public institutions such as hospitals and prisons. Patrick Weil (2004b: 4) wrote:

> my single, strong regret as a result of this commission process does not relate to the headscarf issue as such: it is that the ban on religious signs in public schools is the only one of our twenty-five proposals yet implemented by President Chirac, his government, and the National Assembly.

However, the Commission could hardly blame the media for focusing on the headscarf and, by extension, the ban on religious symbols given the predominance of these issues in their own deliberations – whether it was to do with *laïcité* and challenges to Republicanism or in relation to women's rights, violence against women on inner-city housing estates, Islam and gender relations or the place of Islam in a liberal democracy. The commissioners' preoccupations were reflected not only in their themes of discussion but also their selection of interviewees and questions they asked. For example, Françoise Gaspard was called by the Commission but ended up answering questions about women's rights and Islam rather than about her understanding of why young Muslim women wore the headscarf. The Commission heard from politicians, academics, head teachers and others but the voices of young *hijabis*, their school friends and importantly their non-Muslim supporters were noticeably absent. The accounts of certain commissioners give an insight into the tensions governing the selection of interviewees, discussions and decision-making. Rémy Schwartz, *rapporteur* to the Commission, denied the view that a biased selection took place:

> I've heard a fair bit about the 'pre-selection' of the people interviewed who would have misled and directed the Commission in its work … Each [Commission member] was able to make proposals and we invited people according to the proposals made by the Commission members.
>
> To the question that some people have asked, 'Why did you not interview more young, headscarfed women', the answer is, 'Firstly, the Commission members didn't know many and found it impossible to nominate Mrs "X" or Miss "Y", and besides, we had difficulty in making headscarfed women appear before the Commission.' (Belbah and De Galembert 2008b: 230)

Schwartz's view was not corroborated by Jean Baubérot (2004: 135–141; Belbah and De Galembert 2008a: 237–49), the only Commission member who voted against recommending a law against conspicuous religious symbols in state schools. He explained:

> While maintaining that he was waiting for the Commission's report, Jacques Chirac made comments in favour of a law. Faced with political and media pressure, the Commission felt that if it took a position against this pronounced law, it would give the impression of retreating before the 'Islamic threat', substantiated in various hearings, and which needed a counter-attack. Moreover, the Commission chair and particularly its *rapporteur* skilfully managed the Commission meetings so as to obtain a positive vote. Some were convinced, others were torn within themselves ... As for me, at some point, it seemed to me that it was no longer a question of considering problems linked with *laïcité* but of producing arguments circulating within the Commission in order to justify ... a future vote that was favourable to a pro-ban strategy. So, without any real debate, it was suggested that one couldn't really be in favour of equality between the sexes and [at the same time] put up with the headscarf in state schools. (Baubérot 2004: 139)

Patrick Weil, more pragmatically, defended the commissioners' decisions based on selective hearings:

> We made our choice after long individual and collective hesitations. Were we under pressure, influenced by the impossibility of hearing all the persons interested in giving a testimony or by the lack of time to make a decision based on sufficient evidence? Were we aware of the possibility that some adolescents or their families could perceive our proposal through the prism of discrimination, within the legacy of colonization and racial prejudice? ... I must admit that I have never worked under this amount of public pressure coming from all sides ... But I believe that these pressures did not prevent us from taking all considerations and circumstances into account. The most active opponents to the headscarf did not convince us ... We heard more partisans of the status quo than defenders of a ban. And hearing more girls wearing the headscarf would not have changed our reasoning which was not based on an assessment of a religious sign or its meaning ... we tried to find our way among very complex obstacles, to understand the gaps between the testimonies of the different actors, and finally to propose the least bad choices. (Weil 2004a: 144–5)

Whichever view one feels inclined to favour, the result was that similar accounts and views of the problems surrounding headscarves and Islam – i.e. non-integration in French society, the subordination of women, extremism – were drawn out as in previous media debates and inevitably the commissioners reached conclusions which led to the near unanimous recommendation on a law to ban conspicuous religious symbols in state schools.

Reactions to the law and its implementation

Hostile reactions

While the law was backed by the majority of adults polled – opinion surveys put support at between 57 per cent and 72 per cent (BVA 2003; CSA 2004) – it provoked antagonistic reactions, in France and beyond, both during its passage through Parliament and once it was passed. The hostile response of Muslims in France was to be expected and street protests were organised in Paris and other large French cities. Two of the most notable demonstrations took place in early 2004. On 17 January, a demonstration organised by an obscure group known as the Parti des Musulmans de France (PMF) managed to assemble 10,000–20,000 people, although its impact was lost when it ended in acrimony as numerous marchers, including the PMF leader Latrèche, were accused by both supporters and opponents of the law of expressing a violent *jihadist* message (Chemin 2004). However, the national demonstration of 14 February was presented as a strong anti-law alliance of the broad left, progressive Muslims and adherents of other faiths and succeeded in catching the attention of the media worldwide, thus placing a certain amount of pressure on French deputies and senators as the bill progressed through Parliament, though not enough to cause a significant shift in their attitudes. In addition to street protests, a number of other developments took place; for instance, the creation (by Abdallah Milcent, a French doctor and convert to Islam) of the 'Comité 15 mars et Libertés' which set up a legal helpline to support young women caught up in *hijab* disputes; the formation of Muslim women's groups such as the Collectif Féministe pour l'Egalité; and initiatives to counter increasing public hostility towards Muslims, e.g. the proposal, by the then newly created Conseil Français du Culte Musulman (CFCM), for an Observatoire National de l'Islamophobie.

As far as the main Muslim organisations in France were concerned, the reaction to the new law and its implementation was divided. The

CFCM, keen to remain the main interlocutor between Muslims and government, argued that the headscarf ban provided an opportunity for Muslims in France to fashion a modern form of Islam which could coexist within the bounds of the Republic (Smith 2004) but at the same time it reminded the government to keep up a dialogue with Muslims who wanted a real stake in French society. While the CFCM played a safe game, the Union des Organisations Islamiques de France took a stronger line which consisted not only of urging its followers to join the various street demonstrations but also of instructing headscarfed schoolgirls to test out the law when they returned to school in September 2004. On the more radical side of the UOIF was Abdallah Milcent's Comité 15 mars et Libertés which circulated a revised edition of a handbook Milcent had written in 1994, with guidelines on challenging the 2004 law.

The explosions of discontent over the 2004 law were not confined to France. Demonstrations were held in London, Toronto, Barcelona, Cairo, Kuala Lumpur and several other cities across the world. Moreover, a number of public figures at the time – from former Iranian president Khatami to former London mayor Ken Livingstone – called on the French government to repeal the law. But the most extreme protest against the 2004 law was the kidnapping of French journalists Georges Malbrunot and Christian Chesnot by the 'Islamic Army in Iraq' group, in August 2004. The kidnappers demanded the complete retraction of the law for the release of the journalists who were eventually set free on 21 December 2004. Paradoxically, the pressure on the kidnappers came from another set of intense protests and calls for the release of the journalists from Muslims in France and elsewhere.

Implementation of the law

The law banning conspicuous religious symbols and attire in schools came into effect at the beginning of the academic year 2004/5. In order to guide schools in applying the law, the Ministry of Education had drafted a circular (Circulaire No. 2004-084 Du 18-5-2004, *Journal Officiel*, 22 May 2004) and sent it out to head teachers to be cascaded down. During 2004–5, a total of 639 conspicuous symbols were counted in French schools; 592 of these cases were resolved while 48 were referred to disciplinary councils at school or local education authority level. Of the 48 schoolgirls concerned, all but one were excluded (Chérifi 2005: 41). The main problem for schools was the definition of a 'conspicuous' symbol or attire. In some schools girls replaced their headscarf with a bandana and found that this was tolerated whilst in others they dared not wear anything on the head for fear of being excluded by head teachers who were ardent defenders of the law. The question of what constituted a religious symbol was not easily answered. Given that several high-profile fashion houses such as Hermès and Calvin Klein sell designer headscarves, the question, 'when does a *hijab* become a fashion item?', thus diminishing its religious significance, still remains to be answered.

The other problem, unforeseen when the law was first debated, related to France's small Sikh population and the turban worn by men. A number of Sikh boys argued that the turban carried a cultural rather than religious significance but were turned down. In some instances, even where boys removed the turban but kept on their under-turban (like a hair-net), they were refused teaching – for example, at the Lycée Louise Michel in Bobigny from which three boys were expelled in March 2005. So far there have been no known cases of school boys expelled for wearing dreadlocks (required by Rastafarianism) or a beard (required in Islam).

On the whole, the law has been respected by the majority of Muslim schoolgirls who were its intended target. The expectation of hundreds of expulsions across France was never fulfilled though the law remains as unpopular within French Muslim communities today as it was in 2003–4.

Conclusion

The French headscarf disputes and the debates they have provoked over the past twenty years, leading eventually to a legal ban on conspicuous religious symbols in state schools, have been highlighted here because they produced what some would see as policy solutions based on peculiarly French arguments about maintaining the integrity of the nation-state, through the 'glue' of *laïcité*, in the face of difference marked by religion, culture and ethnicity. However, the French case has a resonance far beyond France's borders and the 2004 law in particular has been both condemned and applauded in other countries where policy- and opinion-makers have been forced to consider issues of religious freedom, human rights, racism, the integration of immigrants and democracy in their own backyards. France is the only EU country which has passed legislation in respect of the headscarf.[9] It therefore provides a window on the potential tensions that could arise within states between different groups of social and political actors and between states and supranational bodies over the interpretation and application of international human rights law and its accommodation of national policies. The headscarf affairs have raised a fundamental question for policy-makers in France and other Western countries: What kind of a democracy do we want in the twenty-first century?

Notes

1. The terms 'headscarf' and '*hijab*' will be used interchangeably in this chapter to denote the scarf worn by Muslim women to cover the hair, ears and neck. The headscarf/*hijab* should not be confused with *niqab* or *burkha*, worn to conceal the face, or *jilbab* which is a loose coat-like dress covering the entire body. In France, the terms '*foulard*' (scarf) and '*voile*' (veil) are used most commonly when talking about *hijab*/headscarf.
2. There is a significant literature, in French and English, on the headscarf controversies in France. See for example Bowen 2006; Gaspard and Khosrokhavar 1995; Nordmann 2004; Rochefort 2002; Scott 2007; Winter 2008.
3. *Laïcité*, translated as 'secularism', has not been explicitly defined in legal-constitutional terms despite its status as a central principle of French Republicanism and mention of the term 'laïque' in the 1946 (Article 1) and 1958 (Article 2) Constitutions.
4. The Concordat regime has continued to apply in Alsace and parts of the Lorraine to this day. These regions were not subject to the 1905 legislation as they had become part of Germany in 1871. Although they reverted to France in 1919, under the terms of the Versailles Treaty they were allowed to continue being governed by the 1801 Concordat.
5. The separation of church and state meant, among other things, that bishops were no longer nominated by the state and that clergymen ceased to be salaried state officials.
6. According to Geisser (2003) a peculiarly French fear of Islam has prevailed for decades, fuelled by France's colonial history, the denial of French failures in the Algerian war and an intense anti-clerical Republicanism.
7. The scope of this chapter does not allow a presentation of nuanced positions within the pro-ban camp. However, as an example, it is worth noting that in 2003 Jacques Chirac supported the introduction of a Code de laïcité (covering all principles and rules relating to *laïcité* and which all public sector employees would have to respect) but that, as the Stasi Commission carried out its brief, his position shifted in favour of a law.
8. The eighteen experts were: Mohammed Arkoun (Emeritus Professor of the History of Islamic Thought at the Sorbonne (Paris III)), Jean Baubérot (professor of the Sociology of Religion), Hanifa Chérifi (see above, p. 159), Jacqueline Costa-Lascoux (sociologist and research director at the CNRS), Régis Debray (academic and former state official in the Conseil d'Etat), Michel Delebarre (Socialist politician and ex-minister), Nicole Guedj (ex-municipal councillor and UMP spokesperson on human rights), Ghislaine Hudson (high school head teacher), Gilles Kepel (professor of Muslim and Middle-Eastern Affairs, at the Institut d'Etudes Politiques (IEP) in Paris), Marceau Long (senior civil servant), Nelly Olin (senator and former UMP government minister),

Henri Pena-Ruiz (lecturer in philosophy at IEP, Paris), Gaye Petek (member of the Higher Council on Integration – HCI), Maurice Quenet (Chancellor of the Universities of Paris), the late René Rémond (historian and member of the Académie française), Raymond Soubie (ex-UMP government adviser), Alain Touraine (sociologist and research director at the Ecole des Hautes Etudes en Sciences Sociales) and Patrick Weil (see above, pp. 177, 178).
9. While the French law on conspicuous religious symbols is applicable to state schools nationwide, in Germany eight *Länder* have enacted laws separately, prohibiting state school teachers and civil servants from wearing the headscarf.

Conclusion

As we stated in the Introduction, focusing on major legal reforms or parliamentary debates does not tell the whole story about policy in each of these areas. Much of this is made at the local level, is remade and remodelled in day-to-day interactions, in implementation, in struggles over funding, resources and priorities. In addition, focusing on individual policy issues does not tell the whole story about gender. For example, it is not just domestic violence policy that affects women experiencing domestic violence. The problem is one of gender inequality, and the solution is gender justice. This is why mainstreaming can be such an ambitious radical and overarching approach, and why, in the hands of some, parity had such radical potential. It also explains why framing is so central to gender politics, since it makes the difference in material terms between victim support each time the violence recurs and remodelling society to eradicate the power relations that cause violence towards women. Taking this approach means that policy is no longer regarded as a technical response to pre-existing problems. Instead, it engages at all levels and at all stages with the construction of the problem and the assumptions on which this rests.

This book is about the tension between, on the one hand, the political expediency factors driving the production of gender policy and, on the other hand, the normative, aspirational desires to address issues of equality and rights. France is not short of gender equality legislation, but striking inequalities still exist. We have seen in the case studies that legislation on equal employment, domestic violence and parity have failed to bring about gender equality. Equality policy in relation to employment is advanced and detailed, but gender inequalities persist. France was the first country in the world to introduce a constitutional amendment and subsequent legislation on parity, but still languishes in 64th place in the Inter-Parliamentary Union's table of women in Parliament (Inter-Parliamentary Union 2008). The 1974 abortion law did not mean that all women in France could access an abortion when they needed one. The Council of Europe Human Rights Commissioner and Amnesty International have expressed concerns about the implementation of laws and policy on domestic violence. However, it is difficult to trace causal links between policy and its impact. In the employment chapter, for example, we find that the policies aimed at removing direct hurdles to women's equal employment are far more easily identified than those which would address the indirect hurdles in relation to taxation, benefits or childcare, for example. In relation to domestic violence, it is not just a question of how women who have experienced domestic violence are treated by medical, police and legal professionals, whether they receive protection, accommodation and support, and whether efforts are made to prevent their partners reoffending, it is about how we make domestic violence unthinkable. So ideas and feminist theory matter. It moves beyond equality, although equality comes into it. Feminism is not just about equal rights; it is about human rights, well-being, health, not being the same as men, but having the capacity to flourish as a member of society.

Equality and difference

French gender debates are embedded in a discourse of Republican universalism which denies the public and political relevance of all differences while resting on a highly symbolic gender dichotomy. The French conception of equality does not make room for the recognition of difference, as we see in debates around the headscarf, employment and parity. Supporters of the headscarf ban based their arguments on defence of a fixed and unchanging concept of *laïcité*, which cannot admit signs of religious difference. *Laïcité* is the protection of the individual from any kind of religious pressure rather than just the right to practise the religion of his/her choice (which is American secularism). It is a way of preserving the national unity, as homogeneous and indivisible, and the state education system has played a central role in doing this. This is a view taken by politicians across the spectrum supporting the headscarf ban. It is opposed to the Anglo-Saxon conception of *laïcité* which includes the recognition of difference and multiculturalism. The headscarf debates raised questions about French identity and the space for differences within Republican universalism.

Supporters of parity found that the only way to circumvent opposition by those who hold dear a fixed and unchanging idea of Republican universalism which cannot admit differences was to posit an essential difference between sexual difference (fixed and unchanging) and other differences, which should continue to be denied all public and political relevance. Supporters of equal rights for women in relation to employment have been caught up in the tension between the protectionist, familialist logic and the equal rights, feminist logic. As Abigail Gregory and Jan Windebank (2000) have argued, until the gendered division of domestic labour and caring is addressed as part of the same debate, it will be impossible for women to achieve equality with men in relation to work.

The headscarf ban claims to protect young Muslim women from the patriarchal forces which make them wear it, just as the Domestic Security Law claimed to protect women from sexual exploitation, pimps and traffickers. In both these cases, this 'protection' is played out in punitive measures directed at the girls or women themselves, such as exclusion from school or deportation.

French conceptions of equality (meaning sameness or equality before the law) do not necessarily translate into equality in practice. This is pertinent to employment, parity and headscarves. Denial of difference does not guarantee equality and makes it difficult to address discrimination and inequalities. 'French' notions of equality are opposed to 'Anglo-Saxon' positive discrimination or affirmative action, for example, the Conseil Constitutionnel's ruling on the unconstitutional nature of clauses in the Ameline Law (2006) relating to gender parity in company level voting and jurisdictional bodies and increased access for women to apprenticeship and vocational training schemes. The idea of parity has influenced equal employment policy since the late 1990s. This has been used by the right since 2002, perhaps as a useful 'French' alternative to the Anglo-Saxon or EU concept of gender mainstreaming.

Abortion, violence and prostitution are not about equality. As feminist issues, they are about the body and bodily integrity. As policy issues, they are framed in a more strategic manner in order to achieve resonance with widespread ideas, values and political priorities. Hence abortion, for example, is constructed by some as a right won by women's struggles and by others as a social necessity to reduce the distress and health risks of backstreet abortions.

However, although violence and prostitution are not about equality in the way that employment and parity are, we can nevertheless see in them the production of inequalities, in terms of access to resources and ability to circumvent state limitations (such as private abortion clinics, high class sex clubs, rather than street prostitution, etc.).

We find that the idea of French specificity is frequently evoked and is opposed to the American/Anglo-Saxon Other. The opposition between gender relations in France and the US has been a recurring theme in the French media. Self-proclaimed feminists such as Elisabeth Badinter as well as non- and anti-feminist celebrities, writers and intellectuals, played a prominent part in the criticisms of the ENVEFF (2003), which they argue victimises women; in criticisms of parity proposals in the late 1990s, which, they claim, treat women as in need of special help; in criticisms of sexual harassment legislation, in 1994, on the grounds that it criminalises seduction, at which the French excel; and in prostitution debates. French national identity is constructed and reinforced in this way, in opposition to the US and the rest of the West.

One example of a specifically French characteristic used as a justification for many demands for policy change is France's 'lateness'. In the case of domestic violence, for example, the association Elues contre les Violences Faites aux Femmes (ECVF), formed on 25 November 2003 by Green and Socialist politicians, stated that 'France has been late in putting the prohibition of acts of gender violence on the political and institutional agenda' (Elgie and Griggs 2000: 183–4). In his speech opening the round-table on domestic violence, on 7 March 2006, Nicolas Sarkozy, Minister for the Interior, referred to France's lateness in relation to neighbouring countries in addressing this issue (Sarkozy 2006). Parity activists based their demands on the claim that France lagged behind other Western European countries, firstly, in winning the vote for women, despite being a forerunner in terms of universal male suffrage, and secondly, in terms of women's presence in political institutions.

The international, regional, national and local

The case studies also enable us to look at the relative influence of the international, regional (in this case EU), national and local on policy debates. International influences are particularly pertinent in relation to violence towards women, in contrast to abortion and prostitution, which have been kept off international agendas by fundamental disagreements between and within states. There has been international agreement on trafficking of women and children for sexual exploitation, which is clearly related to prostitution, but there is no agreement on prostitution itself. Abortion is currently perceived as an issue for national policy-making, although there have been attempts to initiate international and European policy in this area. Reference to international conventions and human rights law supports the right of girls to wear headscarves as part of their freedom of religion and their right to express their beliefs. The Ameline Law (2006) on equal employment combined the traditional French statist reflex of preserving a protectionist logic with EU discourse on equal opportunities for women within the demographic and labour market requirements of European economies. We find that the EU supports action against domestic violence when convinced of the savings to be made in terms of assistance to victims and lost working days. It must not be forgotten, however, that feminists are active at all of these levels and that international measures, including UN conferences and conventions, have at their origin the influence of feminist activism.

Feminist activism and opportunities or constraints on influencing policy

We find that feminists have engaged the state and tried to use legislative reform as part of their struggle for gender justice. They have tried to influence policy debates and outcomes. Feminist activists, elite feminists and women's policy machinery have played an important role in putting issues on the agenda, keeping them there, and gendering policy debates. We have found many instances of feminist or women's activism in favour of better policy for women: for example, nineteenth-century feminist demands for equal pay and professional training for women in factories and workshops; 1970s women's movement demands for equality in employment; and feminist activists' insistence that domestic violence belongs on the policy agenda and cannot simply be relegated to the private sphere.

Feminists disagree: they have different goals, different strategies and different ways of framing issues. We find that feminists, whether in civil society or in the elite, have often framed the issues for strategic reasons in such a way that they resonate with current ideas and values. We nevertheless find that strong, feminist women make a difference to policy. Access to decision-making is very unequally distributed, and some groups of women are particularly excluded. Sex workers and their supporters, for example, have no real voice in a series of debates dominated by a French styled version of abolitionism. Headscarfed girls and their supporters have no real voice, despite wide public/media debates. In domestic violence debates, women are often constructed as victims, and the UN commitment to eradicate gender inequalities which cause gender violence have been replaced with individualised criminal justice approaches.

The headscarf debates illustrate clearly the complexity of the relation between gender and ethnicity, but this is not to say that it is absent from other issue areas: employment, prostitution, abortion, violence and parity all raise questions about differences within the category 'women', as well as between women and men, and these differences include, but are not restricted to, ethnicity, nationality and class. The Domestic Security Law targets foreign prostitutes and 'Others' them. Domestic violence policy debates suggest that migrant populations are particularly violent. We see the relation between gender and class in the CGT refusal to support the implementation of the Loi Roudy on the grounds that it would serve the interest of middle-class professional women, while ignoring working-class women in poorly paid insecure jobs; in parity; and in the ability of women to exercise their legal right to abortion, given the uneven provision of resources.

The broad context in which policies are made and implemented is an important factor in establishing opportunities and constraints for influencing policy. State policy on women workers is heavily influenced by the needs of the economy, for example, during and following the two world wars, and by economic constraints, for example the limited implementation of the Loi Roudy (1983). We have found in the case studies presented in this book, that amongst the most important contextualising factors are the presence of a right- or left-wing government and, in the case of the 1997–2002 Socialist governments, the presence of strong women in sites of decision-making committed to a feminist agenda, and the growing securitisation of policy debates and measures. This has had a marked influence on prostitution and headscarf policy in particular, but has also increased the emphasis on criminal justice responses to domestic violence.

Gender and policy: the future

This study of gender and policy has shown that there is already in place an adequate institutional architecture for policy-making and implementation in relation to issues of concern for women in France. It has also revealed that there are large numbers of civil society policy actors who are not only eager to engage with the French state and international organisations but who have also built up a vast store of knowledge and experience of relevant policy areas and of how women's concerns can be articulated in policy-making in order to improve their lives.

However, what we have also learned is that the most efficient policy-making structures and the most eager of policy actors will achieve little without meaningful budgets for the implementation of policy. In the context of the current global economic recession, the prospects for implementing existing legislation and furthering policies in favour of women look bleak. Experience has demonstrated that in periods of economic uncertainty, the strongest of political champions will divert their attention to what are considered more pressing general concerns while so-called 'specialist budgets and services' for women will either be reduced or done away with altogether. In such circumstances, it becomes all the more important for feminist activists and advocates of women's issues to remain visible and to make and maintain strategic alliances within and across national borders. Women's concerns that are ultimately important political and human concerns cannot be pushed back into the domestic sphere.

Bibliography

(2004) Projet de loi des finances pour 2004. Etat des crédits qui concourent aux actions en faveur des droits des femmes.

(2004) Proposition de loi relative à la lutte contre les violences au sein des couples.

(2004) Proposition de loi tendant à lutter contre les violences à l'égard des femmes et notamment au sein des couples par un dispositif global de prévention, d'aide aux victimes et de répression.

(2006) Proposition de loi relative à l'exploitation sexuelle et à la protection de ses victimes.

Act Up (2005) 'Le noir est une couleur: rencontre avec Marianne, membre du collectif de Vincennes', http://www.actupparis.org/article2065.html, accessed 12 September 2005.

Act Up-Paris, PASTT et al. (16 May 2000) 'Press Release', www.actupp.org/news/ news, accessed 10 December 2001.

Agacinsky, S. (2001) *Parity of the Sexes*, trans. L. Walsh (New York: Columbia University Press).

Allen, K. (2007) 'Women's Rights: Facing the Facts'. *Amnesty Magazine* 18.

Allison, M. (1994) 'The Right to Choose: Abortion in France'. *Parliamentary Affairs* 47: 222–37.

Allwood, G. (1995) 'The Campaign for Parity in Political Institutions', in D. Knight and J. Still (eds), *Women and Representation* (Nottingham: WIF Publications).

Allwood, G. (1998) *French Feminisms* (London: UCL).

Allwood, G. and K. Wadia (2000) *Women and Politics in France: 1958–2000* (London: Routledge).

Alvarez, S. E. (1998) 'Latin American Feminisms "Go Global": Trends of the 1990s, Challenges for the New Millennium', in S. E. Alvarez, E. Dagnino and A. Escobar (eds), *Cultures of Politics/Politics of Cultures: Re-visioning Latin American Social Movements* (Boulder, CO: Westview Press, 1998).

Amar, M. (ed.) (1999) *Le Piège de la parité: arguments pour un débat* (Paris: Hachette Littératures).

Ameline, N. (2003) Communication en Conseil des Ministres. Ministère délégué à la parité et à l'égalité professionelle.

Amnesty International (2005) *No Turning Back – Full Implementation of Women's Human Rights Now! 10 Year Review and Appraisal of the Beijing Platform for Action* (London: Amnesty International).

Amnesty International Section Française (2006) *Les violences faites aux femmes en France: Une affaire d'Etat* (Paris: Autrement).

Amnesty International (2007) 'Worldwide: Amnesty International Defends Access to Abortion for Women at Risk' (14 June), www.amnesty.org.uk/news_details_ p.asp?NewsID=17378, accessed 21 November 2007.

Archambault, E. (2001) 'Historical Roots of the Nonprofit Sector in France'. *Nonprofit and Voluntary Sector Quarterly* 30(2): 204–20.

Assemblée-Nationale.fr. 'La citoyenneté politique des femmes', http://www.assemblee-nationale.fr/histoire/femmes/citoyennete_politique_anthologie.asp, accessed 21 June 2008.

Assemblée Nationale (2000) 'Compte rendu intégral de la première séance du 29 novembre 2000. Discussion du projet de loi relatif à l'interruption volontaire de grossesse et à la contraception', http://www.assemblee-nationale.fr/dossiers/ivg.asp, accessed 10 August 2006.

Aubin, C. and H. Gisserot (1994) *Les femmes en France 1985–1995. Rapport établi par la France en vue de la quatrième Conférence mondiale sur les femmes* (Paris: La Documentation française).

Aubry, M. (2000) Projet de Loi relatif à l'interruption volontaire de grossesse et à la contraception. Ministre de l'emploi et de la solidarité, Assemblée Nationale, Onzième législature.

Auge, M. (1989) 'Le Voile de mots'. *Libération* (20 November).

Bacchi, C. L. (1999) *Women, Policy and Politics* (London, Thousand Oaks and New Delhi: Sage).

Badinter, E. (1996) 'Non aux quotas des femmes'. *Le Monde* (12 July).

Badinter, E. (2002) 'Si c'est leur choix'. *Le Nouvel Observateur* (22 August). Paris: 1972.

Badinter, E. (2003a) *Fausse Route* (Paris: Odile Jacob).

Badinter, E. (2003b) 'Le féminisme d'Elisabeth Badinter'. *L'Humanité* (20 June). Paris: 23.

Badinter, E. and M. Iacub (2003) 'Le débat sur le nouveau féminisme', *Le Nouvel Observateur* 2010 (15 May), http://hebdo.nouvelobs.com/hebdo/parution/p20030515/articles/a194715-.html.

Badinter, E., R. Debray, A. Finkielkraut, E. De Fontaney and C. Kintzler (1989) 'L'Affaire du foulard: "profs, ne capitulons pas!"'. *Le Nouvel Observateur* (2 November).

Badinter, R. (2002) 'Senate Debate, 14 February 2002', www.senat.fr, accessed 16 May 2006.

Barbier, M. (2005) 'Pour une définition de la laïcité française'. *Le Débat* 134 (March–April): 129–41.

Barclay, G. and C. Tavares (with S. Kenny, S. Arsalaan and E. Wilby) (2003) *International Comparisons of Criminal Justice Statistics* (Home Office Statistical Bulletin 12/03) (London: Home Office).

Bard, C. (ed.) (1999) *Un Siècle d'anti-féminisme* (Paris: Fayard).

Bard. C. (2001) *Les Femmes dans la société française au 20e siècle* (Paris: Armand Colin).

Batagliola, F. (2004) *Histoire du travail des femmes* (Paris: La Découverte).

Baubérot, J. (1994) 'Les Avatars de la culture laïque'. *Vingtième Siècle. Revue d'Histoire* 44: 51–7.

Baubérot, J. (2003) 'La Laïcité, le chêne et le roseau'. *Libération* (15 December).

Baubérot, J. (2004) 'La Commission Stasi vue par l'un de ses membres'. *Politics, Culture & Society* 22(3): 135–41.

Baubérot, J. (2005) *Histoire de la laïcité en France* (Paris: Presses Universitaires de France).

Baubérot, J. (2006) *L'Intégrisme républicain contre la laïcité* (Paris: Editions de l'Aube, 2006).

Baudelot, C. and R. Establet (1992) *Allez les filles!* (Paris: Seuil).

Baudino, C. (2005) 'Gendering the Republican System: Debates on Women's Political Representation in France', in J. Lovenduski (ed.), *State Feminism and Political Representation* (Cambridge: Cambridge University Press, 2005).

Baudino, C. (2008) 'Parity Reform in France: Promises and Pitfalls'. *Review of Policy Research* 20(3): 385–400.

Baumgartner, F., C. Green-Pedersen et al. (2006) 'Comparative Studies of Policy Agendas'. *Journal of European Public Policy* 13(7): 959–74.

Beckwith, K. (2000) 'Beyond Compare? Women's Movements in Comparative Perspective'. *European Journal of Political Research* 37: 431–68.

Bédouelle, G., H.-J. Gazey, J. Rousse-Lacordaire and J.-L. Souletie (eds) (2003) *Une république des religions. Pour une Laïcité plus ouverte* (Paris: Editions de l'Atelier).

Belbah, M. and C. De Galembert (2008a) 'Dialogue avec l'abstentionniste de la commission Stasi: entretien avec Jean Baubérot', *Droit et Société* 68(1): 237–49.

Belbah, M. and C. De Galembert (2008b) 'Du Palais Royal à la commission Stasi: entretien avec Rémy Schwartz'. *Droit et Société* 68(1): 225–36.

Bell, L. (2001) 'Interpreting Collective Action: Methodology and Ideology in the Analysis of Social Movements in France'. *Modern and Contemporary France* 9(2): 183–96.

Benkimoun, P., S. Blanchard et al. (2003) 'Les questions soulevées par "l'interruption involontaire de grossesse"'. *Le Monde* (1 December): 8.

Bensoussan, D. (2007) 'Triste anniversaire pour les 35 heures'. Challenges.Fr (10 October), http://www.challenges.fr/actualites/business/20071009.CHA1669/triste_anniversaire_pour_les_35_heures.html, accessed 29 January 2007.

Bentbria, M. (1989) 'Otage d'un certain discours laïc'. *Actualité de l'émigration* (9 November).

Bereni, L. (2007) 'French Feminists Renegotiate Republican Universalism: the Gender Parity Campaign'. *French Politics* 5: 191–209.

Berger, S. (1986) 'Postliberal Vision'. *The New York Times* (8 June), http://query.nytimes.com/gst/fullpage.html?res=9A0DE3D8153FF93BA35755C0A960948260, accessed 5 October 2008.

Bertrand, O. (2004) 'Un Foulard déclenche une grève dans un lycée de Lyon'. *Libération* (13 March).

Beveridge, F., S. Nott and K. Stephen (2000) 'Mainstreaming and the Engendering of Policy Making: a Means to an End'. *Journal of European Public Policy* 7(3): 385–405.

Bezat, J.-M. (2001) 'Une France au travail plus qualifiée et plus féminisée'. *Le Monde* (6 July).

Bird, K. (2002) 'Does Parity Work? Results from French Elections'. *Feminist Studies* 28 (Autumn): 691–8.

Bird, K. (2003) 'Who are the Women, Where are the Women, and What Difference Can They Make? Effect of Gender Parity in the French Municipal Elections'. *French Politics* 1: 5–38.

Bird, K. and M. Dubesset (2003) 'La Parité en politique: espoirs et désillusions'. *Regards sur l'Actualité* 289: 65–71.

Blanchard, S. (2003) 'Le vote de l'amendement Garraud suscite les craintes des éministes et des médecins'. *Le Monde* (29 Novemner). Paris: 11.

Blanchard, S. (2004) 'Les femmes pourront désormais avorter chez leur médecin'. *Le Monde* (24 July). Paris: 5.

Borillo, D. (2002) 'La liberté de se prostituer. En l'absence d'exploitation, vendre son corps est un métier comme un autre'. *Libération* (5 July).

Borillo, D., E. Fassin et al. (2002) 'Non à la guerre aux prostituées'. *Le Monde* (7 November).

Borvo, N. (2001) 'Senate Debate, 21 November 2001', http://www.senat.fr/seances/s200111/s20011121/sc20011121042.html.

Borvo, N. (2002) 'Senate Debate, 14 November 2002', http://www.senat.fr.

Bossuyt, M. J. (1987) *Guide to the 'Travaux Préparatoires' of the International Covenant on Civil and Political Rights* (Dordecht, Boston and Lancaster: Nijhoff Publishers).

Bouamama, S. (2004) 'L'homme en question: le processus du devenir-client de la prostitution', Mouvement du Nid and IFAR.

Boucher, C. (2002) 'Défendre les travailleuses du sexe'. *Le Nouvel Observateur* (22 August). Paris: 1972.

Boulangé A. (2004) 'Foulard, laïcité et racisme', *L'Ecole Démocratique* (2 March), http://www.ecoledemocratique.org/spip.php?article155, accessed 22 March 2007.

Bousquet, D. (2000) Rapport d'information fait au nom de la délégation aux droits des femmes et à l'égalité des chances entre les hommes et les femmes sur le projet de loi (no. 2605) relatif à l'interruption volontaire de grossesse et à la contraception, Assemblée Nationale, 2702.

Bowen, J. R. (2006) *Why the French Don't Like Headscarves: Islam, the State and Public Space* (Princeton and Oxford: Princeton University Press).

Bowles, S. and H. Gintis (1987) *Democracy and Capitalism: Property, Community, and the Contradictions of Modern Social Thought* (London: Routledge).

Branger, J.-G. (2005). Rapport d'information fait sur les propositions de loi no. 62 (2004–5) présentée par M. Roland Courteau et plusieurs de ses collègues, tendant à lutter contre les violences à l'égard des femmes et notamment au sein des couples par un dispositif global de prévention, d'aide aux victimes et de répression, et no. 95 (2004–5) présentée par Mme Nicole Borvo Cohen-Seat et plusieurs de ses collègues, relative à la lutte contre les violences au sein des couples. Délégation aux Droits des Femmes, Sénat. Session ordinaire de 2004–5.

Brunel, C. (2005). Rapport d'information fait au nom de la délégation aux droits des femmes et à l'égalité des chances entre les hommes et les femmes sur la proposition de loi (no. 2219), adoptée par le Sénat, renforçant la prévention et la répression des violences au sein du couple. Paris: Assemblée Nationale.

Brunnerie-Kauffmann, J., H. Désir, R. Dumont, G. Perrault and A. Touraine (1989) 'Pour une laïcité ouverte'. *Politis* (9 November).

Bulard, M. (1999) 'What Price the 35-hour Week?' *Le Monde Diplomatique* (English edition, September), http://mondediplo.com/1999/09/12hours, accessed 15 February 2007.

Bunch, C. (1990) 'Women's Rights as Human Rights: Toward a Re-Vision of Human Rights'. *Human Rights Quarterly* 12: 486–98.

BVA (2003) 'L'Opinion en Question: Le Port de Signes Religieux', *BVA Actualité* (21 November), http://www.bva.fr/data/sondage/sondage_sondage/197/sondage_fichier/fichier/portsignesreligieux_6f8a1.pdf, accessed 23 October 2007.

Cabiria (2000) Annual Report 2001, http://perso.wanadoo.fr/cabiria/pagesinenglish.

Campbell, M. (2003) 'Black Widows of Chechnya Take Another Deadly Revenge'. TimesOnline (6 July), http://www.timesonline.co.uk/tol/news/world/article1148586.ece, accessed 12 December 2007.

Cette, G. (1999) *Le temps partiel en France* (Rapport du Conseil d'Analyse Economique) (Paris: La Documentation française).

CFDT (2005) 'Egalité salariale hommes-femmes: un pas de plus dans l'incitation à négocier'. CFDT Salle de Presse (11 May), http://www.cfdt.fr/actualite/presse/comm/comm511.htm, accessed 20 February 2008.

CFTC (2000) 'Les 35 heures et les femmes'. *Liaison Sociale* 13110.

Chaib, S. (2001) *Facteurs d'insertion et d'exclusion des femmes immigrantes dans le marché du travail en France: Quel état des connaissances? Parti 2, La présence des femmes immigrantes dans les pays d'accueil* (Paris: Confédération Française Démocratique du Travail).

Charles, N. (2000) *Feminism, the State and Social Policy* (Basingstoke: Palgrave Macmillan).

Chemin, A. (2004) 'Celui qui nous insulte, il faut le terroriser politiquement'. *Le Monde* (20 January).

Chemin, A. (2006a) 'Le Planning familial: 50 ans et de nouveaux combats'. *Le Monde* (3 March). Paris: 23.

Chemin, A. (2006b). 'Un rapport préconise un suivi d'au moins six mois pour les hommes violents'. *Le Monde* (25 March). Paris: 11.

Chérifi, H. (2005) *Application de la loi du 15 mars 2004 sur le port des signes religieux ostensibles dans les établissements d'enseignement publics* (Paris: Ministère de l'Education Nationale, de l'Enseignement Supérieur et de la Recherche, July).

Chetcuti, N. and M. Jaspard (2007) 'Présentation', in N. Chetcuti and M. Jaspard (eds), *Violences envers les femmes* (Paris: L'Harmattan).

Chirac, J. (2003) 'Discours prononcé par M. Jacques Chirac, Président de la République, relatif au respect du principe de laïcité dans la République' (17 December), http://www.elysee.fr/elysee/interventions/discours_et_declarations/2003/decembre/discours_prononce_par_m_jacques_chirac_president_de_la_republique_relatif_au_respect_du_principe_de_laicite_dans_la_republique-palais_de_l_elysee.2829.html, accessed 20 February 2007.

CNDF (Centre National pour les Droits des Femmes) (2005) 'Egalité salariale entre les femmes et les hommes d'ici cinq ans? C'est mal parti!' *Forum Information Féministe* (10 January), http://forum.aceboard.net/60786-1288-1056-0-.htm, accessed 20 February 2008.

Cockburn, C. (1991) *In the Way of Women: Men's Resistance to Sex Equality in Organisations* (Ithaca, NY: Cornell ILR Press).

Cohen, S. A. and C. L. Richards (1994) 'The Cairo Consensus: Population, Development and Women'. *Family Planning Perspectives* 26(6): 272–7.

Colclough, C. J. (2004) 'Gender Equality Plans at the Workplace'. EIROnline, http://www.eurofound.europa.eu/eiro/2004/02/study/tn0402101s.htm, accessed 21 March 2007.

Comité d'Action Interassociatif Droits des Femmes, Droit au Séjour (2004) *Femmes et Etrangères: Contre la double violence. Témoignages et Analyses.*

Commaille, J. (1993) *Les Stratégies des femmes* (Paris: La Découverte).

Commission of the European Communities (2006) 'A Roadmap for Equality Between Women and Men 2006–2010'. COM (2006) 92.

Condon, S. (2000) 'L'Activité des femmes immigrées du Portugal à l'arrivée en France, reflet d'une diversité de stratégies familiales et individuelles'. *Population* 55(2): 301–30.

Conseil d'Etat (1989) *Avis no. 346.893 du 27 novembre 1989* (Paris: Le Conseil d'Etat, 27 November), http://www.conseil-etat.fr/ce/missio/index_mi_cg03_01. shtml, accessed 20 February 2007.

Conseil Economique et Social (2007) *La Place des femmes dans les lieux de décision: promouvoir la mixité* (Paris: CES/Délégation aux Droits des Femmes et à l'Egalité des Chances entre les Femmes et les Hommes).

Conseil Economique et Social (2008) *Les Femmes face au travail à temps partiel* (Paris: CES).

Coordination Féministe et Laïque (CFL) (2005) *Manifeste laïque féministe républicain* (7 January), http://www.journee-de-la-femme.com/Manifeste-CFL-7-1-2005.htm, accessed 19 June 2008.

Coquart, E. and P. Huet (2000) *Le Livre noir de la prostitution* (Paris: Albin Michel).

Council of Europe (2004) *Gender Mainstreaming: Conceptual Framework, Methodology and Presentation of Good Practices* (Strasbourg: DG Human Rights/COE).

Council of Europe (2006) *Combating Violence Against Women: Stocktaking Study on the Measures and Actions taken in Council of Europe Member States* (Strasbourg: DG Human Rights/COE).

Couret, F. (2004) 'Face à la violence, des femmes vivent le dos au mur'. *La Croix* (25 November). Paris: 3.

Coutanceau, R. (2006) Auteurs de violences au sein du couple: Prise en charge et prévention. Ministère de la Cohésion Sociale et de la Parité. La Documentation française: 27.

Crossette, B. (2004) 'Reproductive Health and the Millennium Development Goals: the Missing Link'. Background Paper, www.countdown2015.

CSA (2004) 'Les Musulmans et la Laïcité'. *CSA* (26 January), http://www.csa-fr. com/dataset/data2004/opi20040121b.htm, accessed 23 October 2007.

Daune-Richard, A.-M. and A.-M. Devreux (1992) 'Rapports sociaux de sexe et conceptualisation sociologique'. *Recherches Féministes* 5(2): 7–30.

Dauphin, S. (2008) 'Promotion de l'égalité des sexes en France', in Sandrine Dauphin and Réjane Sénac-Slawinski (eds), *Gender Mainstreaming: De l'égalité des sexes à la diversité* (Cahiers du genre no. 44).

Delphy, C. (ed.) (1994) 'La Parité "pour"'. *Nouvelles Questions Féministes* (special issue) 15(4) (November).

Delphy, C. (ed.) (1995) 'La Parité "contre"'. *Nouvelles Questions Féministes* (special issue) 16(2) (May).

Delphy, C. (1998) *L'Ennemi principal, 1: économie politique du patriarcat* (Nouvelles Questions Féministes) (Paris: Syllepse).

Delphy, C. (2004). 'Retrouver l'élan du féminisme'. *Le Monde Diplomatique* (May): 24–5.

Delphy, C. (2006) 'Antisexisme ou anti-racisme? Un faux dilemme'. *Nouvelles Questions Féministes* 25(1): 59–83.

Deltombe, T. (2005) *L'Islam imaginaire: la construction médiatique de l'islamophobie en France, 1975 – 2005* (Paris: La Découverte).

Denmard, D. (1981) 'Lettre de Jules Ferry aux instituteurs du 17 novembre 1883', *Dictionnaire d'histoire de l'enseignement* (Paris: J.-P. Delarge), http://hypo.ge.ch/www/cliotexte//html/education.morale.html, accessed 12 December 2007.

Départements (2008) 'Le Nouveau visage des départements'. *Départements* (Review of the Association des Départements de France) 95 (June): 24.

Derycke, D. (2001) 'Rapport d'activité 2000: les politiques publiques et la prostitution'. La Délégation du Sénat aux Droits des Femmes et à l'Egalité des Chances entre les Hommes et les Femmes.

De Troy, C. (1991) 'La Formation professionnelle et les perspectives d'emploi pour les femmes immigrées'. *Femmes Immigrées: quelles chances pour quelles insertions sociales et professionnelles?* (Rencontre-Débat, 13 December) (Paris: Grec).

Direction des Affaires Criminelles et des Grâces (2004) *La lutte contre les violences au sein du couple. Guide de l'action publique.*

Dollar, D., S. Fisman and R. Gatti (2001) 'Are Women Really the "Fairer" Sex? Corruption and Women in Government'. *Journal of Economic Behavior & Organization* 46: 423–9.

Dreyfus-Schmidt, M. (2001) 'Senate Debate, 21 November 2001', http://www. senat.fr/seances/s200111/s20011121/sc20011121042.html.

Dubois, J-P. 'La laïcité au défi de pluralisme culturel', *Hommes et Libertés*, 113/114 (June 2001), http://www.ldh-france.org/docu_hommeliber3.cfm?idhomme= 642&idpere=613, accessed 21 March 2007.

Duchen, C. (1986) *Feminism in France: From May '68 to Mitterrand* (London and New York: Routledge).

Duchêne, L. (2002) 'Le PC dans un processus d'abolition de la prostitution'. *Prostitution et Société* 139 (October–December): 12–13.

Duru-Bellat, M. (1990) *L'école des filles. Quelle formation pour quels rôles sociaux?* (Paris: L'Harmattan).

Education Nationale, Jeunesse et Sports (1989) *Laïcité, port des signes religieux par les élèves et caractère obligatoire des enseignements* (Circulaire de 12 décembre 1989, nor: MENX8910373C) (Paris: Education Nationale, Jeunesse et Sports, 1989), http://www.assemblee-nationale.fr/12/dossiers/documents-laicite/document-2.pdf, accessed 20 February 2007.

Elgie, R. and S. Griggs (2000) *French Politics: Debates and Controversies* (London and New York: Routledge).

Elman, R. A. (ed.) (1996) *Sexual Politics and the European Union: the New Feminist Challenge* (Oxford: Berghahn Books).

Estrade, M.-A., D. Méda and A. Orain (2001) 'Les Effets de la réduction du temps de travail sur les modes de vie'. *Premières Synthèses* (DARES), 21 January.

Europe-Politique.EU (2008) 'Elections européennes 1984'. *Europe-Politique.EU* (26 January), http://www.france-politique.fr/elections-europeennes-1984.htm, accessed 13 March 2008.

European Economic and Social Committee (2006) 'Opinion of the European Economic and Social Committee on Domestic Violence Against Women, European Economic and Social Committee'. SOC/218.

European Foundation for the Improvement of Living and Working Conditions (EFILWC) (2007) *Part-Time Work in Europe* (Dublin: EFILWC).

Fabre, C. (2001) *Les Femmes et la Politique: du droit de vote à la parité* (Paris: Librio).

Fabre, C. and P. Krémer (2002) 'Plusieurs centaines de "personnes prostituées" se sont rassemblées à Paris contre le projet Sarkozy'. *Le Monde* (6 November). Paris.

Fabre, C. and P. Le Coeur (2002) 'Prostitution: Le Sénat veut compléter le projet Sarkozy'. *Le Monde* (31 October). Paris.

Fabre, C. and N. Weill (2003) 'Violences sexuelles: débat autour d'une enquête'. *Le Monde* (4 June). Paris: 22.

Fagnani, J. and M.-T. Letablier (2004) 'Work and Family Life Balance: the Impact of the 35-hour Laws in France'. *Work, Employment, Society* 18: 551–72.

Falconnat, L. (2004). 'Ni putes ni soumises à l'heure du choix'. *Le Monde*: 8.

Fanon, F. (1967) 'Algeria Unveiled', in *A Dying Colonialism* (New York: Grove Press).

Fassin, E. (1997) 'L'Epouvantail américain: penser la discrimination française'. *Vacarme* 04/05 (Autumn), http://www.vacarme.eu.org/article1159.html, accessed 21 June 2008.

Fassin, E. (2007) 'Une enquête qui dérange', in N. Chetcuti and M. Jaspard (eds), *Violences envers les femmes* (Paris: L'Harmattan).

Fayol, M.-L. (2006) 'La Place des femmes dans les conseils municipaux: enquête départementale', report for the Association des Maires et des présidents de communautés de l'Allier, the Délégation départementale aux droits des femmes et à l'égalité and the Préfecture de l'Allier.

Fayol, M.-L. (2007) 'La place des femmes dans les conseils municipaux de la Haute-Loire', report for Association des Maires and the Mission Départementale aux Droits des Femmes et à l'Egalité de Haute-Loire, http://www.haute-loire.pref.gouv.fr/plugins/fckeditor/userfiles/file/DROITS%20FEMMES%20VIE%20POLITIQUE%20ENQUETE.PDF, accessed 5 October 2008.

Fédération nationale solidarité femmes (2006) 'Qui sommes-nous?' http://solidaritefemmes.asso.fr/, accessed 19 October 2006.

Flottes, A. (2006) 'RTT et santé: petite chronique d'un égarement collectif'. *Pistes* 8(1), http://www.pistes.uqam.ca/v8n1/articles/v8n1a5.htm, accessed 20 February 2008.

Fondation Scelles (2000) *Actes du colloque du 16 mai 2000, tenu à l'UNESCO. Le peuple de l'abîme. La prostitution aujourd'hui* (Paris: UNESCO).

Fondation Scelles (2005) 'La Fondation Scelles présente la première déclaration de sensibilisation des clients de personnes prostituées: "Et si on parlait prostitution"', www.fondationscelles.org, accessed 1 September 2005.

Fong, D. (2007) 'Common Abortion Policy Remains Out of Reach in EU'. *Deutsche Welle* (21 October).

Gardiner, F. (ed.) (1997) *Sex Equality in Western Europe* (London and New York: Routledge).

Gaspard, F. (2001) 'The French Parity Movement', in J. Klausen and C. S. Meier (eds), *Has Liberalism Failed Women? Assuring Equal Representation in Europe and the United States* (New York: Palgrave Macmillan).

Gaspard, F. and F. Khosrokhavar (1995) *Le Foulard et la république* (Paris: La Découverte).

Gaspard, F., A. Le Gall and C. Servan-Schreiber (1992) *Au pouvoir, citoyennes: Liberté, Egalité, Parité* (Paris: Seuil).

Geddes, A. and V. Guiraudon (2004) 'British, French and EU Anti-Discrimination Policy: the Emergence of an EU Policy Paradigm'. *West European Politics* 27(2): 334–53.

Geisser, V. (2003) *La Nouvelle islamophobie* (Paris: La Découverte).

Gelb, J. (1989) *Feminism and Politics: a Comparative Perspective* (Berkeley and Los Angeles: University of California Press).

Génisson, C. (1999) *Femmes-hommes, quelle égalité professionnelle?* (Paris: La Documentation française).

Gil-Robles, A. (2006). Report on the Effective Respect for Human Rights in France following his visit from 5–21 Septebmer 2005 (Strasbourg: Council of Europe).

Giroud, F. (1976) *Cent mesures pour les femmes* (Paris: La Documentation française).

Goetz, A.-M. (2007) 'Political Cleaners: Women as the New Anti-Corruption Force?' *Development and Change* 38(1): 87–105.

Gordon, D. C. (1962) *Women of Algeria: an Essay on Change* (Cambridge, MA: Harvard University Press).

Gray, J. (1996) *Post-liberalism: Studies in Political Thought* (London: Routledge).

Gregory, A. and J. Windebank (2000) *Women's Work in Britain and France: Practice, Theory and Policy* (Basingstoke: Palgrave Macmillan).

Grémillet, M. (2005) 'Parité ne rime pas avec l'égalité'. *Libération* (10 May), http://www.liberation.fr/page.php?Article=295328, accessed 20 February 2008.

Grosjean, B. (2003) 'Des filles de joie bien à la peine'. *Libération* (13 June). Paris.

Guigou, E. (1998) 'Egalité Hommes Femmes'. *Compte rendu analytique officiel* (Archives de la onzième législature, session ordinaire de 1998–1999, 46ème jour de séance, 119ème séance, 2ème séance du mardi 15 décembre), http://www.assemblee-nationale.fr/11/cra/1998-1999/98121515.asp#P295_79259, accessed 21 June 2008.

Handman, M.-E. and J. Mossuz-Lavau (eds) (2005) *La Prostitution à Paris* (Paris: Editions de la Martinière).

Hanley, D., P. Kerr and N. Waites (1984) *Contemporary France: Politics and Society since 1945* (London and New York: Routledge & Kegan Paul).

Harding, J. (2004) 'What to Wear to School'. *London Review of Books* (19 February), http://www.lrb.co.uk/v26/n04/print/hard01_.html, accessed 12 February 2007.

Hayden, A. (2006) 'France's 35-Hour Week: Attack on Business? Win-Win Reform? Or Betrayal of Disadvantaged Workers?' *Politics and Society* 34: 503–42.

Hearn, J. and L. McKie (2008) 'Gendered Policy and Policy on Gender: the Case of "Domestic Violence"'. *Policy and Politics* 36(1): 75–91.

Helft-Malz, V. and P.-H. Lévy (2003) 'La victimisation est aujourd'hui un outil politique et idéologique'. *L'Arche*: 549–50, http://www.pensamientocritico.org/elisbad0105.htm, accessed 20 February 2007.

Heller, H. (1991) *Iron and Blood: Civil Wars in Sixteenth-Century France* (Montreal: McGill-Queen's University Press).

Henry, M. (2007) 'La Lapidation de Ghofrane aux assises'. *Libération* (11 April), http://www.liberation.fr/actualite/societe/246736.FR.php, accessed 12 December 2007.

Hessini, L. (2005) 'Global Progress in Abortion Advocacy and Policy: an Assessment of the Decade since ICPD'. *Reproductive Health Matters* 13(25): 88–100.

Hirata, H. and C. Rogerat (1988) 'Technologie, qualification et division sexuelle du travail'. *Revue Française de Sociologie* 15: 171–92.

Holt, M. P. (1995) *The French Wars of Religion, 1562–1629* (Cambridge: Cambridge University Press).

Hoskyns, C. (1996) *Integrating Gender: Women, Law and Politics in the EU* (London and New York: Verso).

Huet, M. (1982) 'La Progression de l'activité féminine: est-elle irréversible?' *Economie et Statistique* 145: 3–17.

Iacub, M., C. Millet et al. (2002) 'Ni coupables ni victimes: libres de se prostituer'. *Le Monde* (8 January). Paris.

Iacub, M. and H. Le Bras (2003) 'Homo mulieri lupus?' *Les Temps Modernes* 623 (February–April): 112–32.

INSEE (1995) *Les Femmes: contours et caractères* (Paris: INSEE, Service des Droits des Femmes).

INSEE (1997) *Les Immigrés: portrait social* (collection contours et caractères). (Paris: Institut National de la Statistique et d'Etudes Economiques).

INSEE (2006) 'Population active et taux d'emploi dans l'Union européenne'. *France, portrait social*, http://www.insee.fr/fr/ffc/chifcle_fiche.asp?ref_id= CMPFPS03138andtab_id=200andsouspop=2, accessed 13 March 2007.

INSEE (2007) 'Résultats de l'enquête Emploi – Le chômage baisse depuis début 2006'. *Insee Première* (November), http://www.insee.fr/fr/ffc/figure/ NATCCF03302.XLS, accessed 19 February 2008.

INSEE and Service des Droits des Femmes (1997) *Les Femmes: portrait social* (collection contours et caractères). (Paris: Institut National de la Statistique et d'Etudes Economiques).

Institut Européen en Sciences des Religions (2008) 'Bibliothèque virtuelle – Laïcité', updated January–February 2008, http://www.iesr.ephe.sorbonne.fr/index. html?id=436&offset_3792f=0, accessed 13 March 2007.

International Planned Parenthood Federation (2008a) 'Global Gag Rule', http://www.ippf.org/en/What-we-do/Advocacy/Global+gag+rule.htm, accessed 9 May 2008.

International Planned Parenthood Federation (2008b) 'Legal Abortion Throughout Europe?' http://www.ippf.org/en/What-we-do/Abortion/Legal+abortion+ throughout+Europe.htm, accessed 9 May 2009

Inter-Parliamentary Union (2008) 'Women in National Parliaments: Situation as of 30 September 2008', http://www.ipu.org/wmn-e/classif.htm, accessed 23 October 2008.

Jackson, A. (2001) 'Globalization and Progressive Social Policy', paper presented to the Tenth Biennial Conference on Canadian Social Welfare Policy, Calgary, 18 June, http://www.ccsd.ca/pubs/2001/ajglob.htm, accessed 23 May 2008.

Jankowski, P. (2007) *Shades of Indignation: Political Scandals in France, Past and Present* (Oxford and New York: Berghahn Books).

Jaspard, M., E. Brown and S. Condon (2003) *Les Violences envers les femmes en France: Une enquête nationale* (ENVEFF) (Paris: La Documentation française).

Jaspard, M. (2005) 'Les violences envers les femmes: une reconnaissance difficile', in M. Maruani (ed.), *Femmes, genres et sociétés: L'Etat des savoirs* (Paris: La Découverte).

Jaspard, M. (2007) 'L'enquête nationale sur les violences envers les femmes en France (ENVEFF): Historique et contextes', in N. Chetcuti and M. Jaspard (eds), *Violences envers les femmes* (Paris: L'Harmattan).

Jenson, J. (1996) 'Representations of Difference: the Varieties of French Feminism', in M. Threlfall (ed.), *Mapping the Women's Movement* (London and New York: Verso).

Joachim, J. (2002) 'Comparing the Influence of NGOs in Transnational Institutions: the UN, the EU and the Case of Gender Violence', paper presented to the 43rd Annual Convention of the International Studies Association, New Orleans.

Johnstone, H. (2004) 'Human Rights Court Upholds Headscarf Ban'. *The Independent* (30 June), http://www.independent.co.uk/news/world/europe/human-rights-court-upholds-headscarf-ban-734059.html, accessed 12 March 2007.

Journal Officiel de la République Française (JORF) (1983) 'Loi no. 83-635 du 13 juillet 1983 portant modification du code du travail et du code pénal en ce qui concerne l'égalité professionnelle entre les femmes et les hommes'. 14 July: 2176–9, http://la_pie.club.fr/loi/egalprof_loi1983.htm, accessed 20 March 2007.

Journal Officiel de la République Française (JORF) (1999) 'Loi constitutionnelle no. 99-569 du 8 juillet 1999 relative à l'égalité entre les femmes et les hommes'. *JORF* 157 (9 July): 10175, http://www.legifrance.gouv.fr/affichTexte.do?cidTexte=JORFTEXT000000396412&dateTexte=&fastPos=1&fastReqId=172288262&oldAction=rechTexte, accessed 21 June 2008.

Journal Officiel de la République Française (JORF) (2000) 'Loi no. 2000-493 du 6 juin 2000 tendant à favoriser l'égal accès des femmes et des hommes aux mandats électoraux et fonctions électives'. *JORF* 131 (7 June): 8560, http://www.legifrance.gouv.fr/affichTexte.do;jsessionid=E514657349BFF8A636F6E241FD537B81.tpdjo17v_1?cidTexte=LEGITEXT0000 05629480&dateTexte=, accessed 21 June 2008.

Journal Officiel de la République Française (JORF) (2003) 'Loi no. 2003-327 du 11 avril 2003 relative à l'élection des conseillers régionaux et des représentants au parlement européen'. *JORF* 87 (12 April): 6488, http://www.legifrance.gouv.fr/affichTexte.do?cidTexte=JORFTEXT000000237704&dateTexte=&fastPos=2&fastReqId=260162721&oldAction=rechTexte, accessed 21 June 2008.

Journal Officiel de la République Française (JORF) (2004) 'Loi no. 2004-228 du 15 mars 2004 encadrant, en application du principe de laïcité, le port de signes ou de tenues manifestant une appartenance religieuse dans les écoles, collèges et lycées publics' *JORF*, 65 (17 March): 5190. http://www.legifrance.gouv.fr/affichTexte.do?cidTexte=JORFTEXT000000417977&dateTexte=, accessed 20 February 2007.

Journal Officiel de la République Française (JORF) (2004) 'Circulaire N° 2004-084 du 18-5-2004 Respect de la laïcité· port de signes ou de tenues manifestant une appartenance religieuse dans les écoles, collèges et lycées publics' (22 May), in H. Chérifi, *Application de la loi du 15 Mars 2004 sur le port des signes religieux ostensibles dans les établissements d'enseignement publique* (Paris: Ministère de l'Education Nationale, de l'Enseignement Supérieur et de la Recherche).

Journal Officiel de la République Française (JORF) (2007) 'Loi no. 2007-128 du 31 janvier 2007 tendant à promouvoir l'égal accès des femmes et des hommes aux mandats électoraux et fonctions électives'. *JORF*, 27: 1941, http://www.legifrance.gouv.fr/affichTexte.do?cidTexte=JORFTEXT000000273404&dateTexte=&fastPos=3&fastReqId=428474263&oldAction=rechTexte, accessed 21 June 2008.

Journal Officiel de la République Française (JORF) (2008) 'Loi du 26 février 2008 facilitant l'égal accès des femmes et des hommes au mandat de conseiller général'. *JORF* 49 (27 February): 3370, http://www.legifrance.gouv.fr/affichTexte.do?cidTexte=JORFTEXT000018169045&dateTexte=&fastPos=1&fastReqId=2074912174&oldAction=rechTexte, accessed 21 June 2008.

Karam, A. (2000) 'Beijing + 5: Women's Political Participation: Review of Strategies and Trends', in UNDP, *Women's Political Participation and Good Governance: 21st Century Challenges* (New York: UNDP).

Kergoat, D. (1982) *Les Ouvrières* (Paris: Le Sycomore).

Kergoat, D. (1998) 'La Division du travail entre les sexes', in J. Kergoat, J. Boutet, H. Jacot and D. Linhart (eds), *Le Monde du travail* (Paris: La Découverte/Syros).

Kergoat, D. (2005) 'Penser la différence des sexes: rapports sociaux et division du travail entre les sexes', in M. Maruani (ed.), *Femmes, genre et sociétés* (Paris: La Découverte).

Khosrokhavar, F. (1997) *L'Islam des jeunes* (Paris: Flammarion).

Klejman, L. and F. Rochefort (1989) *L'Egalité en marche. Le féminisme sous la Troisième République* (Paris: Presses de la FNSP).

Knecht, R. J. (2000) *The French Civil Wars, 1562–1598* (Oxford: Osprey Publishing).

Krémer, P. (2002) 'La loi autorisant les avortements tardifs n'est que partiellement appliquée'. *Le Monde* (4 February). Paris: 10.

Krémer, P. and M. L. Phelippeau (2002) 'Présidentielle. Le Programme Le Pen'. *Le Monde* (29 April). Paris: 4.

Kriesi, H., R. Koopmans, J. W. Duyvendak and Mario Giugni (eds) (1995) *New Social Movements in Western Europe* (London: UCL Press).

Krook, M. L. (2007) 'National Solution or Model from Abroad? Analyzing International Influences on the Parity Movement in France'. *French Politics* 5: 3–19.

Krook, M. L. and J. Squires (2006) 'Gender Quotas in British Politics: Multiple Approaches and Methods in Feminist Research'. *British Politics* 1(1): 44–66.

Laborde, C. (2005) 'Secular Philosophy and Muslim Headscarves in Schools'. *The Journal of Political Philosophy* 13(3): 305–29.

La Délégation de l'Assemblée Nationale aux Droits des Femmes et à l'Egalité des Chances entre les Hommes et les Femmes (2000a) Audition du professeur Bernard Glorion, Président du Conseil National de l'Ordre des Médecins, Assemblée Nationale. Compte Rendu no. 26: 2.

La Délégation de l'Assemblée Nationale aux Droits des Femmes et à l'Egalité des Chances entre les Hommes et les Femmes (2000b) Audition du professeur Jacques Milliez, chef de service de gynécologie-obstétrique de l'hopital Saint-Antoine à Paris, Assemblée Nationale: 2.

La Délégation de l'Assemblée Nationale aux Droits des Femmes et à l'Egalité des Chances entre les Hommes et les Femmes (2002) 'Compte rendu no. 2, 15 October, Présidence de Marie-Jo Zimmermann', www.assemblee_nationale.fr/12/cr-delf/02-03/c0203002.asp.

La Ministre de l'Emploi et de la Solidarité, Le Garde-des Sceaux, Ministre de la Justice, Le Ministre délégué à la Santé (2001) 'Communiqué: L'accueil en urgence dans les établissements, de santé des personnes victimes de violences ainsi que de toutes personnes en situation de détresse psychologique', Paris, 24 October, http://www.sante.gouv.fr/htm/actu/31_011024.htm, accessed 28 April 2009.

Landrin, S. (2004) 'Un Bandeau porté en guise de voile sème le trouble dans un lycée lyonnais'. *Le Monde* (25 February).

Latour, P., M. Houssin and M. Tovar (1995) *Femmes et Citoyennes: du droit de vote à l'exercice du pouvoir* (Paris: Editions de l'Atelier).

Laufer, J. (2003) 'Equal Employment Policy in France: Symbolic Support and a Mixed Record'. *Review of Policy Research* 20(3): 423–42.

Laufer, J. and R. Silvera (2005) *Les Accords égalité professionnelle suite à la loi du 9 mai 2001, premiers éléments d'analyse* (Etude Equal Timetis).

(Paris: Emergences), http://www.emergences.fr/upload/ress_generales/emer-bilan-accords.pdf, accessed 19 February 2008.

Lazreg, M. (1994) *The Eloquence of Silence: Algerian Women in Question* (London: Routledge).

Lebranchu, M. (2001) 'Senate Debate, 21 November 2001', http://www/senat.fr/seances/s200111/s20011121/sc20011121042.html.

Le Bras-Chopard, A. and J. Mossuz-Lavau (eds) (1997) *Les femmes et la politique* (Paris: L'Harmattan).

Le Doeuff, M. (2000) 'Feminism is Back in France or is it?' *Hypatia* 5(4) (Autumn): 243–55.

Legardinier, C. (2002) 'Audition de Claudine Legardinier, journaliste, par la Délégation de l'Assemblée nationale aux droits des femmes et à l'égalité des chances entre les hommes et les femmes' (Paris: Assemblée Nationale)

Leicke, R. and M. Schreiber (1989) 'Eine Flurbereinigung ist unvermeidbar: der scheidende EG-Kommissar Karl-Heinz Narjes über den Binnenmarkt und die Bonner Europa-Politik'. *Der Spiegel* (2 January), http://wissen.spiegel.de/wissen/dokument/84/92/dokument.html?titvel=%22Eine+Flurbereinigung+unvermeidbar%22andid=13492948andtop=SPIEGELandsuchbegriff=ist+karl-heinz+narjesandquellen=andvl=0, accessed 12 March 2007.

Leitner, B. (2004) 'Un combat pour l'émancipation de l'individu, pour la justice, pour la liberté est un des plus beau' (interview with Fadéla Amara, 9 June 2004, Alice Salomon Archive, Berlin), http://www.asfh-berlin.de/archiv/interview_fr.html, accessed 10 June 2008.

Lemettre, B. (2002) 'Audition de Bernard Lemettre, président du Mouvement du Nid par la Délégation de l'Assemblée nationale aux droits des femmes et à l'égalité des chances entre les hommes et les femmes' (Paris: Assemblée nationale).

Le Monde (1986) *Les Elections législatives du 16 mars 1986* (dossiers et documents) (Paris: Le Monde).

Le Pen, M. (2007) 'Elections 2007 TFI', http://tf1.lci.fr, accessed 8 August 2007.

Lépinard, E. (2006) 'Identity without Politics: Framing the Parity Laws and their Implementation in French Local Politics'. *Social Politics: International Studies in Gender, State and Society* 13(1) (Spring): 30–58.

Lépinard, E. (2007) 'The Contentious Subject of Feminism: Defining Women in France from the Second Wave to Parity'. *Signs: Journal of Women in Culture and Society* 32(2): 375–403.

Lesselier, C. (2005) 'Prostitution et Violence contre les femmes'. *Forum national de la Fasti: Prostitution: L'exploitation des femmes étrangères*. Paris.

Létard, V. (2007). Présentation du plan contre les violences faites aux femmes. Discours de Valérie Létard, 21/11/07, Ministère du travail, République française.

Lévy, A., L. Lévy, Y. Sintomer and V. Giraud (2004) *Des filles comme les autres: au-delà du foulard* (Paris: La Découverte).

Lévy, G. (2003) 'Alma, Lila, le voile'. *Le Monde* (10 October).

L'Express (1994) 'Foulard: le complot. Comment les islamistes nous infiltrent' (special pull-out section), *L'Express* (17 November).

Lignières-Cassou, M. (2000) Rapport fait au nom de la commission des affaires culturelles, familiales et sociales sur le projet de loi (no. 2605) relatif à l'interruption volontaire de grossesse et à la contraception. Commission des affaires culturelles, Assemblée Nationale.

Lignières-Cassou, M. (2001) Rapport d'activité de la Délégation aux Droits des Femmes et à l'Egalité des Chances entre les Hommes et les Femmes, Assemblée Nationale.

Liepietz, A. (2003) 'Le Débat sur le foulard islamique: ce que j'en pense actuellement', *Prochoix* 26 (December). http://lipietz.net/spip.php?article1123, accessed 13 February 2007.

Ligue des Droits de l'Homme, Syndicat des Avocats de France et al. (2002) 'Lettre ouverte à Monsieur Sarkozy', http://www.ldh-france.asso.fr/actu, accessed 29 October 2002.

Ligue des Droits de l'Homme, Syndicat de la Magistrature et al. (2007) 'Des nouvelles zones de non-droit: Des prostituées face à l'arbitraire policier' (23 February), www.syndicat-magistrature.org, accessed 1 March 2007.

Lim, L. L. (ed.) (1998) *The Sex Sector: the Economic and Social Bases of Prostitution in Southeast Asia* (Geneva: International Labour Office).

Loi no. 2001-588 du 4 juillet 2001 relative à l'interruption volontaire de grossesse et à la contraception. MESX0000140L: 10823.

Lombardo, E. (2008) 'Gender Inequality in Politics: Policy Frames in Spain and the European Union'. *International Feminist Journal of Politics* 10(1): 78–96.

Louis, M.-V. (1990). 'Violences conjugales'. *Les temps modernes* (April): 132–68.

Louis, M.-V. (1998). 'Letter to Dominique Fougeyrollas'. Assessed 19 October 2006.

Louis, M.-V. (1999) 'Le Harcèlement sexuel: sujet privilégié de l'antiféminisme', in C. Bard (ed.), *Un siècle d'anti-féminisme* (Paris: Fayard).

Louis, M.-V. (2000). 'De la femme victime de violence à la citoyenne blessée'. http://www.marievictoirelouis.net/textes_auteure.php, accessed 19 October 2006.

Louis, M.-V. (2001a). 'Audition Assemblée nationale Délégation aux droits des femmes et à l'égalité des chances entre les hommes et les femmes'. Accessed 19 October 2006.

Louis, M.-V. (2001b) 'Pour une critique de la politique pro-prostitution de Cabiria', http://www.penelopes.org, accessed 12 October 2001.

Lovenduski, J. (1986) *Women and European Politics: Contemporary Feminism and Public Policy* (Amherst, MA: University of Massachusetts Press).

Lovenduski, J. (2005a) *Feminizing Politics* (Cambridge: Polity Press).

Lovenduski, J. (2005b) *State Feminism and Political Representation* (Cambridge: Cambridge University Press).

Lovenduski, J. and V. Randall (1993) *Contemporary Feminist Politics* (Oxford: Oxford University Press.

Lurol, M. and M. Pélisse (2001) '35 Heures: les disparités entre hommes et femmes'. *4 Pages* 48.

Mabrouk, D. and L. Berkani (2003) 'Violences sexuelles dans le banlieues'. *Le Monde Diplomatique: Manière de voir* 68: 53–7.

Mahéas, J. (2002) 'Senate Debate, 14 November 2002', http://www.senat.fr, accessed 24 February 2006.

Mahéas, J. (2005) 'Bilan de la loi pour la sécurité intérieure en ce qui concerne la prostitution. Question écrite no. 17416. Publiée dans le JO Sénat du 05/05/2005, page 1245', www.senat.fr, accessed 24 February 2006.

Malle, T. (2008) 'L'Observatoire de la parité appelle les partis à respecter la loi'. Paris: Agence France Press (23 January), http://www.redciudadanas.es/spainpdf/municipales_parite_elections.pdf, accessed 5 October 2008.

Marcel, S. (2000) 'L'Impact des 35 heures sur la vie quotidienne des salariés et sur l'emploi'. TNS-Sofres.com, http://www.tns-sofres.com/etudes/pol/130600_35h.htm, accessed 20 February 2008.

Marcovich, M. (2002) *Le système de la prostitution. Une violence à l'encontre des femmes* (Paris: Commission nationale contre les violences envers les femmes).

Marissal, J.-P. and C. Chevally (2007) *Evaluation des répercussions économiques des violences conjugales en France* (Paris: La Documentation française).

Martin, J. (ed.) (1998) *La Parité: enjeux et mise en oeuvre* (Toulouse: Presses Universitaires du Mirail).

Maruani, M. (ed.) (1998) *Les Nouvelles frontières de l'inégalité. Hommes et femmes sur le marché du travail* (Paris: La Découverte).

Maruani, M. (2006) *Travail et emploi des femmes*, 3rd edition (Paris: La Découverte).

Mathieu, L. (2001) *Mobilisations de prostituées* (Paris: Belin).

Mathieu, M. (2003) 'Après des réticences, les médecins s'adaptent à la prolongation du délai de recours à l'IVG'. *Le Monde* (12 March). Paris: 12.

Mayeur, J.-P. (1985) 'La Guerre scolaire, ancienne ou nouvelle histoire?' *Vingtième Siècle: Revue d'Histoire* 5.

Mazey, S. (2000) 'Introduction: Integrating Gender – Intellectual and "Real World" Mainstreaming'. *Journal of European Public Policy* 7(3): 333–45.

Mazur, A. (1995) *Gender Bias and the State: Symbolic Reform at Work in the Fifth Republic* (Pittsburgh, PA: University of Pittsburgh Press).

Mazur, A. (ed.) (2001) *State Feminism, Women's Movements, and Job Training: Making Democracies Work in the Global Economy* (New York and London: Routledge).

Mazur, A. (2002) *Theorizing Feminist Policy* (Oxford: Oxford University Press).

Mazur, A. (2004) 'Prostitute Movements Face Elite Apathy and Gender-Biased Universalism in France', in J. Outshoorn (ed.), *The Politics of Prostitution: Women's Movements, Democratic States, and the Globalization of Sex Commerce* (Cambridge: Cambridge University Press).

Mazur, A. (2007) 'Introduction: Feminists Engage the Republic: Comparative Lessons from France'. *French Politics* 5(3): 187–90.

McIntosh, C. A. and J. L. Finkle (1995) 'The Cairo Conference on Population and Development: a New Paradigm?' *Population and Development Review* 21(2): 223–60.

Méda, D. (2007) *Le Deuxième âge de l'émancipation: la société, les femmes et l'emploi* (Paris: Seuil).

MEDEF (Mouvement des Entreprises de France) (2006) 'Les Entreprises à la rencontre de la diversité', Diversité dans l'entreprise (28 March), http://www.medef.fr/main/core.php?pag_id=48663, accessed 20 February 2008.

Meilland, C. (2004) 'Intersectoral Agreement Signed on Gender Equality'. EIROnline (29 April), http://www.eiro.eurofound.eu.int/2004/04/feature/fr0404104f.html, accessed 20 February 2008.

Merckling, O. (2000) 'L'emploi des femmes étrangères et issues de l'immigration'. *Hommes et Migrations* 1239: 100–11.

Merckling, O. (2003) *Emploi, migration et genre des années 1950 aux années 1990* (Paris: L'Harmattan).

Michel, S. (2002) 'Dilemmas of Childcare', in Sonya Michel and Rianne Mahon (eds), *Childcare Policy at the Crossroads: Gender and Welfare State Restructuring* (London and New York: Routledge).

Ministère du Travail, des Relations Sociales et de la Solidarité (2007) 'Egalité entre les femmes et les hommes', http://www.femmes-egalite.gouv.fr/le_ministere/la_ministre/axes_politique/index.htm, accessed 21 February 2007.

Minkenberg, M. (2003) 'The Policy Impact of Church–State Relations: Family Policy and Abortion in Britain, France and Germany'. *West European Politics* 26(1): 195–217.

Mission d'information sur la question du port des signes religieux à l'école (2003) *Rapport sur la question du port des signes religieux a l'école* (Paris: Assembly National, 4 December), http://www.assemblee-nationale.fr/12/rapports/r1275-t1.asp, accessed 12 April 2007.

Molyneux, M. (1998) 'Analysing Women's Movements', in C. Jackson and R. Pearson (eds), Feminist Visions of Development: Gender Analysis and Policy (London: Routledge).

Monnet, C. (2003) 'Répression et prostitution'. *Passant* 44 (April–May), http://www.passant-ordinaire.com/revue/44-515.asp, accessed 29 April 2009.

Monnot, C. (1999) '25000 patrons réunis par le MEDEF dénoncent une réforme "archaïque"'. *Le Monde* (6 October).

Morgan, K. (2003) 'The Politics of Mothers' Employment: France in Comparative Perspective'. *World Politics* 55: 259–89.

Morineau, M. (1999–2000) 'L'Accueil de l'Islam en France et la laïcité'. *Confluences Méditerranée* 32 (Winter), www.confluences.ifrance.com/numeros/32.htm, accessed 12 March 2007.

Mossuz-Lavau, J. (1998) *Femmes/hommes pour la parité* (Paris: Presses de Sciences Po).

Mossuz-Lavau, J. (2002) *Les lois de l'amour: les politiques de la sexualité en France 1950–2002* (Paris: Payot).

Mossuz-Lavau, J. (2003) 'Une loi? Non'. *Le Monde* (16 December), http://www.ac-versailles.fr/PEDAGOGI/ses/themes/laicite/mossuz-lavau.html, accessed 22 February 2007.

Mouloud, L. (2005) 'Prostitution. Le racolage à l'index'. *L'Humanité* (29 June).

Murray, R. (2004) 'Why Didn't Parity Work? A Closer Examination of the 2002 Election Results'. *French Politics* 2: 347–62.

Murray, R. (2008) 'The Power of Sex and Incumbency'. *Party Politics* 14(5): 539–54.

Nor, M. (2001) *La Prostitution* (Paris: Le Cavalier Bleu).

Nordmann, C. (2004) *Le Foulard islamique en questions* (Paris: Editions Amsterdam).

Nouvel Observateur (2005) 'L'Assemblée penche sur l'égalité salariale' (10 May). http://permanent.nouvelobs.com/politique/20050510.OBS6202.html, accessed 20 February 2008.

O'Connor, J. S., A. S. Orloff and S. Shaver (1999) *States, Markets, Families: Gender, Liberalism and Social Policy in Australia, Canada, Great Britain and the United States* (Cambridge: Cambridge University Press).

Ognier, P. (1994) 'La Laïcité scolaire dans son histoire (1880–1945)', in Y. Lequin (ed.), *Histoire de la laïcité* (Besançon: CRDP de Franche-Comté).

Oliveira, A. and V. Ulrich (2002) 'L'Effet des 35 heures sur la durée du travail des salariés à temps partiel'. *Documents et Etudes* (DARES) 61.

Opello, K. (2006) *Gender Quotas, Parity Reform and Political Parties in France* (Oxford: Lexington Books).

OPFH (2008a) 'Législation: modifications relatives à la loi du 6 juin 2000', http://www.observatoire-parite.gouv.fr/presentation/list_decrets.htm, accessed 30 August 2008.

OPFH (2008b) *Les Modes de scrutin et la parité entre les femmes et les hommes en 2008* (Paris: OPFH), http://www.observatoire-parite.gouv.fr/portail/guide.pdf, accessed 13 June 2008.

Ourliac, G. (1988) 'The Feminisation of Higher Education in France: Its History, Characteristics and Effects on Employment'. *European Journal of Education* 23(3): 281–92.

Outshoorn, J. (1996) 'The Stability of Compromise: Abortion Politics in Western Europe', in M. Githens and D. Stetson (eds), *Abortion Politics: Public Policy in Cross-Cultural Perspectives* (London and New York: Routledge).

Outshoorn, J. (2000) 'Legalizing Prostitution as Sexual Service: the Case of the Netherlands'. ECPR Joint Session Workshop 12, Copenhagen.

Outshoorn, J. (2001) 'Debating Prostitution in Parliament: a Feminist Analysis'. *European Journal of Women's Studies* 8(4): 472–90.

Parliamentary Assembly of the Council of Europe (2006) 'Parliaments united in combating domestic violence against women'. Council of Europe, Resolution 1512 (2006).

Perben, D. (2005) La lutte contre les violences au sein du couple: Communiqué. Ministère de la Justice, Gouvernement français.

PEW (2005) *Islamic Extremism: Common Concern for Muslim and Western Publics* (Washington DC: PEW Research Centre).

Picq. F. (1993) *Libération des femmes: les années mouvement* (Paris: Seuil).

Poujade, R. (1975) *Le Ministère de l'impossible* (Collections Questions d'Actualité, Paris: Calmann-Lévy).

Presidency of the Intergovernmental Conference (2007) Draft Declarations CIG 3/1/07 REV 1, EU.

ProChoix Collective (2003) 'Islamophobes?' (special issue), *ProChoix* 26–27.

Prost, A. (1987) 'The Educational Maelstrom', in G. Ross, S. Hoffmann and S. Malzacher (eds), *The Mitterrand Experiment* (Cambridge: Polity Press).

Quid.fr (2007) 'Enseignement en France – quelques dates', *Quid.fr*, http://www.quid.fr/2007/Enseignement/Quelques_Dates/3, accessed 20 February 2008.

Ramsay, R. (2008) 'Parity – from Perversion to Political Progress: Changing Discourses of "French Exception"'. *French Politics*, 6: 45–62.

Randall, V. (1987) *Women and Politics: an International Perspective*, 2nd edition (Basingstoke: Macmillan).

Rehfeldt, U. (2007) 'Government Launches Tripartite Conferences and Consultations on Social Reforms', EIROnline, http://www.eurofound.europa.eu/eiro/2007/12/articles/fr0712029i.htm, accessed 21 February 2008.

Rémy, M. (1990) *De l'Utopie à l'intégration: histoire des mouvements des femmes* (Paris: L'Harmattan).

République française (2006) Sixième Rapport périodique national sur l'application de la Convention sur l'élimination de toutes les formes de discrimination à l'égard des femmes.

Reskin, B. and P. Roos (1990) *Job Queues, Gender Queues: Explaining Women's Inroads into Male Occupations* (Philadelphia, PA: Temple University Press).

Reuter, S. and A. Mazur (2003) 'Paradoxes of Gender-Biased Universalism: the Dynamics of French Equality Discourse', in U. Liebert (ed.), *Gendering Europeanisation* (Brussels: Peter Lang).

Révillard, A. (2006) 'La Conciliation travail–famille: un enjeu complexe pour le féminisme d'état'. *Recherches et Prévisons* 85: 17–27.

Révillard, A. (2007) *La Cause des femmes au ministère du travail: le comité du travail féminin* (Paris: CNRS).

Richemont, H. D. (2005) Rapport fait au nom de la commission des lois constitutionnelles, de législation, du suffrage universel, du Règlement et d'administration générale sur la proposition de loi de M. Roland Courteau et plusieurs de ses collègues tendant à lutter contre les violences à l'égard des femmes et notamment au sein des couples par un dispositif global de prévention, d'aide aux victimes et de répression et sur la proposition de loi de Mme Nicole Borvo Cohen-Seat et plusieurs de ses collègues relative à la lutte contre les violences au sein des couples. Commission des Lois du Sénat, Session ordinaire 2004–5.

Ricol, R. (2007) *Perceptions de la corruption et place des femmes dans des dispositifs anti-corruption*, report for the Women's Forum for the Economy and Society, http://www.csa-tmo.fr/dataset/data2007/opi20070915-presentation-perceptions-de-la-corruption-et-place-des-femmes-dans-des-dispositifs-anti-corruption.pdf, accessed 5 October 2008.

Rieu, A., H. Cettolo and Y. Le Quentrec (2003) 'Gender and Politics: Obstacles to the Political Representation and Activity of Women', paper presented at the 6th ESA Conference (Murcia).

Rigourd, D. (2002) 'Audition de M. Daniel Rigourd par la délégation aux droits des femmes et à l'égalité des chances entre les hommes et les femmes. Compte rendu no. 6. Mercredi 13 novembre 2002', http://recherche.assemblee-nationale.fr, accessed 9 May 2006.

Rochefort, F. (2002) 'Foulard, genre et laïcité en 1989'. *Vingtième Siècle* 75 (July–September): 145–56.

Roger, P. (2003) 'Le délit d'"interruption involontaire de grossesse" est créé'. *Le Monde* (29 November). Paris: 11.

Roman, J. (1995) 'Un multiculturalisme à la française'. *Esprit* 212: 145–60.

Roman, J. (1996) 'Pour un multiculturalisme tempéré'. *Hommes et Migrations* 1197: 18–22.

Roman, J. (1998) *La Démocratie des individus* (Paris: Calmann–Lévy).

Roman, J. (2006) *La Reconnaissance: une revendication de dignité?* (Paris: Editions Le Temps des Cerises).

Rouge (1976) 'La déléguée à la Condition féminine Nicole Pasquier nous déclare: "mon mari est plus féministe que moi"'. *Rouge* (15 November).

Roux, C. (1966) 'Population active féminine et travail professionnel de la femme mariée en France depuis la première guerre mondiale'. *Cahiers de l'Institut de Science Economique Appliquée* 6: 1–90.

Royal, S. (2002) 'Senate Debate, 7 February 2002', http://www.senat.fr, accessed 16 May 2006.

Rozier, J. (2002) 'Rapport d'information fait au nom de la délégation du Sénat aux droits des femmes et à l'égalité des chances entre les hommes et les femmes sur le projet de loi no. 30 (2002–3) pour la sécurité intérieure' (Paris: Le Sénat).

Saguy, A. C. (2000) 'Employment Discrimination or Sexual Violence? Defining Sexual Harassment in American and French Law'. *Law and Society Review* 34(4): 1091–1128.

Saguy, A. C. (2003) *What is Sexual Harassment? From Capitol Hill to the Sorbonne* (Berkeley: University of California Press).

Saint-Crin, R. and S. Dauphin (2001) 'Parité et renouveau féministe: Les spécificités françaises d'un changement culturel'. *Contemporary French Civilization* 25(2): 235–49.

Salom, G. and A. Seksig (1999) 'Clarté, fermeté, laïcité'. *Libération* (12 September).

Samir, D., P. Hüküm, D. Le Saout and W. Yalaz (2002) 'Les Femmes migrantes et la création d'activité. Un apport à l'economie française'. *Migrations Etudes* 104: 1–12, http://www.adri.fr/me/pdf/me104.pdf, accessed February 2007.

Sanchez, R and J.-C. Santana (2003) 'Laicité, cécité'. *Le Monde* (22 May), http://www.ac-versailles.fr/PEDAGOGI/ses/themes/laicite/sanchez_santana. html, accessed 21 February 2007.

Sarde, M. (1988) 'L'Action du ministère des droits de la femme, 1981–86: un bilan'. *The French Review* 61(6): 931–41.

Sarkozy, N. (2002a) 'Exposé des motifs, Projet de loi pour la sécurité intérieure No. 30, 2002–3', presented to the Senate, 23 October 2002, www.senat.fr.

Sarkozy, N. (2002b) 'Senate Debate, 13 November 2002', www.senat.fr, accessed 13 November 2002.

Sarkozy, N. (2002c) 'Senate Debate, 14 November 2002', http://www.senat.fr, accessed 9 May 2006.

Sarkozy, N. (2005) 'Bilan de la loi pour la sécurité intérieure en ce qui concerne la prostitution. Question écrite no. 17416. Publiée dans le JO Sénat du 05/05/2005, page 2723', www.senat.fr, accessed 24 February 2006.

Sarkozy, N. (2006) 'Intervention lors de l'ouverture de la table ronde sur les violences conjugales le 7 mars 2006'.

Schemla, E. 'Les Femmes et l'islam', *Le Nouvel Observateur*, 1559 (22 September 1994). http://hebdo.nouvelobs.com/hebdo/parution/p1559/articles/a44829-. html, accessed 20 February 2008.

Scott, J. (2005) *Parité! Sexual Equality and the Crisis of French Universalism* (Chicago and London: University of Chicago Press).

Scott, J. (2007) *The Politics of the Veil* (Princeton and Oxford: Princeton University Press).

Sebbar, L. (1989) 'Recluses et fugueuses, les nouvelles délinquantes'. *Libération* (20 November).

Secrétariat d'Etat aux droits des femmes et à la formation professionnelle (2000) *Conférence de Pékin, cinq ans après* (Paris: La Documentation française).

Sénac-Slawinsky, R. (2008) 'Justifying Parity in France after the Passage of the So-called Parity Laws and the Electoral Application of them: the "Ideological Tinkering" of Political Party Officials (UMP and PS) and Women's NGOs'. *French Politics* 6: 234–56.

Sénat (2002a) 'Compte rendu analytique officiel de la séance du 14 novembre'.

Sénat (2002b) 'Compte rendu intégral des débats du Sénat: Séance du 14 novembre 2002', http://www.senat.fr.

Sénat (2008) 'Renouvellement du 21 Septembre 2008. Composition du Sénat: Liste par circonscription après renouvellement', http://www.senat.fr/senateurs/

elections/2008/senatoriales2008/d/liste_par_circonscription_senat.pdf, accessed 10 October 2008.

Service des études juridiques (2005) Etude de législation comparée no. 144 La lutte contre les violences conjugales. Paris: Senate.

Simon, C. (2002) 'Clients de la prostitution'. *Le Monde* (20 May). Paris.

Sineau, M. (2002) 'Institutionnalisation de la parité: l'expérience française'. *Les Femmes au parlement: au-delà du nombre* (Stockholm: International IDEA).

Sineau, M. (2008) 'Mairies et cantons, zones arides de la parité'. *Revue Politique et Parlementaire* 1047 (April–June): 65–71.

Smith, A. (2004) 'France Divided as Headscarf Ban is Set to Become Law'. *The Observer* (1 February), http://www.guardian.co.uk/world/2004/feb/01/france.schoolsworldwide, accessed 23 March 2007.

Smolar, P. (2006) 'Une circulaire demande la garde à vue immédiate pour les auteurs de violences conjugales'. *Le Monde* (30 January). Paris: 9.

Snyder, F. (2000) 'Europeanisation and Globalisation as Friends and Rivals: European Union Law in Global Economic Networks', in F. Snyder (ed.), *The Europeanisation of Law: the Legal Effects of European Integration* (Oxford: Hart Publishing), pp. 294–320.

Sparrow, A. (2008) 'MPs to Vote on Abortion Time Limit Tonight', www.guardian.co.uk (20 May), accessed 24 June 2008.

Stasi, B. (2004) (Commission de réflexion sur l'application du principe de laïcité dans la République) *Laïcité et République* (Paris: La Documentation française, 2004).

Stein, R. and M. Shear (2009) 'Funding Restored to Groups that Perform Abortions, Other Care'. *Washington Post*, 24 January.

Steinberg-Ratner, R. (1980) 'The Policy and Problem: Overview of Seven Countries', in R. Steinberg-Ratner (ed.), *Equal Employment Policy for Women* (Philadelphia: Temple University Press).

Stetson, D. McBride (1987) *Women's Rights in France* (New York, Westport and London: Greenwood Press).

Stetson, D. McBride (ed.) (2001) *Abortion Politics, Women's Movements and the Democratic State: a Comparative Study of State Feminism* (New York: Oxford University Press).

Stetson, D. McBride and A. Mazur (eds) (1995) *Comparative State Feminisms* (Thousand Oaks, London and New Delhi: Sage).

Stewart, M. L. (1989) *Women, Work and the French State: Labour Protection and Social Patriarchy, 1897–1919* (Kingston, Montreal and London: McGill-Queen's University Press).

Storti, M. (1976) 'La déléguée à la Condition Féminine n'a rien à dire'. *Libération* (15 November).

Stratigaki, M. (2004) 'The Cooptation of Gender Concepts in EU Policies: the Case of "Reconciliation of Work and Family"'. *Social Politics* 11(1): 30–56.

Sullerot, E. (1968) *Histoire et sociologie du travail féminin* (Paris: Gonthier).

Sung, H.-E. (2003) 'Fairer Sex or Fairer System? Gender and Corruption Revisited'. *Social Forces* 82(2) (December): 703–23.

Surduts, M. (2000) 'Evidence to Délégation aux droits des femmes. Séance du 18h30. Mardi 19 septembre', http://www.assemblee-nationale.fr/11/cr-delf/00-01/c9900019.asp#P43_259, accessed 14 June 2001.

Swamy, A., S. Knack, L. Young and O. Azfar (2001) 'Gender and Corruption'. *Journal of Development Economics* 64: 25–55.

Tapinos, G. (1992) 'Immigration féminine et statut des femmes étrangères en France'. *Revue Française des Affaires Sociales* 46: 29–60.

Terrade, O. (2001) Rapport d'information fait au nom de la délégation du Sénat aux droits des femmes et à l'égalité des chances entre les hommes et les femmes sur le projet de loi, adopté par l'Assemblée nationale, après déclaration d'urgence, relatif à l'interruption volontaire de grossesse et à la contraception, Sénat.

Terrail, J.-P. (1992a) 'Destins scolaires de sexe: une perspective historique et quelques arguments'. *Population* 3: 645–76.

Terrail, J.-P. (1992b) 'Réussite scolaire: la mobilisation des filles'. *Sociétés Contemporaines* 11–12: 53–89.

Tévanian, P. (2005a) *Le Voile médiatique: un faux débat* (Paris: Raisons d'Agir).

Tévanian, P. (2005b) *La Parole confisquée (première partie): analyse des pages 'Débats' du Monde et de Libération consacrées au 'débat sur le voile'*, Collectif Les Mots Sont Importants (12 August), http://lmsi.net/spip.php?article450, accessed 23 March 2008.

Tévanian, P. (2005c) *La Parole confisquée (deuxième partie): analyse de la composition des émissions de 'débat' télévisées consacrées au 'problème du voile'*, Collectif Les Mots Sont Importants (14 August), http://lmsi.net/spip.php?article451, accessed 23 March 2008.

Thiercé, A. (1999) 'La pauvreté laborieuse au XIXème siècle vue par Julie-Victoire Daubié'. *Travail, Genre et Sociétés* 1: 119–46.

Threlfall, M. (ed.) (1996) *Mapping the Women's Movement: Feminist Politics and Social Transformation in the North* (London and New York: Verso).

Toutain, J. C. (1963) 'La Population de la France de 1700 à 1959'. *Cahiers de l'Institut de Science Economique Appliquée* 133: 1–250.

Trotignant, Y. (1985) *La France au XXe siècle – tome 1: jusqu'en 1968* (Paris: Dunod).

UNESCO (2000) *Peuple de l'Abîme: la prostitution aujourd'hui* (Paris: La Fondation Scelles).

United Nations (1948) *Universal Declaration of Human Rights*. http://www.un.org/Overview/rights.html, accessed 22 March 2007.

United Nations (1995) *Report of the Fourth World Conference on Women* (New York: UN), http://www.un.org/esa/gopher-data/conf/fwcw/off/a–20.en, accessed 21 June 2008.

United Nations General Assembly (2006) *In-depth Study on all Forms of Violence against Women*. Report of the Secretary-General. Advancement of Women, United Nations: 139.

Vautrin, C. (2005) 'Pourquoi un label égalité' (Brochure, Ministre déléguée à la Cohésion Sociale et à la Parité), http://www.femmes-egalite.gouv.fr/se_documenter/operations_de_communication/label_egalite.pdf, accessed 21 February 2008.

Vernier, J. (2005a) 'La Loi pour la sécurité intérieure: punir les victimes du proxénétisme pour mieux les protéger?' in M.-E. Handman and J. Mossuz-Lavau (eds), *La Prostitution à Paris* (Paris: Editions de la Martinière).

Vernier, J. (2005b) 'La pénalisation des prostitués selon la LSI'. *Plein Droit* (65–6).

Vidalies, A. (2002a) 'L'Expression "travailleur du sexe" ne doit pas être taboue'. *Le Monde* (20 October). Paris.

Vidalies, A. (2002b) 'Rapport d'information par la mission d'information commune sur les diverses formes de l'esclavage moderne'. Assemblée Nationale, No. 3459.

Vigerie, A. and A. Zelensky (2003) '"Laïcardes" puisque féministes'. *ProChoix*, 25: 11–14.

Walby, S. (2005) 'Introduction: Comparative Gender Mainstreaming in a Global Era'. *International Feminist Journal of Politics* 7(4): 453–70.

Waters, S. (2003) *Social Movements in France: Towards a New Citizenship* (Basingstoke: Palgrave Macmillan).

Waylen, G. (2002) 'Gender, Feminism and the State: an Overview', in V. Randall and G. Waylen (eds), *Gender, Politics and the State* (London: Routledge).

Weil, P. (2004a) 'Lifting the Veil'. *French Politics, Culture & Society*, 22(3): 142–9.

Weil, P. (2004b) 'A Nation in Diversity: France, Muslims and the Headscarf'. *OpenDemocracy* (25 March), http://www.opendemocracy.net/content/articles/PDF/1811.pdf, accessed 24 June 2007.

Welzer-Lang, D. (2003) 'Quand le sexe travaille ou Une loi peut en cacher une autre', www.multisexualites-et-sida.org/yapasque/client.html, accessed 3 February 2003.

White, L. A. (2004) 'Ideas and Normative Institutionalism: Explaining the Paradoxes of French Family and Employment Policy'. *French Politics* 2: 247–71.

Wieviorka, M. (2006) 'Comment les minorités peuvent-elles concilier valeurs universelles et identités particulières? Le modèle néorépublicain'. *Libération* (13 November).

Willaime, J.-P. (2007) 'Teaching Religious Issues in French Public Schools: From Abstentionism to a Return of Religion in Public Education', in R. Jackson (ed.), *Religion and Education in Europe: Developments, Contexts and Debates* (New York and Berlin: Waxmann Verlag).

Windebank, J. (1994) 'Explaining Women's Relationship to Domestic Labour: Individualism, Structuralism and Empiricism in the French Debates'. *Women's Studies International Forum* 17(5): 499–509.

Windebank, J. and A. Gregory (2000) *Women and Work in France and Britain: Theory Practice and Policy* (Basingstoke: Palgrave Macmillan).

Winter, B. (2008) *Hijab and the Republic: Uncovering the French Headscarves Debate* (NY: Syracuse University Press).

Zimmerman, M.-J. (2005) *Effets directs et indirects de la loi du 6 juin 2000: un bilan contrastée* (Report) (Paris: OPFH).

Zimmerman, M.-J. (2008) *Elections municipales et cantonales 2008: les partis politiques résistent encore à la parité* (Report) (Paris: OPFH).

Index